Georges Bernage & Dominique François

Utah Beach
Sainte-Mère-Eglise
Sainte-Marie-du-Mont

HEIMDAL

– Based on an idea by Georges Bernage.

– Written by Georges Bernage (for most of the text, the design and captions) and Dominique François (for the American personal accounts and the part of the iconography marked "D.F.").

– English translation: John Lee.

– Reportage in the field : Erik Groult (photos marked E.G.).

– Maps : Bernard Paich.

– Art work : Erik Groult.

– Composition and layout : Christel Lebret.

– Photoengraving : Christian Caïra, Philippe Gazagne.

– Computer graphics : Philippe Gazagne.

– – Iconography : Bundesarchiv, Koblenz, IWM.

Editions Heimdal
Château de Damigny - BP 61350 - 14406 BAYEUX Cedex
Tél. : 02.31.51.68.68 - Fax : 02.31.51.68.60 - E-mail : Editions.Heimdal@wanadoo.fr

ISBN 2 84048 193-6

Preface

Some places are steeped in history. Thanks to a book – "The Longest Day" – and the film of the book, Sainte-Mère-Eglise is now world-famous, with its sturdily built church topped by a bell-tower with a saddle-back roof forming the outline we all know so well.

This airborne bridgehead also faced a very unusual type of terrain which has become familiar to us: a vast, low beach with a long overhanging dune, and behind it a then flooded area drained by ditches, and a hinterland of dense hedgerow country. Dominating this whole Plain area were two small towns tightly packed around their church, with one airborne division assigned to each: Sainte-Mère-Eglise for the 82nd, Sainte-Marie-du-Mont for the 101st. Sainte-Mère and Sainte-Marie, two names that sound alike and have entered the history books together. But the Plain area at the time was a peninsula, with the sea and inundated land to the east, the Carentan marshes to the south, the flooded Merderet to the west, and in the middle, this bocage country with its thick hedgerows and sunken lanes, surprising and mysterious terrain which saw worried US paratroopers losing their bearings upon landing on the ground. One just needs to read William Tucker's account (see page 79) to understand: hedges five to seven feet high covered from top to bottom with a jungle of bushes and rows of trees. While this mysterious landscape has regained its peaceful beauty, we must remember that on 6 and 7 June 1944 it was the scene of all the horrors of war. Civilians caught up in the battle and mown down by war, friends and enemies alike pinned down inextricably in a beachhead where there was no such thing as a front line for the first thirty hours, hand-to-hand fighting with knives or bayonet. Many dead, paratroopers drowning in the marshes, soldiers mown down along some lane, cumbersome prisoners quickly liquidated. The picture we get from the movies should not let us forget the terrible reality that war is an appalling slaughter. It hit this peaceful land, then, three days later, after a rapid offensive surge, the troops carried on towards Carentan and Sauveur-le-Vicomte. The civilian population was at last able to enjoy the return to peace in an area that had not suffered from the destructive bombardments seen all too often elsewhere in Normandy.

After this short battle, the countryside, the towns and villages mostly spared by the war and rampant progress, remained a scene tied to History and Memory. After the war, through the work of Alexandre Renaud, who was mayor of Sainte-Mère-Eglise on 6 June 1944, and his wife, American veterans were taken in each year and later welcomed by the entire population, setting a unique example in Normandy which now also sees young paratroopers of the 505th welcomed each year into families. Two places of remembrance: the Airborne Troops Museum at Sainte-Mère-Eglise, which was run by its curator, American veteran Philip Jutras [who, sadly, died on 4 April], and the Utah Beach D-day Museum, brought about through the efforts of its curator, the late Michel de Valavieille. Today, in a moving setting that has remained untouched, these places of History and Remembrance attract visitors in their thousands.

These places also mean a great deal to the present author. As a young historian and publisher in 1976, Madame Auvray, who ran a bookshop at Sainte-Mère-Eglise, put me in touch with Philip Jutras, who wrote the first guide I brought out. This marked the starting point for many other books, and turned me into a Battle of Normandy specialist. We built up a good team and published three more books on Sainte-Mère-Eglise and Utah Beach, and many others on the fighting in the Cotentin and in Normandy. Thus a quarter of a century of work and experience have gone into the present book which offers a lavishly documented overview for younger generations to grasp the many facettes of this great chapter in history.

Georges Bernage
Historian and publisher
Damigny, 20 March 2004

Books on the airborne bridgehead published by Editions Heimdal:

- P. Jutras, *Guide Sainte-Mère-Eglise,* 1976. Numerous reprints.

- P. Jutras, *Les paras US dans le canton de Sainte-Mère-Eglise,* 1979. Numerous reprints.

- G. Bernage, *Débarquement à Utah Beach,* 1984.

- G. Bernage, *Première victoçre américaine en Normandie*, 1990.

- G. Bernage, Ph. Lejuée, L. Mari, H.-J. Renaud, *Objectif Sainte-Mère-Eglise, Jour J, les paras US*, 1993.

- Ph. Esvelin, *D-Day Gliders,* 2001.

- D. François, *508th Parachute Infantry Regiment,* 2001.

- D. François, *507th Parachute Infantry Regiment,* 2002.

• *Command and staff* (commandement et état-major) :

— **Commanding General** : Major General Raymond O. Barton (28 Jan. 44 - 18 Sep. 44).

— *Assistant Division Commander* : Brigadier General Henry A. Barber (28 Jan. 44 - 9 Jul. 44).

— **Artillery Commanded** : Brigadier General Harold W. Blakeley (28 Jan. 44 - 28 Dec. 44).

— **Chief of Staff** (chef d'état-major) : Colonel James S. Rodwell (28 Jan. 44 - 2 Jul. 44).

— *Assistant Chief of Staff G-1* : Lieutenant-Colonel Garlen E. Bryant.

— *Assistant Chief of Staff G-2* : Lieutenant-Colonel Harry F. Hansen.

— *Assistant Chief of Staff G-3* : Lieutenant-Colonel Orlando C. Troxel, Jr. (28 Jan. 44 - 13 Jun. 44).

— *Assistant Chief of Staff G-4* : Lieutenant-Colonel John Richard S. Marr (28 Jan. 44 - 2 Jul. 44).

— *Assistant Chief of Staff G-5* : Lieutenant-Colonel Dee W. Stone (31 May 44).

— *Adjutant General* : Major George H. Garde (15 May 44 - 28 Aug. 44).

— *Commanding Officer, 8th Infantry* : Colonel James A. Van Fleet (28 Jan. 44 - 2 Jul. 44).

— *Commanding Officer, 12th Infantry* : Colonel Russell P. Reeder, Jr. (28 Jan. 44 - 11 Jun. 44).

— *Commanding Officer, 22d Infantry* : Colonel Hervey A. Tribolet (28 Jan. 44 - 26 Jun. 44).

• **Composition**

— 8th Infantry Regiment

— 12th Infantry Regiment

— 22d Infantry Regiment

— 4th Reconnaissance Troop (Mechanized)

— 4th Engineer Combat Battalion

— 4th Medical Battalion

— *4th Division Artillery*

• 29th Field Artillery Battalion (105 mm Howitzer)

• 42d Field Artillery Battalion (105 mm Howitzer)

• 44th Field Artillery Battalion (105 mm Howitzer)

• 20th Field Artillery Battalion (105 mm Howitzer)

— *Special Troops*

• 704th Ordnance Light Maintenance Company

• 4th Quartermaster Company

• 4th Signal Company (transmissions)

• Military Police Platoon

• Headquarters Company (compagnie de QG)

• Band (fanfare)

Maj. Gen. Raymond O. Barton

- *Command and staff* (commandement et état-major) :
- **Commanding General** : Major General Matthew B. Ridgway (9 Dec. 44 - 27 Aug. 44).
- *Assistant Division Commander* : Brigadier General James M. Gavin (9 Dec. 43 - 26 Aug. 44).
- **Artillery Commander** : Colonel Francis A. March (22 May 44 - 16 Nov. 44).
- **Chief of Staff** (chef d'état-major) : Colonel Ralph P. Eaton (9 Dec. 43 - 28 Aug. 44).
- *Assistant Chief of Staff G-1 :* Lieutenant-Colonel Frederick M. Schillhammer (i.e., *Schellhammer*) (9 Dec. 43 - 28 Aug. 44).
- *Assistant Chief of Staff G-2 :* Lieutenant-Colonel Jack Whitefield (9 Dec. 43 - 28 Aug. 44).
- *Assistant Chief of Staff G-3 :* Lieutenant-Colonel Robert H. Wienecke (17 Febr. 44 - 28 Aug. 44).
- *Assistant Chief of Staff G-4 :* Lieutenant-Colonel Bennie Zinn (17 Febr. 44 - 7 June 44).
- *Assistant Chief of Staff G-5 :* Capt. Peter Shouvaloff (22 May 44 - 13 Dec. 44).
- *Adjutant General :* Lieutenant-Colonel Raymond M. Britton (9 Dec. 43 - 23 Febr. 45).
- *Commanding Officer, **505th Parachute Infantry*** : Lieutenant-Colonel William E. Ekman (22 March. 44 - 22 July 44).
- *Commanding Officer, **325th Glider Infantry*** : Colonel Harry L. Lewis (9 Dec. 43 - 22 Aug. 44).

- **Composition**
- 325th Glider Infantry Regiment
- 505th Parachute Infantry Regiment
- 507th Parachute Infantry Regiment
- 508th Parachute Infantry Regiment
- 307th Airborne Engineer Battalion
- 80th Airborne Antiaircraft Artillery Battalion
- 307th Airborne Medical Company

- *82d Airborne Division Artillery*
- 319th Glider Field Artillery Battalion
- 320th Glider Field Artillery Battalion
- 376th Parachute Field Artillery Battalion
- 456th Parachute Field Artillery Battalion
- *Special Troops*
- 782d Airborne Ordnance Company
- 407th Quartermaster Company
- 82d Airborne Signal Company (transmissions)
- Military Police Platoon
- Headquarters Company (compagnie de QG)

Maj. Gen. Matthew B. Ridgway

101st Airborne Division « Eagle Division »

- *Command and staff* (commandement et état-major) :
— **Commanding General** : Major General Maxwell D. Taylor (14 Mar. 44 - 5 Dec. 44).
— *Assistant Division Commander* : Brigadier General Don F. Pratt (15 Sep. 43 - 6 June 44).
— **Artillery Commander** : Brigadier General Anthony C. Mc Auliffe (15 Sep. 43 - 5 Dec. 44).
— **Chief of Staff** (chef d'état-major) : Colonel Gerald J. Higgins (15 Sep. 43 - 11 Aug. 44).
— *Assistant Chief of Staff G-1* : Lieutenant-Colonel Ned D. Moore (15 Sep. 43 - 14 Dec. 44).
— *Assistant Chief of Staff G-2* : Major Arthur M. Sommerfield (17 Apr. 44 - 7 July 44).
— *Assistant Chief of Staff G-3* : Lieutenant-Colonel Raymond D. Millener (15 Sep. 43 - 1 July 44).
— *Assistant Chief of Staff G-4* : Lieutenant-Colonel Carl W. Kohes.
— *Assistant Chief of Staff G-5* : Major General C. Erbele (6 May 44 - 18 June 44).
— *Adjutant General* : Lieutenant-Colonel Edward Schmitt (15 Sep. 43).
— *Commanding Officer, **327th Glider Infantry*** : Colonel George S. Wear (15 Sep. 43 - 10 June 44).
— *Commanding Officer, **501st Parachute Infantry*** : Colonel Howard R. Johnson (1 Feb. 44 - 7 Oct. 44)
— *Commanding Officer, **502d Parachute Infantry*** : Colonel George V.H. Moseley (15 Sep. 43 - 9 June 44).
— *Commanding Officer, **506th Parachute Infantry*** : Colonel Robert F. Sink (15 Sep. 43).

- **Composition**
— 501st Parachute Infantry Regiment
— 502d Parachute Infantry Regiment
— 506th Parachute Infantry Regiment
— 327th Glider Infantry Regiment
— 101st Parachute Maintenance Battalion
— 326th Airborne Engineer Battalion
— 81st Airborne Antiaircraft Artillery Battalion

— *101st Airborne Division Artillery*
- 321st Glider Field Artillery Battalion
- 377th Parachute Field Artillery Battalion
- 907th Glider Field Artillery Battalion
— *Special Troops*
- 801st Ordnance Company
- 426th Quartermaster Company
- 101st Signal Company (transmissions)
- Military Police Platoon
- Headquarters Company
- Reconnaissance Platoon

Maj. Gen. Maxwell D. Taylor

Contents

Paratroopers over the Cotentin

In 1944, the Germans had used locks to inundate the lowlying areas behind the sand dunes and the marshy meadowland around the Douve and Merderet rivers, so as to create obstacles and make the eastern seaboard of the Cotentin peninsula easier to defend. Today winter rains flood these marshlands, turning them "white" as in 1944 (**1** and **2**). A Schwimmwagen amphibious vehicle, probably belonging to 13./919, a heavy company of IR 919, whose regimental marking is on the rear of the vehicle, driving along an inundated roadway (**3**). This American map (**4**) sets out D-day objectives and indicates inundated areas. (**1** and **2**: EG/Heimdal, **3** and **4** : B. Paich coll.)

In May 1943, at the *Trident* Conference in Washington, the D-day landing sector for *Overlord was chosen: Normandy rather than the* Pas-de-Calais. It was then planned in the area between the mouths of the Orne and the Vire, with five divisions in the first wave, two airborne and three infantry divisions. But these resources were deemed inadequate. Late in January **1944**, Eisenhower gave final figures for the resources that would actually be committed: three airborne divisions and five seaborne divisions. In the west, between Port-en-Bessin and the Cotentin peninsula, the landing sector was given to the **First US Army**. On its left flank, V *Corps was to land at Omaha Beach.* On the right flank **VII Corps** was to land at *Utah Beach* with the *4th Infantry Division* in the first wave, followed by the *9th Infantry Division*, the *90th Infantry Division* and the *79th Infantry Division*. To establish this beachhead and secure the beach exits, two airborne divisions were to be dropped in the sector: the *82nd Airborne Division* and the *101st Airborne Division*. This sector was much more favorable than the one given to *V Corps* (Omaha Beach) (1), (*VII Corps* came ashore on a low beach with two airborne divisions in support!)

Lowlying flooded land

The Cotentin peninsula dips into the sea with its northern section completely edged with rocky coasts and plateaux rising to 178 meters above sea level. The south-east section however, between Valognes in the north and Carentan in the south, tails off down to the sea in a low plain aptly called **Le Plain**. This large plain stretching in a north-south direction is surrounded by marshlands to the west (Merderet marshes), south (Douve marshes) and east (between the plain and the dune ridge). Usually these **marshy areas** are drained and sealed off, and dry out for much of the year although crisscrossed with small drainage channels. In winter, on the other hand, with the much heavier rainfall, the marshes flood, and are then said to be "white". The Germans saw how these marshlands could be turned to their advantage and decided as a defensive measure to inundate them permanently, using a system of locks and sluices. Thus by an unfortunate coincidence the Allied airborne troops encountered inundated areas on both flanks of the landing sector, with the Dives marshes awaiting the British paratroops and the Cotentin marshes the Americans.

In the center of the Plain was a small town – **Sainte-Mère-Eglise** – astride Highway 13, a major crossroads between Carentan and Cherbourg; already two millennia ago there was a Roman road here and there is a Roman milestone (converted into a cross) near the church. Later, King Louis XIII authorized a Thursday market at Sainte-Mère, which is still operating today.

The Plain is fine bocage country, with all the mystery of the hedgerows and sunken lanes, numerous manors nestling in the green countryside, winding roads and lanes sometimes leading only to the marshes, or eastwards to the sea. Southeast of Sainte-Mère-Eglise, going towards the sea, stands the village of **Sainte-Marie-du-Mont** snuggling up to its fine medieval church surmounted by a tall Renaissance tower. On the south side of the village lies the old castle of the powerful Aux Epaules family of the Cotentin which died out in the 17th century.

To the north, the road to Valognes and Cherbourg is blocked by a ridge of high ground preceded by the village of **Montebourg**. South of the marshes, the small town of **Carentan** lies outside the planned

1

2

beachhead but remained a vital objective for the *VII Corps which* was to link up, starting there, with the *V Corps* on the high ground at Isigny. To the west, **La Fière** (a hamlet with its manor house) and the village of Chef-du-Pont were major D-day objectives opening up a way across the Merderet marshes to another D-day objective, **Pont-l'Abbé,** on the other side. From there, the *VII Corps* would be able to advance on Saint-Sauveur-le-Vicomte then Barneville-Carteret so as to cut off the Cotentin peninsula before moving back up north on Cherbourg.

Thus, despite the serious obstacle presented by the marshlands, and the maze of greeenery of the hedgerow country, the zone chosen to establish VII Corps' beachhead was relatively favorable. The land was flat with hardly any hilly areas, the soft sandy beach was also flat and it extended over a vast distance from north to south.

(1) On this subject, see the book on Omaha Beach, Editions Heimdal.

3

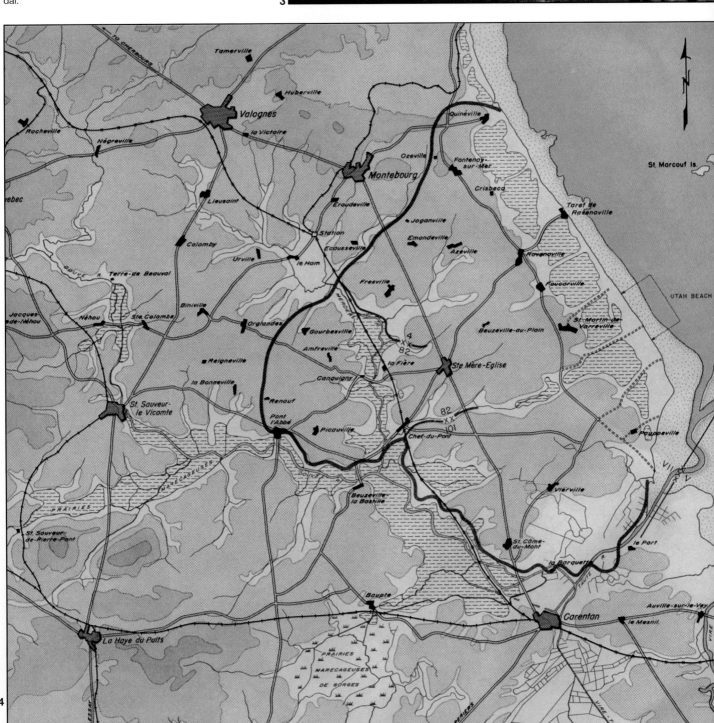

4

Generalmajor Wilhelm Falley. (Coll. Charita.)

Due to the strategic position of the Plain in the south-east Cotentin (Cherbourg, as a major wartime port, was a crucial objective for the Allies who came across with substantial supplies), the Allied command decided to commit the US VII Corps there on D-day with three divisions, including two airborne, and a further three divisions in reinforcement, for a total of six divisions. To face these forces, the Germans could only line up three divisions in the Cotentin Peninsula: *243. Infanterie-Division* in the west, *709. Infanterie-Division* in the east and *91. (Luftlande) Infanterie-Division* in the center. Only elements of two of them faced the airborne and amphibious attack on D-day.

91. (LL) Infanterie-Division's commanding officer was *Generalmajor* Wilhelm **Falley**, who had taken over command of the division in April 1944. This division, from Wave 25, was raised at Baumholder, in *Wehrkreis XII*, in January 1944. It had originally been intended as an airborne division, hence its initials *LL* for *Luftlande*, but it was used as a standard infantry division. Upon completing training, on Hitler's orders, the division was allocated as of 14 May 1944 to the central Cotentin Peninsula, with *LXXXIV. Armee-Korps* under *General* Marcks to reinforce the troops in that sector. Contrary to his generals' opinion, Hitler believed the Allies would land in Normandy and just a few weeks before D-day had brought up several divisions to reinforce what would be the Normandy front. The *352. Infanterie-Division* was now facing the future Omaha Beach.

This division had just two infantry regiments, *Grenadier-Regiment 1057* and *Grenadier-Regiment 1058*, along with a mobile infantry group, *Divisions-Füsilier-Bataillon 91*. It also had an artillery regiment (*Gebirgs-Artillerie-Regiment 91*), a "mountain" regiment, an engineers battalion (*Pionier-Bataillon 191*) and an antitank group (*Panzerjäger-Abteilung 191*).

The division was not full-strength; as we have seen, it only had two infantry regiments, with a total strength of just 10 555 men, i.e. 60% of the strength of an Allied division. The artillery regiment had two battle-groups each with twelve 10.5 cm guns, and one with twelve 15.5 cm guns. *Generalmajor* Wilhelm Falley had set up his HQ at the château at Picauville. **GR 1058** was in position west of the Merderet in the sector where the 82nd Airborne Division was to land. The regimental staff was at Fauville, on Highway 13, south of Sainte-Mère-Eglise. The staff of the 3rd Battalion (*III./1058*) was also on Highway 13, in the southern part of the sector, opposite Carentan, at Saint-Côme-du-Mont. The staff of the 1st Battalion (*I./1058*) was in the far north of the sector, west of Montebourg. Thus the 1st Battalion was to prove a threat to the US paratroopers of the 101st Airborne Division for its parachute drops (506th PIR) and the advance on Carentan. In the north, *III./1058*, reinforced by the anti-tank group of *709. ID, Panzerjäger-Abteilung 709*, proved a serious threat to US paratroopers dropped over Sainte-Mère-Eglise. **GR 1057** was west of the Merderet, from where it could launch counter-attacks against the airborne beachhead. Its *II./1057* was in position north-west of Picauville. Its *I./1057* was south-west of that locality, where it received support from *Panzer-Abteilung 100*, of which more later.

This division had the advantage of surprise because the Americans had not expected it to be there, having only arrived three weeks before D-day. But it was under-strength, and took the full blast of the airborne assault. By 10 June it was down to 6 596 fighting men, a figure that had dropped to 1 250 after another month.

On the peninsula's eastern side of the, **709. Infanterie-Division** covered the entire coastal sector. This Wave 15 division was raised on 2 May 1941 in the Kassel area (*Wehrkreis IX*), in Hesse. It was a static division with a high proportion of older soldiers. In November 1941, it went to occupy Brittany in the area around Saint-Brieuc and Saint-Malo. It was transferred to the Cherbourg peninsula in December 1943 to hold the Carentan-Valognes-Barfleur-Cherbourg sectors. It then received a regiment in reinforcement, *Infanterie-Regiment 919*. But here again, the men were on the mature side, with an average age of 36 in 1944.

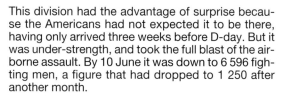

Château de Bernaville at Picauville, the *91. Infanterie-Division's* prewar HQ (B. François coll.) and as it is today. (E. Groult/Heimdal.)

Unconfirmed emblem of the *91. Infanterie-Division* based on the unit's name of Haudegen Division, the Rapier division.

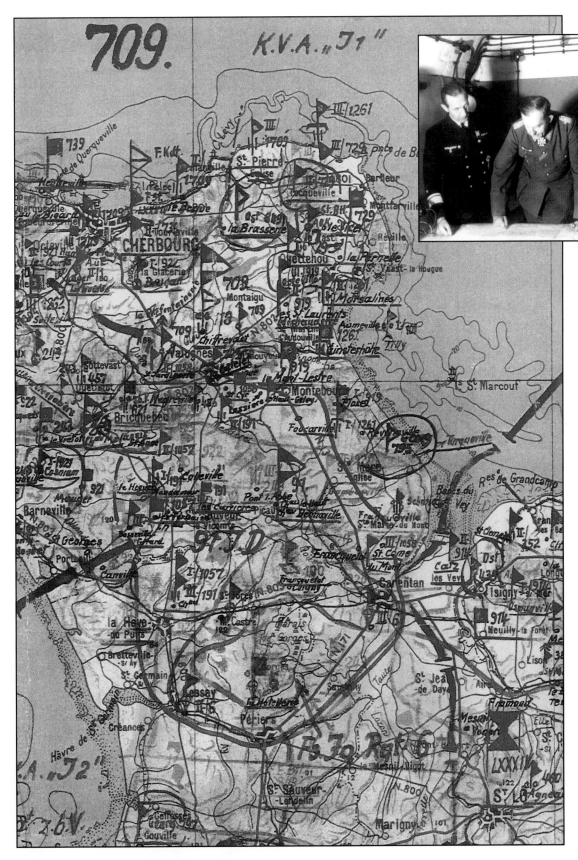

At Cherbourg, *709. ID* CO *Generalleutnant* Karl-Wilhelm von Schlieben discusses coastal defenses with Seekommandant Normandie (naval commander in Normandy), Konteradmiral Walter Hennecke, left, and the commader of fortress Cherbourg, *Generalmajor* Sattler, right. (BA.)

Emblem of the *709. Infanterie-Division* seen in Brittany in the summer of 1942.

In December 1943, the division also came under the command of *Generalleutnant* Karl Wilhelm **von Schlieben**. The son of a Prussian officer, he was born on 30 October 1894 at Eisenach, in Thuringen. A cadet in 1914, he became a *Leutnant* in a foot grenadier regiment a year later. He continued his career in the infantry and the cavalry after the war, becoming a captain in the cavalry in 1929, with promo-tion to colonel on 1st August 1941. In February 1943, he assumed command of *208. Infanterie-Division* and was promoted to *Generalmajor* on 1st May. At that same date, he took over command of *18. Panzer-Division* which took part in the Battle of Kursk in July. This tank division was disbanded on 20 October 1943 and he was put in command of *709. Infanterie-Division* on 12 December 1943. He was promoted to the

5

rank of *Generalleutnant* on 1st May 1944. One of his subordinates, Lieutenant-Colonel Keil, described him as follows: *"He was an old soldier from the front line and a practitioner. He was an astute psychologist and knew how to use his wealth of experience. He had natural humour, and had a bearlike calmness in tough situations. He was warm-hearted with his subordinates. Being of ancient noble stock, he required from his officers the same feeling of responsibility that he demanded from himself, and he left them the necessary freedom. When he took over the divisional command in January, he said to me: "you are in charge of your sector, I have nothing further to say." The tragedy of his situation was that he found himself in positions that were hopeless from the outset."*

709. Infanterie-Division had three infantry regiments. On first arriving in Normandy, it had two regiments, **IR 729** and **IR 739**. The latter was in position in *Festung* Cherbourg with its CP at Querqueville, west of Cherbourg. *IR 729* was in position in the Val de Saire, with its CP at Le Vicel, east of Cherbourg and north of Valognes and Montebourg. These two regiments were chiefly involved in the final battle for Cherbourg. The third regiment, **Infanterie-Regiment 919**, was attached to the division in October 1943 and was sent to the east coast of the Cotentin peninsula. This was the regiment that faced the assault of three Alied divisions on D-day, along with *GR 1057* already mentioned above.

IR 919 faces its destiny

Commanded by Lieutenant-Colonel Günther **Keil**, this regiment was raised on 17 July 1943, at the parade ground at Gross-Born in West Prussia, as part of *241. Infanterie-Division*. It was then made up of older recruits, with 75% of the NCOs and men aged between 35 and 45. During their peacetime military service, they had only been given a short eight-week training course. They were now called up again to make up numbers. On the other hand, 25% of them were veterans of the Eastern front and being experienced soldiers made up for their age. The regimental *Kommandeur*, Günther Keil, and his battalion commanders were experienced officers. The rest were reserve officers with no military experience. On the other hand, half of the company commanders were former NCOs in the regular army with proper military training. On 1st August 1943, the regiment moved to the Charleroi area in Belgium for further training. Forty kilometer hikes with a complete pack were hard going for soldiers over forty. In October, the regiment and an artillery battalion had been detached from *241. ID* and allocated to *709. ID*. It was then that it moved up to the Cotentin. The regimental HQ was

initially set up at Sainte-Mère-Eglise and the regiment was scattered from Montebourg and La Haye-du-Puits to cut off the entire peninsula; as yet it only had two divisions. Sometime around Christmas, the best elements, those who had already seen action on the Eastern front, left the regiment and were sent back to Russia. The young soldiers also left, to be replaced by even younger men (18 and 19 year-olds) with very little military training. Among these, 10% were "ethnic Germans" (*Volksdeutsche*, foreigners to the Reich). In January 1944, the regiment was moved, abandoning the marshlands in the south of the peninsula for the Plain. Here it took up the position it would have on D-day to face the Allied assault.

The regiment stretched from the Baie des Veys (the bay north of Carentan), in the south, as far as the cove at Saint-Vaast-la-Hougue (and more specifically up to and including Belle Croix). This was a vast sector 35 kilometers long. For such a broad front, two or three divisions would normally be needed in the east, or even three or four divisions depending on your training manual!

In the north, the dividing line between *IR 729* in position in the Val de Saire area and *IR 919* passed through Belle Croix (included), Crasville (excluded), the Quettehou-Valognes crossroads, Montaigu and Saint-Germain-de-Tournebu.

The regimental HQ was now set up at **Montebourg**; the combat CP was in a quarry northeast of that locality (le Mont). Lieutenant-Colonel Keil placed his 1st Battalion, *I./919*, to the south, the 2nd (*II./919*) in the north of the sector, with *III./919* held in reserve with its CP at Saint-Floxel.

In the south, *I./919* was commanded by Captain Fink, with its CP at Beuzeville-au-Plain and Foucarville. This is the battalion that faced the landings and Keil had no trust in his battalion commander. Captain **Fink** was a young officer in the regular army who had been committed on the Finland Front and fought the partisans. Then he was ill for a long time and sent home. Keil felt he was too inexperienced. In April 1944, he wanted to get rid of him, but refrained on General von Schlieben's advice: *"You're right, but how do you know you will get someone better? The Invasion is coming any time now, at least Fink is familiar with his sector."*

When Keil arrived in the sector in January, little progress had been made on the coastal defenses ; two thirds of them were still at the drawing-board stage. He felt that the work should have commenced a year before, and he encountered all kinds of difficulties. He obtained some, but not enough, concrete from members of the Todt Organization and had to build wooden bunkers in his defensive positions. Also, he thought the distance between defensive casemates should be no more than 1 200 or 1 400 meters at the outside for them to cover each other, otherwise the enemy could pass between them, with nothing but a few narrow minefields to stop him. The distances were in fact anything from 1 200 to 3 000 meters! This meant that each of these defenses was left to fend for itself, and the landing troops just skirted round them, there being no continuous defensive line. The idea of a Wall was one great scam!

Keil only left a skeleton garrison at these coastal strongpoints, with the main body of his troops in "alert units" (*Alarmeinheiten*) to the rear. So there were only about ten men in each defensive position. And the men exhausted themselves planting beach obstacles and "Rommel's asparagus" while the paperwork came in from above. Lieutenant-Colonel Keil's desk was buried under a pile of regulations and orders. His deputy officer, *Oberleutnant* Saul,

GRENADIER REGIMENT 919

6 JUNE 1944

took over these duties to give his commander time to get into the field.

As stated above, the Plain is a low-lying area extending eastwards, its highest point some thirty meters above sea level. In front of it lies a vast sandy beach, then a **dune ridge** up to four meters high, and lastly **a depression** between the dune ridge and the hinterland. This depression is furrowed with numerous streams known as "Tarets", flowing through the dunes into the sea. It was inundated by the Germans. It was 1.5 to 2.5 kilometers wide and so formed quite a considerable obstacle. The **water** was about a meter deep but numerous **ditches** crisscrossing the watery expanse were two to four meters wide and took the depth of the water to two or three meters, making them formidable traps. Also, the **roadways** were under about ten centimeters of water. There were six of them: one heading northwest from Pouppeville (the Americans knew it as **Exit 1**); - another went from Sainte-Marie-du-Mont to La Grande Dune **(Exit 2)**; a third from Audouville-la-Hubert to La Madeleine **(Exit 3)**; a fourth from Saint-Martin-de-Varreville to Les Dunes de Varreville **(Exit 4)**; a fifth from Saint-Germain-de-Varreville to the coast; and one last road went from Ravenoville to Le Grand Hameau des Dunes.

In front of this flooded area were the "Atlantic Wall" defenses. These came in two types of defensive emplacements: - the strongpoints (*Stützpunkter, StP* or *S* for short) which were heavy defensive works, built by the Todt Organization and construction companies (*Bau-Kompanien*). They were designed to hold out isolated in hedgehog formation against an enemy assault, and contained three weeks' supplies. There were four of these *StPs* in this sector: **S9, S12, S16** and **S18**. – Resistance nests (*Widerstandnester, Wn* or *W* for short) which were light defensive works built by the troops and contained a week or a fortnight's supplies.

Captain Fink's 1st Battalion, **I./919**, lined up four companies from Le Grand Vey in the south to Le Grand Hameau des Dunes (Ravenoville) in the north. 1st Company (**1./919**) was commanded by *Oberleutnant* Gluba and based at Sainte-Marie-du-Mont. 2nd Company (*2./919*) was commanded by *Leutnant* Rohweder and based at Pouppeville. **3./919** was commanded by *Oberleutnant* Matz and based at La Madeleine. **4./919** was commanded by *Oberleutnant* Werner and based at Ravenoville.

2./919: W 1, W 2, W 2a, W 3, W 6

These four companies were in charge of about ten defensive emplacements. To the south, at **Le Grand**

Field-Marshal Rommel examines the state of progress with the coastal defenses on the eastern Cotentin peninsula, in the future Utah Beach sector, in the spring of 1944. Here we see various beach obstacles, mostly stakes. (Utah Beach Museum.)

Below: Positioning of IR 919 units on the basis of information supplied by Lieutenant-Colonel Keil. (map by B. Paich/Heimdal.)

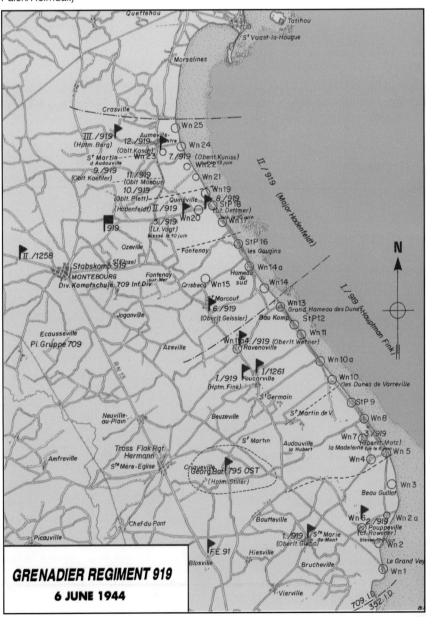

GRENADIER REGIMENT 919
6 JUNE 1944

1

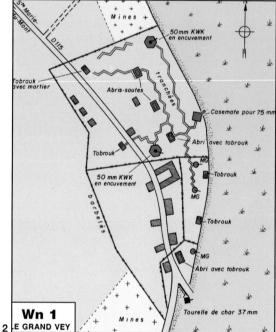

2 LE GRAND VEY

Wn 1

Vey, near Pouppeville, was **W 1** *(100)* controlled by *2./199* under *Leutnant* Rohweder. To the far south of the Banc du Grand Vey, this first link in the defenses of *IR 919*'s sector had to bar access to Carentan canal. The position had two 5 cm *KWK L/42* guns in concrete pits (*Ringstandnester*), a 7.5 cm *FK 235 (b)* gun in a concrete Type H 612 flanker casemate, a *Panzerstellung* R 35 tank turret mounted on a concrete gun stand with its 3.7 cm *KWK 144 (f)* gun capable of firing in every direction, a bunker with a tobruk housing a 50 mm *mle 37* type *Gr. W. 203 (f)* light mortar to the north-west of the position, which enclosed the entire hamlet behind barbed wire. Along with this *Widerstandnest* were four bunkers with tobruks, two ammunition store/shelters and three machine-gun stands. These elements were linked via a trench system.

Further on, before **Pouppeville**, were two emplacements marked 2 and 2a by Keil but actually still under construction (*im Bau*); they are *Wn 101* in the alternative numbering. To the rear, the village where *2./919* under *Leutnant* Rohweder had set up its CP, was placed on the defensive; this was **W 6**.

In the spring of 1944, German soldiers come to fetch water from the pump at Sainte-Marie-du-Mont (1./919's CP) using a water tank belonging to A. Brohier of Sainte-Mère-Eglise. US paratroops would use the same pump a few weeks later, as we shall be seeing further on. (ECPA.)

6

To the north, at **Beau Guillot**, **W 3** (*102*) completed 3
the defensive works covering the mouth of the Vire.
It had a 5cm *KWK L/42* gun and a 4.7 cm *Pak 181
(f)* wheeled antitank gun. Another position of *2./919*
was commanded by *Leutnant* Ritter, one of *Leutnant*
Rohweder's officers.

3./919: W 4, W 5, W 7, W8, StP 9

At **La Madeleine**, **W 4** (*103*) was a resistance nest
located behind the coastal defense emplacement,
W 5 (or *104*) which was soon destined to enter the
history books in this month of May 1944. It was pla-

W1 at Le Grand Vey.

Located at the southern end of the Banc du Grand Vey,
strongpoint W1 was the first link in the chain of German
defenses allocated to *709. ID*, to which Infanterie-Regiment
919 belonged. This "resistance nest" (Widerstandsnest)
was to bar access to the Carentan canal. It had two 5 cm
KwK guns in tobruk pits and a 7.5 cm gun in a casemate.
To the south, a concrete-lined tobruk pit **(photo 1)** overlooking the river mouth. It was topped by a R35 tank turret
armed with a 3.7 cm gun. It can be seen on the site plan
(2) and still in place in this American photograph taken in
1944 **(3).** These two presentday photos **(4 and 5),** taken at
the same spot, show how it covered the slipway down to
the sea. From there **(photo 6),** the Germans controlled the
whole vast estuary of the Vire and the Carentan canal.
(EG/Heimdal : **photos 1, 4, 5, 6.** Plan by B. Paich/Heimdal.
2. Heimdal coll. **3.** ECPAD.)

5

5

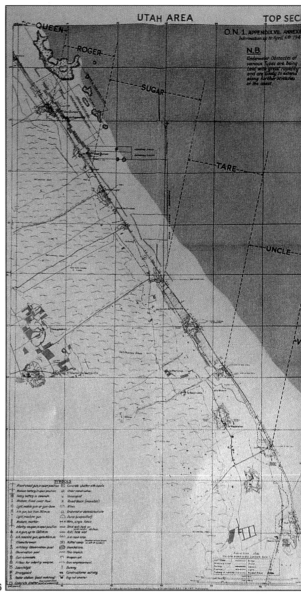

6

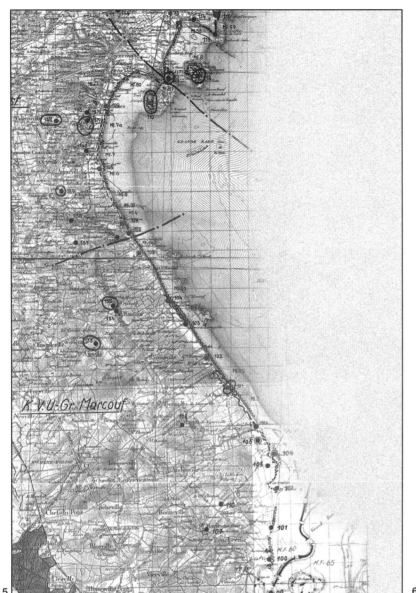

1

2

On around 20 May 1944, at the time of the ceremony at W5 (see following pages), a German war correspondent produced a reportage in the sector, showing how work was far from complete, with D-day just two weeks away. Here we see a minefield **(photo 1)** then soldiers busy setting up anti-glider obstacles **(photos 2** and **3).** A little farther into the dunes, probably near W5, some trenches have been dug **(4).** (ECPA.)

Document 6 : the Americans were thoroughly familiar with the layout of the German positions as can be seen from this "Top Secret" Bigot map of the Utah sector. (B. Paich coll.)

The mystery of the "W" numbering system

Various German documents, including ordnance survey maps of the Küsten-Ver-teidigungs-Gruppen (coastal defense groups) of the Cotentin peninsula and building programs report numbering of "Wn" and "StP" as starting at N° 100 (W1, Grand Vey), as shown in the map reproduced here **(doc. 5)** and counting up from 100. Also on this map, the numbering from 100 starts further up, thus making for some confusion. Lieutenant-Colonel Keil for his part, in his report, numbers the positions starting from Grand Vey, which is his usual numbering, the one he used on 6 June 1944 and which is recorded in history books. It is the method used here, with the other numbering indicated in brackets.

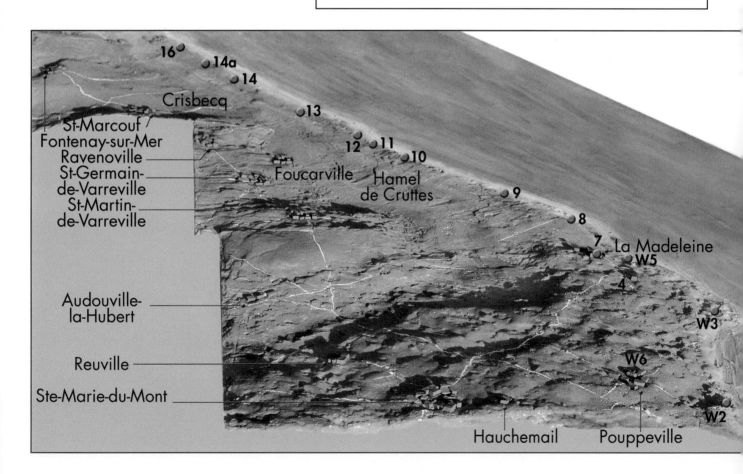

Opposite and below: two views of a Type H 667 casemate for a 5 cm KwK gun on the south side of W5. The embrasure on this casemate, turned southwards, is now completely buried in the sand as the dune has moved since 1944. It is now near the Utah Beach museum. (Photos E. Groult/Heimdal.)

Generalleutnant von Schlieben decorating Leutnant Jahnke. (ECPA.)

W5 on 20 May 1944. On that day, a
fortnight before D-day, a ceremony was held at W5, which was to feel the full blast of the Utah landings. On that day Generalleutnant von Schlieben, commander of *709. Infanterie-Division*, awarded a Knight's Cross of the Iron Cross (Ritterkreuz) to the position's commander, Leutnant Arthur Jahnke. This young officer of 3./919 had won this decoration as commander of the *5th Company*, GR 572, *302. ID* on the eastern front early in 1944. He had fought bravely with the VI Army in the Nikolaievsk area. Here General von Schlieben awards him this prestigious decoration **(photo 1)** then, to the sound of the brass band, the general, accompanied by Leutnant Jahnke, inspects the troops **(2)**. We see Leutnant Janhke with some of his men **(3)** after the ceremony. (ECPA.)

W5

1. The 5 cm KwK tobruk, oto the south of the position, overlooking the Type H 667 casemate seen on the previous page, where a 4.7 cm Pak 181 (f) Mle 37 A antitank gun has been placed. (EG/Heimdal.)

2. The other 5 cm gun tobruk still houses a 5 cm KwK gun. (EG/Heimdal.)

3. Between these two tobruks, a Type H 67 (Panzerstellung) concrete gun stand still carries its early model FT 17 tank turret for a machine-gun. Despite the bombing on 6 June 1944, the position is still fairly well preserved. (EG/Heimdal.)

ced under *2./919*, commander *Oberleutnant* Matz, and *Leutnant* Jahnke was the man in charge. It was protected on its seaward side by a concrete antitank wall on which stood a concrete Type H 667 casemate housing a 5 cm *KWK L/42* gun. To the rear, connected by a trench system, were two hardstandings (*Ringstände*) each with a 5 cm *KwK L/42* gun, a Type H67 tobruk for FT 17 tank turret with a 3.7 cm gun, three Type H 69 machine-gun tobruks, a Type H 206 bunker for a 5 cm *Gr.W 278 (f)* mortar, a 4.7 cm *Pak 181 (f)* antitank gun, two Type H 134 ammunition stores, four Type H 702 bunkers, a Type H 501 bunker, and MG positions. To the north of the site, a house was kept within the defensive perimeter. As we shall see, this "red chalet" was used as a landmark on several photos taken on 6 June 1944. *W5/104* was surrounded by barbed wire and covered to the rear by a large minefield. This defensive position, which made history when it took the brunt of the D-day assault, was commanded by a young officer who had won the *Ritterkreuz*, the prestigious Knight's Cross only recently awarded to him at this very position. An appointment with destiny! In fact, *Leutnant* Arthur **Jahnke** had earned his decoration as 5th Company commander with *Grenadier-Regiment 572, 302. ID* on the Eastern front early in 1944. He had fought with bravery with the VI Army in the Nikolaievsk area. His decoration was handed to him by *Generalleutnant* von Schlieben in a ceremony held at *Wn 5* on 20 May 1944, just over a fortnight before D-day! A war correspondent shot a reportage which we still have. To the rear, at the crossroads, **W 4** was still *"im Bau"*.

The *3./919* commander's CP was somewhat to the rear, in the village of La Madeleine where *Oberleutnant* Matz set it up in **W 7** (*Wn 105*). A little further on, to the north-east, on the coast where the Audouville-la-Hubert road comes out, **W 8** (*Wn 106*) was set up at the place named La Redoute d'Audouville.

1

Below: Leutnant Arthur Jahnke was commander of W5. This photo was taken on 20 May 1944. Two weeks later, all hell was let loose on him and his men. (ECPA.)

2

3

6

7

5

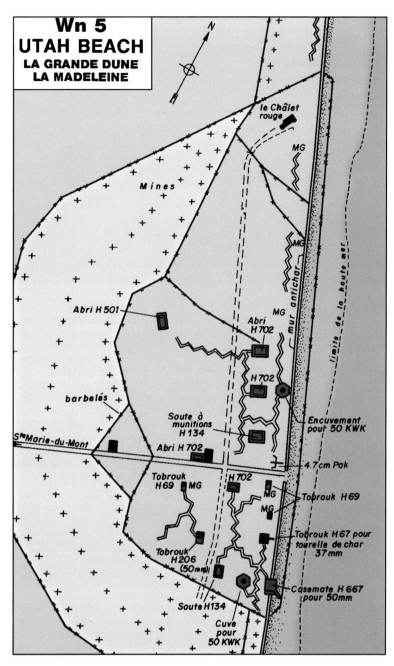

**Wn 5
UTAH BEACH
LA GRANDE DUNE
LA MADELEINE**

N

le Châlet rouge

Mines

MG

MG

MG

Abri H 501

Abri H 702

H 702

barbelés

Soute à munitions H 134

mur antichar

Encuvement pour 50 KWK

limite de la haute mer

Abri H 702

Ste-Marie-du-Mont

H 702

4.7 cm Pak

Tobrouk H 69 MG

MG

MG

Tobrouk H 69

Tobrouk H 67 pour tourelle de char 37 mm

Tobrouk H 206 (50mm)

Casemate H 667 pour 50mm

Soute H134

Cuve pour 50 KWK

4. West of the position stood a Type H 501 shelter.

5. Type H 134 ammunition store allocated to the two guns already seen to the south of the position; today it is a public toilet.

6. This inscription is visible to this day.

7. MG tobruk, with actual barbed wire fence post, part of the position's close defenses. (Photos courtesy E. Groult/Heimdal.)

4

1

against shells from the sea. The casemate on the south side had its embrasure protected by a concrete shoulder facing south towards the mouth of the Vire. An 8.8 cm gun had a maximum range of 15 kilometers. In the middle of the sea front, a tank turret armed with a 3.7 cm *KwK 144 (f)* was mounted on a *Panzerstellung* (fixed tank position) on a concrete pit. It had a tunnel leading to a shelter in the rear. Another similar turret was placed at the position's south-east corner, with a the north-east corner defended by a third. Lastly, two more turrets were spaced behind the position, with 360° firing capacity for close defense. So this strongpoint had five tank turrets defending it, three on the sea front and two to the rear. Towards the north of the emplacement, a 5 cm M 19 mortar under an armored bell was mounted on a Type H 633 bunker also with an MG tobruk. Also there were two observation posts to the north, away from the sea front, plus a 150 cm searchlight in a concrete bunker to the south. Three MG tobruks and various bunkers completed this strongpoint with theoretically enough supplies to hold out for three weeks.

4./199: W 10, W 10a, W 11, W 11a, S 12, W 13

After Saint-Martin-de-Varreville, we come to the coastal sector controlled by *4./919* under *Oberleutnant* Werner with its HQ **(W 11 a)** based at **Ravenoville**. The first position was **W 10** (*101*) at Les Dunes de Varreville (north). This was another strong position. South of the sea front stood two Type H 677 and SK casemates for 4.7 cm *Skoda 36 (t)* guns covering the

It too had the protection of a concrete antitank wall facing out to sea, and this wall extended along most of the beach sector from Le Grand Vey to Saint-Vaast-la-Hougue. This *Wn*, built around an old redoubt, in which an ammunition store and two MG tobruks were erected, had two tobruks with 5cm *KwK L/42* guns, two round observation posts (one at either end), a concrete casemate housing a 4.7 cm *Pak 1981 (f)* antitank gun, a Type H 612 casemate with a 7.7 cm gun, a 5 cm *Gr.W. 203 (f)* mortar tobruk, three bunkers, two of which had MG tobruks, and four machine-gun positions. This *Wn*, which unusually had two round observation posts, was protected behind various minefields.

To the south of **Les Dunes de Varreville**, one of the most powerful strongpoints in the entire sector was built, a *Stützpunkt*, **StP 9** (or *W 100*). Up against a concrete antitank wall overlooking the beach, its perimeter was a huge polygon surrounded by an antitank ditch and flanked by minefields on either side. On the seaward antitank wall were two Type H 677 casemates each housing an 8.8 cm *Pak 43/41*. Like any other coastal casemate, these two were positioned so as to enfilade the beaches. The embrasure of the northernmost one was aimed northwards to sweep across the beach towards Saint-Vaast. Its aperture was protected by a concrete shoulder

4

3

W8 - The Audouville redoubt

This position was defended by the men of 3./919, commander Lieutenant Matz, and was just north of the D-day landing sector. In fact, had the landing craft not drifted off course on D-day, the assault should have taken place opposite this W8 and opposite the position a little further north, S9, which we shall be seeing in following pages.

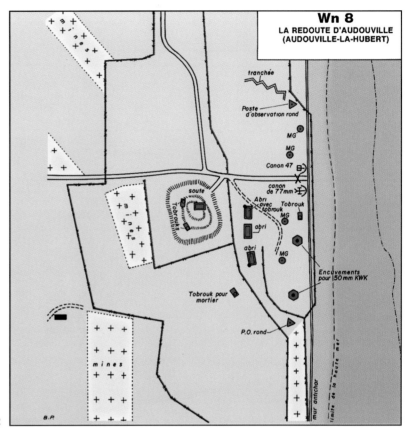

Wn 8
LA REDOUTE D'AUDOUVILLE
(AUDOUVILLE-LA-HUBERT)

tranchée

Poste d'observation rond

MG

MG

Canon 47

canon de 77mm

soute

Tobruk

Abri avec tobrouk

Tobrouk

MG

abri

MG

abri

Encavements pour 150 mm KWK

Tobrouk pour mortier

P.O. rond

mines

mur antichar

limite de la haute mer

B.P.

1 and 2. One of the two 5 cm KwK gun tobruks overlooking the beach. On the second photo, to the rear, a small concrete MG position (see plan) and the corner of the shelter we shall be seeing in photo "5".

3. One of the two shelters with MG tobruk pit, the northernmost one.

4. Embrasure for machine-gun covering the entrance to the shelter.

5. The other, southernmost one, with tobruk. (Photos courtesy EG/Heimdal.)

6. Example of everyday life in a personnel shelter. (BA.)

7. This position had two observation posts. (B. Paich/Heimdal.)

Observation Post

P.O. SUR LE TERRAIN (ENTERRÉ)

0.5

2.18

1.45

1.95

2.75

Coupe A-B

0.6

A

B

0   1   2

Vue en plan

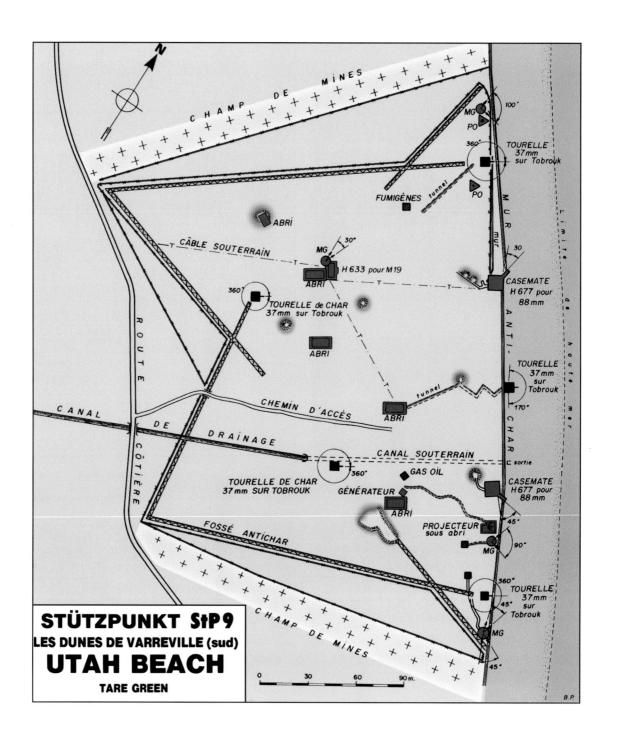

CHAMP DE MINES

MG
PO
TOURELLE
37mm
sur Tobrouk
100°
360°
FUMIGÈNES
PO
tunnel

ABRI

CÂBLE SOUTERRAIN

MG
30°
ABRI
H 633 pour M19

TOURELLE de CHAR
37mm sur Tobrouk
360°

ABRI

ROUTE CÔTIÈRE

CANAL DE DRAINAGE

CHEMIN D'ACCÈS

tunnel

ABRI

CANAL SOUTERRAIN

TOURELLE DE CHAR
37mm SUR TOBROUK
360°

GAS OÏL

GÉNÉRATEUR

ABRI

FOSSÉ ANTICHAR

MUR ANTI-CHAR

mur

CASEMATE
H 677 pour
88 mm
30

TOURELLE
37mm
sur
Tobrouk
170°

sortie

CASEMATE
H 677 pour
88 mm

PROJECTEUR
sous abri
45°

MG
90°

TOURELLE
37mm
sur
Tobrouk
360°
45°

MG
45°

Limite de haute mer

CHAMP DE MINES

STÜTZPUNKT StP 9
LES DUNES DE VARREVILLE (sud)
UTAH BEACH
TARE GREEN

0   30   60   90 m.

B.P.

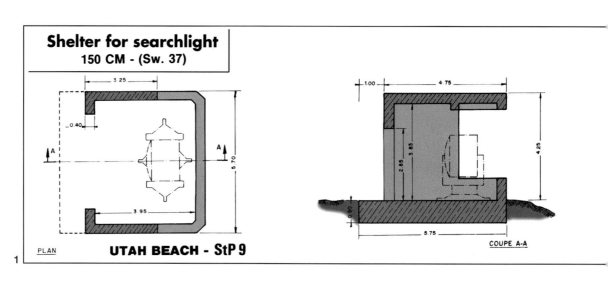

Shelter for searchlight
150 CM - (Sw. 37)

3 25
0.40
5.70
3 95

A   A

PLAN

1.00   4.75
2.85
3.85
4.25
0.90
5.75

COUPE A-A

UTAH BEACH - StP 9

1

18

2 Type H 653 shelter:

2. The rear of the shelter shortly after the battle with its masked emplacement with flanking wall on the right. (NA/Heimdal.)

3. The site has changed little although the armored cupola was reinforced after the war. (B. Paich.)

4. Plan of this shelter. (BP/ Heimdal.)

S9, Dunes de Varreville.

Here is another position, one of the biggest in the sector, a strongpoint (Stützpunkt). It is also one of the two positions that should have taken the brunt of the D-day assault. We find the usual personnel shelters, MG tobruks, bunkers with tank turret and also (document 1, B.P./Heimdal.) a light shelter for a searchlight and a Type H 633 shelter for M19 mortar, something of a rarity on the Normandy coast.

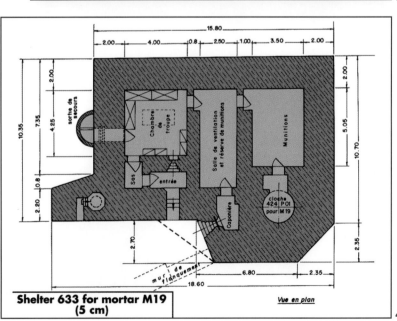

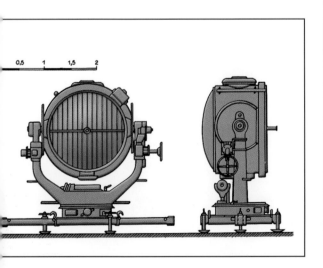

Shelter 633 for mortar M19 (5 cm)

Vue en plan

S9, Dunes de Varreville

This strongpoint also had two powerful Type H 677 casemates, each housing a potent 8.8 cm Pak 43/11 gun.

1. This rare color photo was taken from inside the casemate facing south, enfilading Utah Beach. (A. Chazette coll.)

2. The same casemate. (NA.)

3. Photo showing the inside of the casemate facing north with its 8.8 cm gun in position. (NA.)

4. The same casemate, outside view. (NA.)

2

3

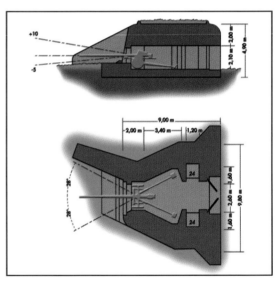

W10, Dunes de Varreville, north

Slightly further north, this was a relatively powerful position. To the south, two casemates (photo 5) housing 4.7 cm Skoda 36 (t) guns are aimed southwards to sweep the beach and cross fire with the northernmost casemate of S9. Saint-Vast-la-Hougue can be seen in the distance. (EG/Heimdal.)

4

beach towards the south. At the other end, a Type H 677 casemate armed with an 8.8 cm *Pak 43/41* flanked the beach to the north. Also on the sea front were two Panzerstellung 3.7 cm *KwK 144 (f)* tank turrets. Then there were two tobruks for 5 cm *KwK L/42* guns, one on the sea front, the other to the rear, and two Type Vf 69 double tobruks for MG and 8.14 cm *Gr.W 34* mortar. On the sea front, there was a 4.7 cm *Pak 181 (f)* gun in an open unconcreted emplacement. In addition to these defensive works, there were numerous MG tobruks, bunkers, ammunition stores, a kitchen, four observation posts and a number of automatic flame-throwers along the boundary fence. To complete the disposition, further north, in the sand dunes, was **W 10a**, a lighter position but which had a flanker casemate.

After Saint-Germain-de-Varreville, the roadway from Foucarville leads to **Hamel-Mauger** and Hamel des Cruttes and **W 11** (*102*) which had a tobruk for a 5 cm KwK L/42 gun, two tank turrets with 3.7 cm guns built into the concrete antitank wall, a double hardstanding (*Ringstand*) for 8.14 cm *Gr.W. 34* mortar and machine-gun, a bunker with tobruk, two machine-gun positions and various shelters and ammunition stores. In front of the position there were barbed wire and minefields.

S 12 was set up a short distance to the north, at « chalet de Ravenoville », south of Petit Hameau des Dunes. This strongpoint was small but defended on the seaward side by two flanker casemates and three tobruks leaning up against the antitank wall and each topped with a tank turret containing a 3.7 cm gun. The flanker casemate facing south was derived from the H 667 type, for a 5 cm gun and two MG tobruks. The casemate facing north was even more original, being a Type H 612 for 8.8 cm *43/41* gun with a 60 cm searchlight on the roof. Within the defensive area,

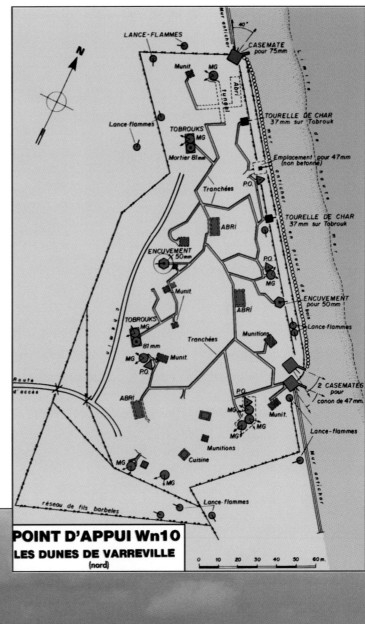

POINT D'APPUI Wn10
LES DUNES DE VARREVILLE
(nord)

5

W10

4. One of the shelters located south of the position. (EG/Heimdal.)

5. A simple close defense MG tobruk west of the position. The fields visible in the background were inundated in 1944. (EG/ Heimdal.)

6. The double tobruk west of the position, the one on the right for a machine-gun, the one on the left for a mortar. (EG/Heimdal.)

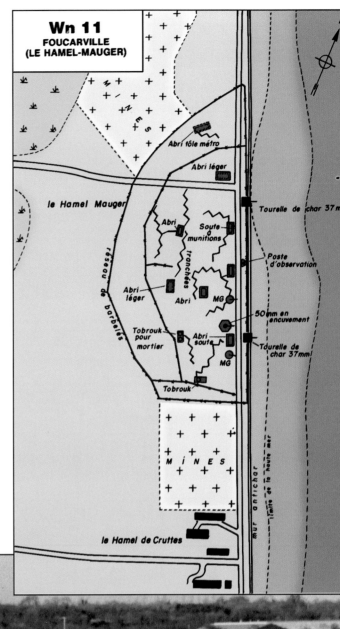

W 10, Dunes de Varreville (north)

This position had relatively strong firepower but the guns were arranged in such a way as to be vulnerable from the rear, which may explain how American troops had captured the strongpoint by D-day evening. **1.** and **2.** Comparative view, the Type H 677 flanking casemate armed with a 8.8 cm Pak 43/41 gun extended northwards by an antitank wall is now completely cleared of sand. (A. Chazette and DR.) South of the position, we see a number of MG nests and an observation post **(3)**, notice the second 4.7 cm gun casemate in the background on the left.

23

S12, Ravenoville.

1. Facing the sea and the Saint-Marcouf Islands, this concrete pillbox carried a tank turret with a 3.7 cm gun. (EG/Heimdal.)

2 and **3.** Site plan and aerial view taken by the Allies showing how work was progressing. We see very clearly the anti-tank ditches, one of the tank turrets, and the Type H 644 shelter. Detailed documents such as this were used to draw the Bigot maps. (B.P./ Heimdal. and Heimdal coll.)

4. Type H 644 shelter, rather rare in Normandy, with the armored bell-shaped cone with six

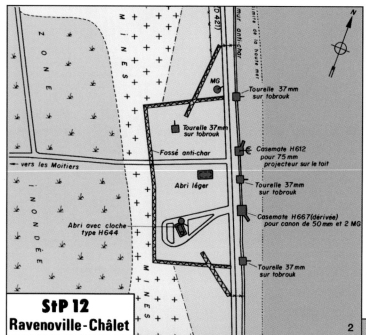

MG

Tourelle 37mm
sur tobruk

Tourelle 37mm
sur tobruk

Fossé anti-char

Casemate H612
pour 75 mm
projecteur sur le toit

Abri léger

Tourelle 37mm
sur tobruk

Abri avec cloche
type H644

Casemate H667(dérivée)
pour canon de 50 mm et 2 MG

Tourelle 37mm
sur tobruk

vers les Moitiers

**StP 12
Ravenoville-Châlet**

2

ther was also a tobruk with a tank turret armed with a 3.7 cm gun and a Type H 644 bunker with armored bell dome with six apertures for two machine-guns. This position extended northwards with a light gun emplacement set around Petit Hameau des Dunes.

The sector held by *4./919* ended with **W 13**, at Grand Hameau des Dunes.

6./919: W 14, W 14a, StP 16

North of Ravenoville and Grand Hameau des Dunes, we enter the sector held by the 2nd Battalion **(II./919)** placed under the command of Major **Hadenfeldt**, who set up his CP at Octeville-l'Avenel. The sector's first company was **6./919** under *Oberleutnant* Geissler, who set up his CP at Saint-Marcouf. It was in charge of three defensive coastal batteries. The first of these, **W 14** (*104*) was at Chalet de Gouville and included an old fort south of the position. It had chiefly one very unusual SK (*Sonderkonstruktion*) case-

embrasures reinforced, is still visible south-west of the position. (EG/ Heimdal.) Here we see a detail **(5)** of the cone shortly after the battle showing numerous impacts (US Army), and a plan **(6)** of this shelter. (BP/Heimdal.)

7. Type H 612 casemate, located north of the position; in 1944 it had a searchlight on the roof. (SHM.)

4

3

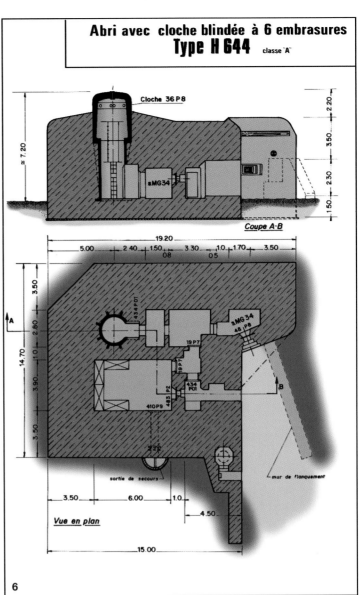

Abri avec cloche blindée à 6 embrasures
Type H 644 classe "A"

Cloche 36 P 8

sMG34

Coupe A-B

≈ 7.20 · 2.20 · 3.50 · 2.30 · 1.50

19.20
5.00 · 2.40 · 1.50 · 08 · 3.30 · 0.5 · 1.70 · 3.50

3.50
2.80
14.70
1.0
3.90
3.50

434 P01
19 P7
sMG 34
49 P8
19 P7
434 P01
48.5 P2
410 P9

232
sortie de secours
mur de flanquement

Vue en plan

3.50 · 6.00 · 1.0 · 4.50

15.00

6

5

7

8. This Type H 667 case-mate for a 5 cm KwK L/42 gun has an odd design, with a machine-gun embrasure in the basement. It is aimed southwards. (BP/Heim-dal.)

8

25

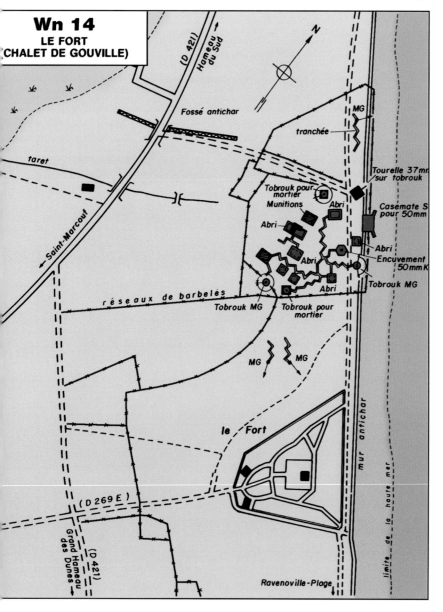

mate, a special construction that did not take the standardized Type H plans into account. This casemate had a double embrasure for 5 cm *KwK L/42* guns. It also lined up a tobruk for 5 cm *KwK L/42* gun, a tobruk for a tank turret with a 3.7 cm gun, two 5 cm *Gr.W* mortar tobruks, two MG tobruks, shelters and ammunition stores. A light position stood nearby, **W 14a.**

Moving up north, and passing through Crisbecq and Saint-Marcouf (with its battery), along the sea front, we come fo the old fort of Saint-Marcouf, at Hameau du Nord and **Les Gougins** where **StP 16** was built. This heavy gun emplacement had two Type H 671 flanker casemates containing 8.8 cm *Pak 43/47* guns, a Type H 634 bunker surmounted with an armored bell dome for two (*s.MG 34*) machine-guns, four tank turrets, a 60 cm searchlight and several shelters.

8./919 and 5./919: W 17, StP 18, W 19, W 20

We now come to the sector of *8./919* commanded by *Leutnant* Dettmer, who set up his CP west of Quinéville. To the rear was *5./919* commanded by *Leutnant* Vogt (who was wounded on 10 June). On the dunes at Fontenay stood **W 17** (*106*) with two tobruks for 5 cm *KwK L/42* guns, 8.14 cm mortar and MG tobruks. At **Quinéville**, at the mouth of the Sinope, **StP 18** was protected by a powerful concrete anti-tank wall with firing slits, reinforced by a Type H 612 casemate camouflaged to look like a house and carrying a horse-drawn 76.2 cm *FK* gun, Somua tank turrets armed with a 3.7 cm *KwK*, a 150 cm searchlight, and a Type H 621 bunker. On the other bank of the Sinope, to the north overlooking the river mouth, the old **Lestre fort** had been converted into **W 19** (*107*). Two tobruks for 5 cm *KwK L/42* guns, others for 8.14 cm (*Vf 69*) and for (*Vf 58 c*) MG were set up, along with a few shelters. To the east, on the high ground where the church at Quinéville stood, **W 20** (*136*) comprised two Type H 680 casemates containing 7.5 cm *Pak 40* guns covering the sector, and a bunker.

III./919: W 21, W 22, W 23, W 24, W 25

Further on, we come to a narrow section where the 3rd Battalion **(III./919)**, commanded by Captain **Berg**, was held in reserve. Here he concentrated four infantry companies, *9./919* (*Oberleutnant* Kaehler), *10./919* (*Oberleutnant* Plett), *11./919* (*Oberleutnant* Moebius), *12./919* (*Oberleutnant* Kasch). These four companies controlled *W 21, 22, 23, 24* and *25*. Beyond, it was *Regiment 729*.

IR 919 also had support from its heavy companies:
- **13./919** (*Oberleutnant* Schön) with two platoons in position north of Audouville-la-Hubert, with four 76.2 mm infantry guns to monitor the coast. Its third platoon (*Leutnant* Saturnus) was at Cauvin (commune of Brucheville) with two 76.2 mm guns covering the Baie des Veys (the Vire estuary) and Carentan canal.
- **14./919** (antitank company) put some of its platoons in this sector, i.e a standard platoon (with an extra antitank gun) spread over the high ground at the Audouville-la-Hubert crossroads, one on the coast road from Saint-Germain-de-Varreville, another on the coast road from Ravenoville (2).

Soldiers from the Caucasus

On 11 May 1944, Field-Marshal Rommel, whom Hitler appointed inspector general of the coastal defenses in November 1943, ended a tour of ins-

S18, Quinéville

1. Here we see, to the east of this position, an R 35 tank turret mounted on a Ringstand to cover the beach. (NA.)

2 and **3, 4, 5.** A Type H 612 casemate camouflaged as a house, flanking the position on the northern side - in 1944, today, embrasure and rear, location model. (**2** : ECPA, **3, 4, 5**: Heimdal).

pection in the Cotentin peninsula. On taking over, he realized that the much-vaunted *Atlantikwall* of the propaganda was just so much wool over the eyes. Apart from the coastal artillery batteries (particularly in the Pas-de-Calais) and the ports, which were relatively well fortified, the rest was mostly made up of field positions - trenches and log shelters, with

(2) All this invaluable information regarding IR 919 is taken from the detailed report drawn up by Günther Keil in captivity on his regiment's action in the battle of 1944. MS. C. 018. (Bundesarchiv Freiburg.)

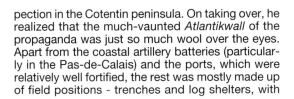

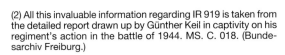

6. Firing slits through the antitank wall. (EG/Heimdal.)

7. Another flanking casemate with embrasure in the anti-tank wall – but at the defensive point at Saint-Marcouf/Les Gougins.

concrete casemates still few and far between. He then launched a program with just about everything still to do. Concrete was frantically mixed, he had obstacles set up on the beaches and others to prevent gliders from landing (the famous "Rommel's asparagus"). But things had gotten so behindhand that, as Lieutenant-Colonel Keil stated for his own sector, the program required months more work; this was in May 1944, with D-day less than a month away.

On that day, **11 May**, at the soldiers' home at Urville-Hague, west of Cherbourg, in the presence of Seventh Army commander *Generaloberst* Dollmann and *General der Artillerie* Erich Marcks (commander of *LXXXIV. A.K.,* the corps controlling German troops in western Normandy), Rommel reported what he seen on his visit. The details of what was said at that meeting remained secret; the two generals in command of the divisions then stationed in the Cotentin (*243. ID* and *709. ID*) did not attend. However, after this conference, Generals Hellmich and von Schlieben were informed of the decisions taken by their superiors and of the modifications to their disposition.

Generalleutnant **Hellmich**, commander of *243. Infanterie-Division*, stationed on the west coast of the Cotentin, had had an unusual career for a general officer. Born in Karlsruhe on 9 June 1890 and commissioned as a lieutenant with the infantry on 22 March 1910, he rose up through the ranks, taking over command of *23. ID* on 1 June 1940. The division (which had returned to the traditions of the Prussian Imperial Guard) was wiped out before Moscow during the winter of 1941-1942. Heinz Hellmich had a nervous breakdown and was sent home to Germany, his career at an end. But on 15 December

1. *Field-Marshal* Rommel on a tour of inspection of the Cotentin on 10 and 11 May 1944, less than a month before D-day. This was his second inspection of the sector since the start of the year. He examines a map handed to him by an officer. On the left (wearing a mountain cap), corps commander General Marcks. General von Schlieben is on the far right.

3

1

1942, he became a *General der Osttruppen* (General of the Eastern troops) supervising training of volunteers enlisted from among Soviet citizens (POWs or volunteers, whether Russian or members of one of the national minorities). On 10 January 1944, he received a new command with a fighting unit ; he arrived in the Cotentin peninsula and became *Kommandeur* of *243. ID*. There he came across soldiers he already knew well, as his division had several *Osttruppen* battalions, including *Ost-Bataillon 561* (in position in the Cap de Flamanville sector) and *Ost-Bataillon 795* (in position in the Cap de la Hague sector), this last

battalion being made up of Georgian – Caucasian – volunteers.

Georgia was then a republic in the western Caucasus and part of the USSR. The Caucasus, with its many valleys, was peopled with a mosaic of different ethnic groups, all with their own languages, cultures and religions. There were often very marked antagonisms between them. These have now come to the fore with the current Chechnya crisis. Muslims live alongside Armenian Catholics or orthodox Catholics, including **Georgians**. Even in Georgia, there a range of different peoples: Adjarians, Gurians, Imeretins, Kakhetins, Laz, Mingrelians, Svans and south Ossetians. They speak Georgian but are orthodox like the Russians. The then Soviet head of state, Josef Dzhugashvili, aka "Stalin", was himself a Georgian. In 1942, Georgia rose up against the central Soviet power. Many Georgians were liquidated in the ensuing repression, including the philosopher Tsereteli, the orientalist A. Tsereteli, the economist Akhmeteli, the poets Javakhishvili, Iashvili, Tabidze, Tombili, the literary critic Kochishvili and many more. This is how thousands of Georgians came to join the Germans as volunteers, thinking they would help them to free their country.

As of the summer of 1941, when the German army invaded the USSR, the front line troops recruited volunteers from among Soviet citizens. At first, Hitler was hostile to such local initiatives, but gradually the *Osttruppen* were raised. The Germans recruited over a million volunteers in this way, during the war years. Not only did they come from a variety of backgrounds, they all had very different motivations as well.

Soon after the invasion of the USSR, a **Georgian Legion** was set up to muster volunteers from that republic ; their distinguishing badge was a red shield with a white stripe and a black stripe in the top left canton, with the inscription "*Georgien*" woven along the top of the badge. Two Georgian battalions were raised at Kruszyna late in the fall of 1942: the **795th** and 796th. There were more to follow early in 1943: battalions 797, 798, 799 and 822, then battalions 823 and 824 in the second half of the year, with another five battalions raised elsewhere. Thus, by the end of 1943, a total fourteen Georgian battalions, totalling

2. Georgia lies along the western flank of the Caucasus. The republic was then part of the USSR, and supplied fourteen battalions of volunteers for the German army: they were recruited from POW camps. One of those battalions, the 795th, had to face the American assault. (BP/Heimdal.)

some 14 000 men, had been raised by the Germans. These battalions were not brought together into a "Georgian division" but spread throughout the German army. Thus, on that 11 May, *Georgische Bataillon 795* was attached to *243. ID* under General Hellmich. This was the first battalion raised. Its commander was Captain **Stiller**, a German who had led his men ever since the unit was formed and so had won their confidence. The unit had three combat companies and a heavy machine-gun company commanded by a lieutenant who had previously been a staff officer in the Russian army. The German propaganda services provided these men with a newspaper in Georgian: "*Sakharthvelo*" (meaning "Georgia").

Following the **11 May** meeting, reinforcements arrived. First came *91. (LL) Infanterie-Division*, presented at the beginning of this chapter, and which took up position in the center of the peninsula as of **14 May**. Lastly came **Ost-Bataillon 795** to reinforce *Infanterie-Regiment 919*'s disposition in the Plain, which pleased Lieutenant-Colonel Keil. This battalion was placed around the village of **Turqueville**, between Sainte-Mère-Eglise and Sainte-Marie-du-Mont, right in the middle of what would soon be the airborne bridgehead! This battalion was in place sometime in mid-May, three weeks before D-day…

Artillery and heavy units

While the coastal defensive positions only had light ordnance, mostly 3.7 cm, 5 cm (plenty of these), 7.7 cm and 8.8 cm guns, the coastal artillery was spread back off the coast, between the main highway and the inundated low ground. Three powerful coastal artillery batteries watched over the sea between La Baie des Veys and Val de Saire. They belonged to **Heeres-Küsten-Artillerie-Regiment 1261** (*HKAR 1261* for short), an artillery regiment with eight batteries placed along the east coast of the Cotentin. Its commander was *Oberst* Triepel and it lined up three battalions from south to north.

3. General Hellmich, commander of *243. ID*, on a general inspection of Ost-Bataillon 795 on the west coast of the Cotentin (at Les Asselins near Digulleville), in La Hague before this Georgian battalion's transfer to the east coast as of 14 May 1944. This general was an Eastern troops specialist. Here he is examining a Soviet machine-gun, a 7.62 mm MG 216 (r) made from 1940 to 1943. (BHVP.)

4. A Georgian sergeant and platoon commander with the battalion. They are wearing German decorations awarded to Eastern troops, proof that they have already seen action. (BHVP).

On this map of the units positioned in the eastern Cotentin on the eve of D-Day, the units of 709. ID (mainly IR 919) are shown in blue, as is the "second line of defense" backing up against the marshes. In red are the coastal artillery batteries of HKAR 1261. Marked in green are the units of 91. ID and its attached units (Pz. Abt. 100, FSR6). All units marked in green arrived just three weeks before D-day. (Map by BP/ Heimdal.)

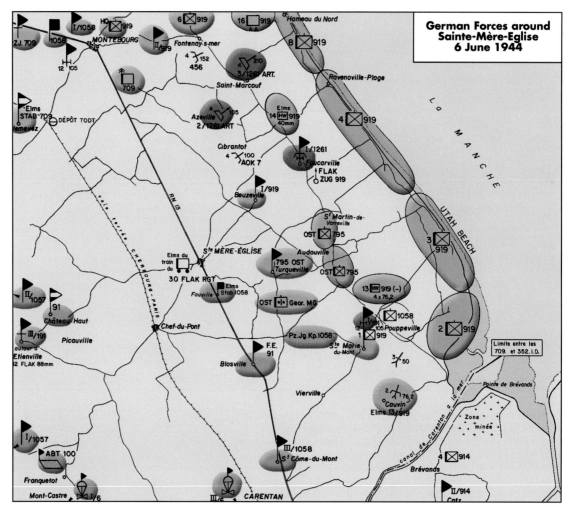

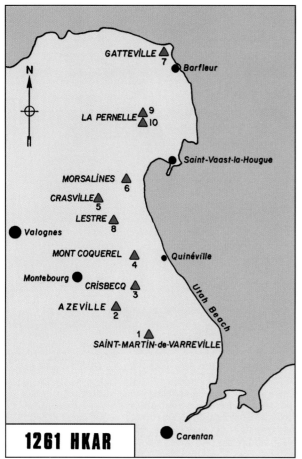

1. On this other photo from a reportage by French photographer Zucca during a general inspection of Ost-Bataillon 795 by General Hellmich in La Hague, we see a second-lieutenant from this unit using a binocular telescope. Notice his "Georgien" shoulder flash. (BHVP.)

2. Shoulder flash worn by Georgian volunteers on their right sleeve.

3. This Georgian staff lieutenant commanding the battalion's machine-gun company poses proudly for Zucca's photograph; we find him a few weeks later as a prisoner of the Americans! (BHVP.)

To the south, we come first to the **Saint-Martin-de-Varreville** battery, **1./1261**. It was set up in this locality back in 1941. It was then mobile and changed emplacements several times over. In May 1944, its commander was *Oberleutnant* **Erben** and it had four Russian 12.2 cm *K 390 (r)* guns. It became a static unit positioned at a height of 25 meters at the hamlet of La Croix aux Berlots, to the west of the village. Tobruks were built for the guns and also various concrete constructions - two personnel bunkers, a garage, nine bunkers for active or defensive purposes. Behind the four tobruks, some Type H 669 casemates were under construction but were never finished. The Americans were worried about this bat-

tery, thinking it had 150 mm guns, and during the night of 28 to 29 May 1944, sixty-four RAF Lancaster bombers dropped several hundred tons of 500 kg bombs on the site; the village was not badly hit. The Americans planned to attack the position during the D-day assault: a massive bombing raid by RAF Bomber Command was scheduled, to be followed by an American attack by Lieutenant-Colonel Robert G. Cole's parachute battalion at a place called Les Mézières (the hamlet slightly further west). Northeast of this battery was **I./1261's** CP at **Foucarville**, near Captain Fink 's own command post (*I./919*).

Moving up nord-eastwards, we come to **Azeville** where the second battery was, **2./1261**, under the command of *Leutnant* **Kattnig**. The four French Schneider 10.5 cm *K331 (f)* guns were set on either side of the D 269 road from Azeville village to Saint-Marcouf. They were placed in two different types of concrete casemate. On the south side of the road, two guns were inside Type H 671 casemates with a 120° aperture Todt front (naval type). On the north side of the road, the other two Schneider 105 mm guns were set in imposing Type H 650 casemates along with a shell store, a cartridge store and a room for the men. These two casemates were also topped by a tobruk for 3.7 cm *Flak 36* AA guns. These four casemates, covered with camouflage paint (which fooled nobody…) imitating stonework, were linked by a concrete tunnel system and two Type H 132

Oberst Gerhard Triepel commanded the coastal artillery regiment *HKAR* 1261 in position on the east coast of the Cotentin; he was promoted to *Generalmajor*.

Azeville Battery

1. The battery had two types of casemate to house its 10.5 cm K 331 (f) guns. Here we see one of the guns still in place, after the battle in one of the two imposing Type H 650 casemates topped by a Flak gun pit. (SHM.)

2. The same casemate today. (EG/Heimdal.)

3. These casemates were camouflaged as houses. He we see the remains of this disguise around a caponière to the rear of a Type H 650 casemate. (EG/Heimdal.)

4. These casemates, their shelters and ammunition stores were linked together by concrete underground passages. (EG/Heimdal.)

of the threat from the air, they were gradually housed in huge Type H 683 casemates. On the eve of D-day, just two (of the planned four) of these Type H 683 casemates had been completed, along with the Type M 272 casemate (for the 15 cm *SKL/45* gun). Also two control bunkers (one for the battery, the other for the Azeville *HKB*) were ready. The Saint-

bunkers, a Type H 621 shelter, a Nissen hut and an MG tobruk. This Azeville *HKB* also had two observation posts, a factory shelter, and two water tanks. Its control bunker was to the front, along with the Saint-Marcouf battery control bunker we come to now.

The 3rd Battery **(3./1261)** was set up ahead of the Azeville Battery, north of the village of **Saint-Marcouf** and west of the hamlet of Crisbecq, hence the names "*Batterie Marcouf*" for the Germans and "Crisbecq Battery" for the Americans. It was commanded by *Oberleutnant zur See* Walter **Ohmsen**. It was in fact a naval battery attached to this land army unit, the artillerymen were sailors and their commander was a lieutenant junior grade. Ohmsen, a workman's son, was born on 7 June 1911 at Elmshorn (near the Danish border). He had four powerful Czech-made guns, 210 mm (21 cm K *39/40 L/52*) Skodas with a range of 27 kilometers, and a 150 mm gun. Initially these guns were placed in tobruks. But on account

6. Example of camouflage on the northernmost Type H 650 casemate: notice the water tank in the foreground. As can be seen in the above photo, the camouflage has washed off except for parts out of the rain. (NA.)

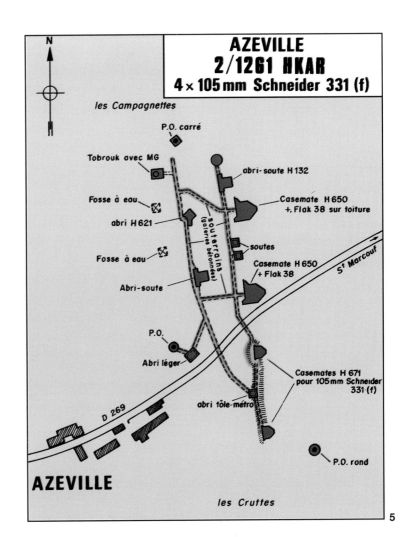

**AZEVILLE
2/1261 HKAR**
4 × 105mm Schneider 331 (f)

N

les Campagnettes

P.O. carré

Tobrouk avec MG

abri-soute H 132

Fosse à eau

Casemate H 650
+ Flak 38 sur toiture

abri H 621

souterrains
(galeries bétonnées)

soutes

Fosse à eau

Casemate H 650
+ Flak 38

St Marcouf

Abri-soute

P.O.

Abri léger

Casemates H 671
pour 105mm Schneider
331 (f)

abri tôle-métro

D 269

P.O. rond

AZEVILLE

les Cruttes

5. This site plan plainly shows the distribution of the two types of casemate. (Plan by B. Paich/Heimdal.)

1. Perspective view of the two Type H 650 casemates. Notice the traces of camouflage still visible in the embrasure. (EG/Heimdal.)

2. Plan and cross section of a large Type H 650 casemate. (B. Paich/Heimdal.)

3. Painted decor of a dummy house on the side of one of these casemates, photo taken after the battle. Notice the flak gun emplacement. (NA.)

4. The underground sections looked like this. (EG/Heimdal.)

5 and **6.** The two Type H 671 casemates, south of the position, photographed after the battle. Here again we see the concrete painted to look like stonework. (NA.)

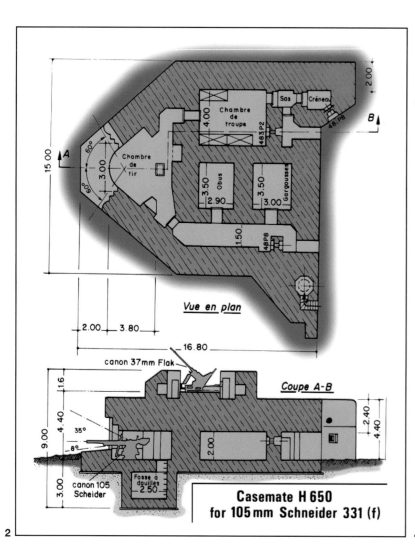

Vue en plan

Coupe A-B

canon 37mm Flak

canon 105 Scheider

Fosse à douilles

Casemate H 650 for 105 mm Schneider 331 (f)

5

6

8

7. Detail of a Type H 650 casemate embrasure showing remains of vestiges dummy stonework camouflage. (EG/Heimdal.)

8. One of the observation posts. (EG/ Heimdal.)

7

Saint-Marcouf Battery

1. This battery was commanded by Oberleutnant zur See Walter Ohmsen seen here photographed late in June 1944, wounded and decorated with the Knight's Cross following his action against the Allied fleet. (Heimdal coll.)

2. This propaganda photo shows the size of the 21 cm guns in their Type H 683 casemates, photo taken in the spring of 1944. (ECPAD.)

Marcouf battery control bunker was a complex affair, on two levels, surmounted by an armored dome with a rangefinder slit and protected by a 2 cm *Flak Oerlikon* gun, and two Type H 621 and H 622 bunkers, Type H 134 ammunition stores, six French 7.5 cm AA guns, another two 2 cm *Flak* guns, eight MG tobruks (plus the ones placed on top of various bunkers). The whole setup was surrounded by barbed wire entanglements and minefields. This powerful battery was a veritable entrenched camp which also had considerable antiaircraft firepower. These were the most formidable defenses the Germans had on this Cotentin coast and they gave the American troops a very hard time …

Further north, there were further batteries as far as Gatteville. West of Quinéville, on Hill 69 at Le Poteau, a Type H 608/SK bunker was used as a CP by *Oberst* Gerhard Triepel, the colonel commanding the regiment. The Germans knew the place as *Ginsterhöhe* (broomy high ground). **4./1261** (Quinéville *HKB*, CO *Oberleutnant* Schulz) was stationed nearby at Mont Coquerel, and had four French 10.5 cm *K 331 (f)* guns in Type H 671 casemates. Further north, at Lestre,

1

8./1261, there since 1942, was no longer on duty in May 1944. Further on, at Crasville, **5./1261** (Crasville *HKB*), commanded by *Oberleutnant* Franz Kerber, also had four French 10.5 cm *K 331 (f)* guns in Type H 650 and H 671 casemates. Coming to the edge of the beach sector, at Morsalines, before you come to Saint-Vaast-la-Hougue, **6./1261** had six bigger 15.5 cm *K 416 (f)* guns, again French, placed in large tobruks, with concreting work still in progress on four casemates. Also at Morsalines was the 2nd Battalion's **(II./1261)** CP. In the Val de Saire, overlooking the sea from the high ground at La Pernelle, were **9./1261** and **10./1261**, respectively the Hessen bat-

2

3

Casemate Type H 683
for 210 mm gun

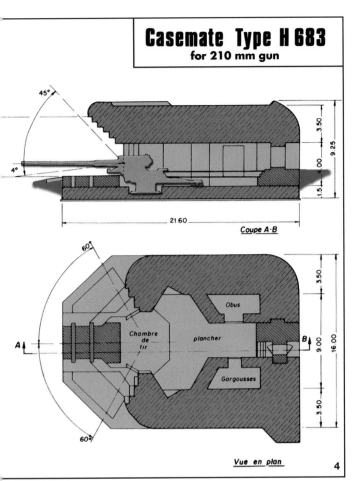

Coupe A-B

Vue en plan

4

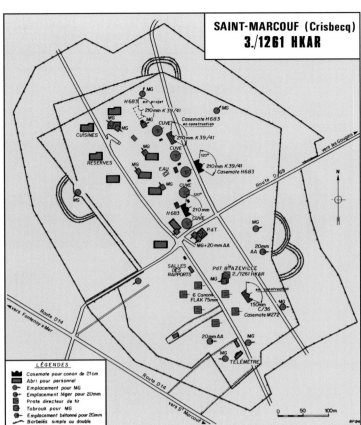

SAINT-MARCOUF (Crisbecq)
3./1261 HKAR

LÉGENDES
- Casemate pour canon de 21cm
- Abri pour personnel
- Emplacement pour MG
- Emplacement léger pour 20mm
- Poste directeur de tir
- Tobrouk pour MG
- Emplacement bétonné pour 20mm
- Barbelés simple ou double

5

6

3. But two of these casemates were still awaiting concrete when the Americans arrived, photo taken on 2 August 1944. (Heimdal coll.)

4. Plan and cross section of a Type H 683 casemate. (B. Paich/Heimdal.)

5. This view of one of the Type H 683 casemates after the battle and the capture of the battery by US troops gives some idea of its sheer volume. (NA.)

6. The Americans tested explosives on one of the casemates. The roof slab tipped over into the gun chamber. (EG/Heimdal.)

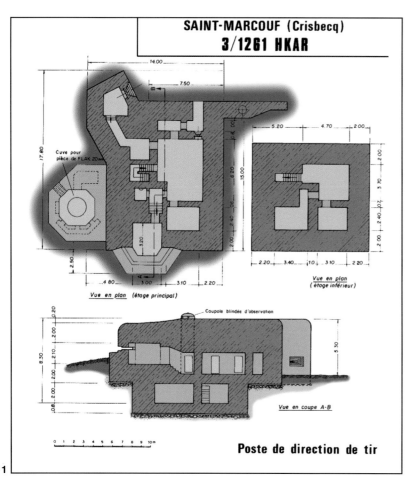

SAINT-MARCOUF (Crisbecq)
3/1261 HKAR

Cuve pour pièce de FLAK 20...

Vue en plan (étage principal)

Vue en plan (étage inférieur)

Coupole blindée d'observation

Vue en coupe A-B

Poste de direction de tir

Saint-Marcouf Battery

1. The battery's highly complex control bunker was constructed on two levels. It had an armored observation cupola on top. The Azeville battery's control bunker was close by. (Maps by B. Paich/Heimdal.)

2. Here we see the control bunker with its foundations laid bare by the bombing. (Heimdal coll.)

3. … and today. (EG/Heimdal.)

4. The battery was also defended by heavy flak relying notably on 2 cm Flak Oerlikon guns. (ECPA.)

5. Aerial view, after the battery was taken. The land has been churned up in the bombing but one of the two Type H 683 casemates has emerged unscathed. (NA.)

3

5

Major Friedrich von der Heydte commander of *Fallschirmjäger-Regiment 6*, based between Lessay, Périers and Carentan, the only German crack unit in the sector. It was attached to *91. ID*. (ECPAD.)

teries (called *Pernelle I* and *HKB Pernelle II*). *Pernelle I* also had six French 10.5 cm *K 331 (f)* guns in Type H 671 casemates. South of that battery, near the church at La Pernelle, there was a Type H 120 control bunker, a Type H 608 battalion command post for *I./729* and a Type H 637 artillery observation bunker. Certainly, the view was outstanding from the site. The *Pernelle II* position (*10./1261*) was behind the village with three 17 cm *K 18* guns awaiting their Type H 688 casemates still under construction. Lastly, **7./1261** was stationed at Gatteville, north-west of the tiny port of Barfleur, and lined up six French 15.5 cm *K 420 (f)* guns, some of them in four Type H 679 casemates. The 3rd Battalion also had its CP in the sector.

So this artillery regiment provided considerable firepower in supporting the troops defending the coast. But as we have seen, these batteries were using captured, mostly French, but also Czech and Russian guns. The batteries' commitment against a landing was however considerably reduced by their being too thin on the ground, and mostly placed in casemates with narrower firing slits whereas the guns had initially been placed in all-directional tobruks. Bombing raids faled to destroy these batteries, but the mere threat was enough to force the Germans to protect their guns in concrete casemates, thereby greatly reducing their effectiveness, short of bringing them out of the casemates during the battle.

There were also other units in this sector. One such, the 1st Battery of *Sturm-Bataillon AOK 7*, was stationed west of Foucarville, with its combat supply line at Cibrantot. It had its guns trained on the sea. South of Brucheville, a smoke-thrower battery of *I./Nebelwerfer-Regiment 100* was set up. Other static *Nebelwerfers* were installed near Les Dunes de Varreville. Also, in the southern part of the peninsula, a tank battalion was held in the army reserve. This **Panzer-Abteilung 100**, or rather *Panzer-Ersatz-und-Ausbildungs-Abteilung 100* (100th replacement and training tank battalion) was commanded by Major Bardenschlager and tactically attached to *91. Infanterie-Division*. It had its CP at Château de Francquetot at Coigny and its companies were spread across the Saint-Jores, Baupte and Carentan area. This unit was raised in April 1941 and a year later sent to Satory camp near Versailles; this dépôt battalion was made available to the "Gross Paris" command. It was used as a training school teaching would be tank crews to steer, fire onboard weapons, and operate onboard radios. But the tanks they used had no turrets and were driven by gas generator! Most of the officers were wounded and finishing their convalescence there. The NCOs were veterans who had long since quit the front line. When the unit moved up to Nor-

mandy, again on 10 May 1944, it was not operational, and its most serviceable vehicles were obsolete French Renault tanks. The command company (*Stabs-Kompanie*), stationed at **Francquetot**, included a light troop with five Renault R 35 tanks with short 37 mm guns. The 1st Company, stationed at **Baupte**, had one troop with five Renault R 35 tanks and two infantry platoons. The 2nd Company, stationed at **Coigny**, had one Somua tank (armed with a 47 mm gun) and four R35 tanks for its 1st Troop, one Renault B1 Bis tank and four Hotchkiss tanks (armed with 37 mm guns) for its 2nd Troop, one *Panzer III* (armed with a 5 cm gun) and four Hotchkiss tanks for its 3rd Troop. The 3rd Company, stationed at **Auvers**, also had a troop with five R35 tanks and two infantry platoons. Altogether, this made up a mixed bag of completely outdated, mostly French, tanks: 19 R 35s, 1 Somua, 1 B1bis, 8 Hotchkisses and 1 *Panzer III*! The men of the battalion were spending all their time planting stakes – "Rommel's asparagus". On the evening of 4 June, the sky over Carentan was lit up by explosions, tracer in thousands rising up in a dreadful din. The next day, it started all over again, and 1st Company commander Lieutenant Weber reassured his men, saying: *"Zirkus! Nicht für uns bestimmt!"* (this circus has nothing to do with us!).

Finally, one unit was sent up to reinforce the sector, but it was a crack unit, **Fallschirmjäger-Regiment 6**, a parachute regiment commanded by *Major* Friedrich **von der Heydte**. It was based between Lessay, Périers and Carentan, south of the Gorges marshes. It was detached from *2. Fallschirmjäger-Division*, after its ordeal on the Eastern front. The regiment was reconstitued at Köln-Wahn, near Cologne. When it arrived for its Normandy assignment, it too was attached to *91. Infanterie-Division*. *FSR 6*'s 1st Battalion was commanded by Captain Preikschat, the 2nd Battalion by Captain Mager and the 3rd Battalion by Captain Trebes.

So just a few weeks before D-day, major reinforcements had been brought up to the Cotentin peninsula. However, despite this recent upheaval, the balance of forces remained heavily in favor of the Americans, who would commit ten infantry regiments on D-day itself. That day, the defending Germans could only oppose three infantry regiments (*GR 1058*, *IR 919* and *FSR 6*). As for the coastal defenses, the assault was only opposed in places, and the resources of the other batteries could not be engaged. As we have seen, the coastal artillery was in the same position, and only two or three batteries could respond. In any battle, a surprise attack is often decisive, and this time it was to come from the sky, by night!

Prelude to Invasion

The Normandy landings in June 1944 finally proved to the Allies how useful and effective the airborne troops were. Three full-strength divisions, the US 82nd and 101st Divisions, and the British 6th Division, were to be dropped behind the Normandy beaches just a few hours before the seaborne troops came ashore.

The airborne troops' objective was to prevent German counter-attacks aimed at pushing back the landing troops while they were vulnerable arriving on five beaches. This plan was codenamed Neptune. However, some chiefs of staff like British Air Chief Marshal Leigh-Mallory tried to have the plan abandoned owing to the most pessimistic forecasts in terms of casualties among the airborne troops. Fortunately, General Eisenhower saw how useful these ground troops would be, and so confirmed the plan and the dropping zones.

For the Normandy invasion, the 82nd Airborne Division's assignment involved taking a whole string of roads and crossroads and bridges behind the Utah beachhead, whilst the 101st Airborne Division was to concentrate its efforts on the roads to the north and east of Carentan.

The Allies were aware of the existence of numerous obstacles and booby-traps littering the Normandy hedgerow country and designed to deter any airborne operations – low-lying land inundated to prevent gliders and paratroops landing, and covering the drop and landing zones, stakes nicknamed "Rommel's asparagus", topped with barbed wire or mines.

Despite the risk involved in taking on the enemy defenses, Operation Neptune was to go ahead, and was ready by early June.

The Neptune plan

The Neptune plan was the assault and support phase of the Overlord plan, chiefly involving the paratroops and gliderborne infantry. Neptune was broken down into three forces:

- Force A included all the paratroopers due to land in drop zones marked out earlier by the
Pathfinders.

- Force B was made up of reinforcements brought in by glider and responsible for bringing the first vehicles to the two airborne divisions, heavy weapons, special equipment and advanced medical units.

- Force C, the seaborne troops, included non-commissioned personnel and any heavy equipment for the airborne divisions that could not be brought in by air.

Lightnin' Joe for Utah Beach

The amphibious and airborne assault on the east coast of the Cotentin was the task of **VII Corps**. This

was a large force of four infantry divisions and two airborne divisions. This powerful army corps had as its commander one of the greatest of all the US World War II generals. Joseph Lawton **Collins's** was an extraordinarily rapid and brilliant career. The son of an Irish emigrant who served in the Unionist army, and Catherine Lawton, Joseph Collins was born on 1 May 1896 in Algiers, Louisiana. After studying at Louisiana University, he went to West Point Military Academy in 1913. He then joined the 22nd Infantry Regiment in New York; he was to have been one of the first to enlist for the Great War but remained in the USA. From May 1919 to the summer of 1921, he took part in the occupation of Germany. In 1933, he was promoted to Major, stationed in the Philippines. He later rose to the rank of colonel in January 1941 and became chief-of-staff of the VII Corps (already!) in Alabama. He was promoted to Major General in May 1942 and took over command of the 25th Division which was sent ot the south Pacific to relieve the 1st Marine Division at Guadalcanal; it went onto the attack on 10 January 1943 and crushed the Japanese forces within the month. It was here that General Collins earned the nickname "Lightnin' Joe" recalling the lightning on the division's shoulder flash. After further battles leading to ultimate victory, Joseph Collins was dispatched to England on 14 February 1944; there he was put in command of the VII Corps. For four months, he supervised training of the divisions placed under him. This period was marked by the tragic deaths of 700 seamen and soldiers at Slapton Sands, when German E-Boats attacked and sank several landing craft taking part in an exercise.

The **VII Corps** was raised on 26 January 1918 and equipped at Remiremont on 19 August 1918; it was demobbed on 11 July 1919 in New York state and later re-formed in the reserve on 29 July 1921, passing into the regular army on 18 October 1927. It was

Opposite and below : General Joseph L. Collins was one of the most brilliant American World War II generals. He commanded VII Corps which he led to victory. (DAVA/ Heimdal.)

VII Corps

Shoulder flash worn by the men of the 4th Infantry Division.

then reactivated at Fort McClellan, Alabama, regaining its name of VII Corps, on 19 August 1942. It arrived in England in October 1943, where it came under the command of Major General Collins on 14 February 1944. On the eve of D-day, it comprised six divisions, the 4th, 9th, 79th and 90th Infantry Divisions and 82nd and 101st Airborne. It was assigned four tasks: to land at Utah Beach, link up with the forces landing at Omaha Beach (V Corps), cut off the Cotentin peninsula and capture Cherbourg. One infantry division landed on Utah Beach on D-day; this was the 4th Infantry Division, the Ivy Division, with a regiment of the 90th Infantry Division in support.

The Ivy Division

This map (below) shows the 4th Infantry Division's D-day objectives.

General Collins gave Major General Raymond O. Barton the honor of landing in his assigned sector on D-day. General Barton led in the **4th Infantry Division**,

also known as the *Ivy Division*, on account of the unit's badge with four ivy leaves in a cross shape, indicating the division's number; and of course Ivy is pronounced IV, which is 4 in Roman numerals.

This 4th Division was fitted out at Camp Greene in 1917, under its CO *Major General* George H. Cameron. It landed in France on 5 June 1918 having already suffered some early casualties on 23 May when the *Maldovia*, the ship carrying the unit, was torpedoed by a German submarine, killing 56. Later it took part in the Aisne-Marne, Saint-Mihiel and Meuse-Argonne offensives. Following the armistice, it stayed on for six months occupying Germany, until it was sent home to the USA for demobilization.

The *4th Infantry Division* was then reactivated on 1 June 1940 at Fort Benning, Georgia. On 15 November 1941, it was transferred to Camp Gordon, also in Georgia, where it came under the *2nd Army*. *Major General* Barton took over command in June 1942. It

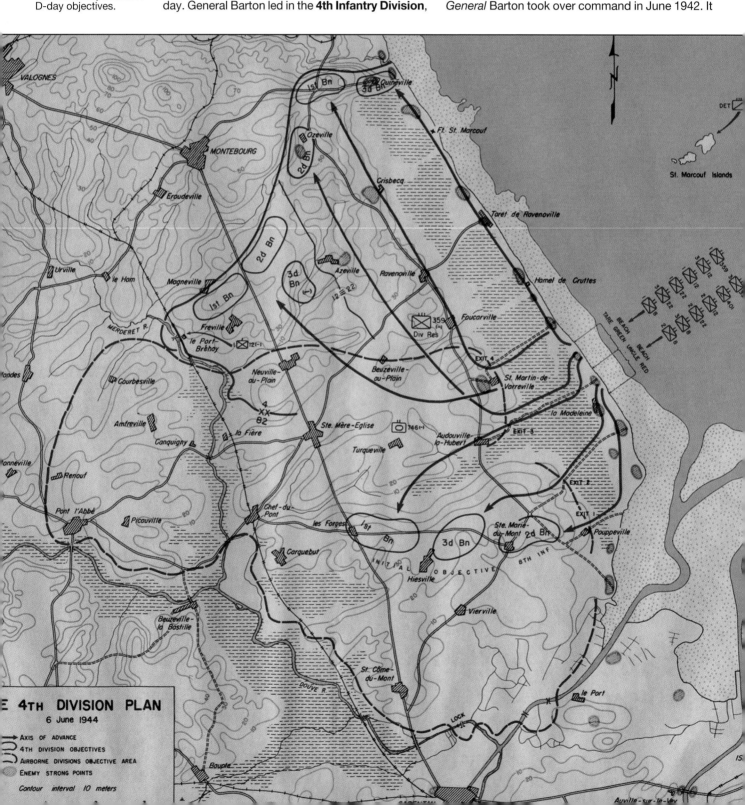

E 4TH DIVISION PLAN
6 June 1944

→ AXIS OF ADVANCE
⬭ 4TH DIVISION OBJECTIVES
⬭ AIRBORNE DIVISIONS OBJECTIVE AREA
▨ ENEMY STRONG POINTS

Contour interval 10 meters

was transferred to Fort Dix, New Jersey, in April 1943, where it continued training until September, when it returned to Camp Johnston in Florida to take part in amphibious exercises; its preparation covered every tiny detail. In December, it was assigned to Fort Jackson, South Carolina, and was later transferred to the UK, in January 1944 in the buildup to Operation Overlord. Once there, it carried on training in Devon and took part in further amphibious exercises at Slapton Sands. The division may have had no battle experience, but according to General Bradley, *"it was a superbly trained outfit"*.

It had three infantry regiments. The **8th Infantry Regiment** was commanded by Colonel James A. Van Fleet. The **12th Infantry Regiment** was commanded by Colonel Russel P. Reeder. The **22nd Infantry Regiment** was commanded by Colonel Hervey A. Tribolet. Supporting the division were four artillery battalions: the **20th Field Artillery Battalion**, the **29th F.A.B.**, the **42nd F.A.B.** and the **44th Self-Propelled (L) Field Artillery Battalion**. For D-day, it was further reinforced by the 87th Heavy Mortar Battalion, the 1106st Engineer Group, the *801st Tank Battalion* (TDM10 tanks), a troop of 980th F.A.B. (155 mm guns), anti-aircraft units and a detachment of the 13th Field Artillery Observation Battalion. Also, one of the *90th Infantry Division's* regiments, the *359th Infantry Regiment*, landed with the 4th Division on D-day and during the early hours these shock troops were crucial in establishing a foothold.

Raymond O. Barton was just the man for the job of commanding this fine infantry unit. Born on 22 August 1889, at Granada, Colorado, to Conway O. Barton and Carrie Mosher, he graduated from West Point Military Academy in 1912. He was assigned to the *30th Infantry Regiment* in Alaska. Then in 1917-1918 he was an instructor and went to France in August 1919 where he served as a captain with the *8th Infantry Regiment*. From then on, his career was up all the way, taking in this regiment and the division to which it was attached. He gained a place at the General Staff school in 1924 then at *Army War College* in Washington. He was *VII Corps* chief-of-staff from 1924 to 1928. Promoted to the rank of lieutenant-colonel in 1935, he took over command of the *8th IR* from the end of 1938 until July 1940, when he became chief-of-staff of the *4th Infantry Division*, the division to which this regiment was attached. A *brigadier general* then major-general in June 1942, Barton commanded the *4th Infantry Division* from June 1942. He held onto that command until late December 1944. *General* Barton was a good teacher and helped to turn the *Ivy Division* into a superbly trained outfit. Back in the USA, he commanded the Fort McClellan infantry training center (March 1945). He left the army in 1946 and died at Fort Gordon, Georgia on 27 February 1963.

General Barton also had by his side a deputy with excellent experience of amphibious operations: Brigadier General **Theodore Roosevelt Jr**. He was the son of Theodore Roosevelt, the 26th President of the USA (who was a cousin of the incumbent 32nd President, Franklin Delano Roosevelt). "Teddy" Roosevelt was born in 1887, frail and poor-sighted, but that did not prevent him from fighting bravely in World War I with the *26th Infantry Division* (1st Infantry Division); he was wounded twice! Back in civvy street after the war, he wrote books, led archaeological expeditions to Asia, and dabbled in politics. Then war broke out again, and he re-enlisted with his old regiment, the 26th. He went on to fight in North Africa and Sicily, again with the *1st Infantry Division*, becoming its deputy commander. With the benefit of his combat experience as an officer in the Great

War, he insisted on taking part in the assault up with the first wave, which he did with courage, calm and composure. In Sicily he led in the assault waves armed with nothing more than his 45 colt, and afterwards took part in his third amphibious operation on the beaches of Corsica, which he helped to liberate. On joining up with the *4th Infantry Division* in Britain, *Brigadier General* Roosevelt filed a written request to be allowed to take part for the fourth time in the first wave of an amphibious assault, and his request was finally granted.

The boys from Texas and Oklahoma

However on D-day, the *4th Division* had support from two battalions of a regiment of the **90th Infantry Division**. This division was raised at Camp Travis in Texas in August 1917, with men from Texas and Oklahoma, and landed in France in June and July 1918. It took part in the Saint-Mihiel offensive and later broke through the Hindenburg Line. It was sent home to the US in mid-June 1919, and disbanded shortly afterwards. It was reactivated on 25 March 1942 at Camp Barkeley in Texas. After training in Louisiana (February-March 1943) and in the desert (September 1943), it moved to New Jersey then left the USA in March 1944, bound for England where it trained in amphibious operations. It lined up three infantry regiments *(357th, 358th* and *359th)* and four artillery battalions. It was known as the "Texas Oklahoma Division". The divisional badge in fact interlaces a letter T and a letter O, referring to the initials of the men's two home states, and the initials were combined to stand for their nickname, Tough 'Ombres. The division was then under Brigadier General Jay W. McKelvie who was a controversial leader and was relieved of his command immediately on 12 June, to be replaced by *Major General* Eugene M. Landrum.

Two battalions of the **359th Infantry Regiment** landed on D-day in support of the 4th Division. The remaining elements of the 90th Division followed on 7 and 8 June; the division was up to full strength in Normandy by 9 June. As for the other infantry divisions belonging to VII Corps, the 9th Infantry Division landed on 10 June (its 39th Infantry Regiment was committed first to capture Quinéville), and the 79th Infantry Division landed from 12 to 14 June.

The airborne troops

The beach sector chosen for the amphibious operation carried out by the *VII Corps* was codenamed *Utah Beach*. The low, soft sandy beach was a particularly suitable spot for a landing but the inundated

4th Inf. Div.

Major General Raymond O. Barton.

Brigadier General Theodore Roosevelt Jr.

90th Inf. Div.

9th Inf. Div.

79th Inf. Div.

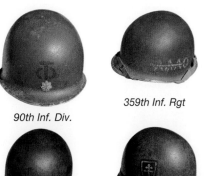

90th Inf. Div.

359th Inf. Rgt

9th Inf. Div.

79th Inf. Div.

43

1. Before arriving in England, the airborne troops followed special training in the US. The school for US airborne troops at Fort Benning took in thousands of young paratroopers, who would fight in every theater of war. (D. François coll.)

2. The four training towers at Fort Benning; only three are still standing today. (D. François coll.)

3. One of the 250-foot towers used for training paratroopers. During its sixty years of service, millions of paratroopers will have admired the Georgia countryside on their way up. (D. François.)

5. The tower for training to jump out of the aircraft. (D. François.)

4. 508th commander Colonel Roy Lindquist inspects training jumps at Fort Benning. His regiment dropped a few months later in the Picauville sector. (D. François.)

6. These paratroops are ready to board a C-47. (D. François.)

1. Rare color photo of two paratroopers of the *82nd Airborne Division* on a training drop in the US. (D. François coll.)

2. These two paratroopers of *508th PIR* have Griswold bags, used to carry a dismantled Garand gun. (D. François coll.)

3. This paratrooper of *507th PIR* is preparing to jump, the Fort Benning DZ is just below. (D. François coll.)

In England: 4. This paratrooper of 507th PIR, carrying a bazooka, will soon be leaving the canvas camp at Nottingham to take part in Operation Neptune. 5. Dropping containers was the only way of bringing in supplies to the airborne troops during the early days of the battle. 6. Inventory of a paratrooper's kit. 7. .30 caliber machine-guns are oiled before being sent to the airfields for dropping by parachute along with their servers. (Photos D. François coll.)

1. This paratrooper/wireless operator is carrying the base of the radio antenna for a transmitter and not for the Eureka radio beacon. (D.F.)

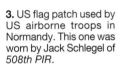

2. Shoulder flash worn by members of the *82nd Airborne Division.*

3. US flag patch used by US airborne troops in Normandy. This one was worn by Jack Schlegel of *508th PIR.*

1

3

6

4

4. *82nd Airborne Division* commander Major General Ridgway. (Ass. 82nd).

5

5. *Brigadier* James M. Gavin was the division's second-in-command.

6. Colonel Ekman, 505th PIR. (D.F.)

area coming off the beach formed a serious obstacle. Also, as we have seen, the Plain where the beachhead was to form was surrounded by more flooded land. The landing troops were in danger of being pinned down by the Germans behind this flooded area. Also, as Lieutenant-Colonel Keil mentions in his report, a second line of resistance was planned west of the Douve and Merderet marshes, from Carentan to Montebourg.

To avoid this trap, the Allied commanders planned to commit two airborne divisions. In the north-west around Sainte-Mère-Eglise, the *82nd Airborne Division* was assigned to take that locality, which was at a major crossroads, establish a defensive front north of the town, capture the bridges over the Merderet with a bridgehead to the west of that inundated valley, and establish a bridgehead over the River Douve. The *101st Airborne Division* was to be dropped in the south-east of the sector, around Sainte-Marie-du-Mont, and its assignment involved neutralizing an artillery battery, clearing the beach exits and capturing the bridges north of Carentan before entering the town.

The **82nd Airborne Division** was already an experienced outfit. During World War I, the *82nd Infantry Division* was raised with soldiers from Georgia, Alabama and Tennessee. It was reactivated on 25 March 1942 and became an airborne division on 15 August as the *82nd Airborne Division*. It was called the All American Division for drawing men from every state in the Union. On 16 August 1942, it was split into two airborne divisions, the *82nd Airborne Division* and the *101st Airborne Division*. It trained initially at Camp Clairborn, in Louisiana, then at Fort Bragg, in North Carolina. It was transferred to the

UK in April 1943, where it continued training. The *82nd Airborne Division* landed at Casablanca on 10 May 1943 for a month's training in Morocco. It made its first parachute landing on 9 June 1943, in the Gela sector in Sicily, where it fought for seven days. It captured Trapani in August, returning to Morocco to refit on 22 August. It was then committed again in Sicily and Italy (September 1943). It was dropped into the Salerno sector and went on to fight near Naples before being committed in the Anzio sector. The division left Italy in November 1943 for Belfast, arriving in December. It was transferred to England and the Leicester area north-west of London. The *504th Parachute Infantry Regiment*, which had stayed behind in Italy, joined the division in April; it took no part in Overlord and was replaced by two other regiments, the *507th* and *508th PIR*. So the *82nd Airborne Division* was to be committed with three parachute infantry regiments, **505th PIR**, **507th PIR** and **508th PIR**, one gliderborne infantry regiment, the **325th Glider Infantry Regiment**, one airborne artillery battalion, the **456th Parachute Field Artillery Battalion**, two gliderborne field artillery battalions, the **319th** and **320th Glider Field Artillery Battalions**, and one AA battalion, the **80th Antiaircraft Battalion**.

The division was commanded by *Major General* Mathew B. **Ridgway**. He was born on 3 March 1895 at Fort Monroe, Virginia. He graduated from West Point in 1917. He was then posted to China, the Philippines, Nicaragua, West Point and Fort Benning. He attended staff college in 1935, held various posts on the general staff, and in June 1942 took over command of the division he was to lead into battle. In August 1944 he was put in command of the *XVIII Airborne Corps*.

Brigadier General James M. **Gavin** was the division's second-in-command. Il He was born in Brooklyn on

22 March 1907 and joined the army when he was 17; he attended West Point. A second lieutenant in 1929, he served in the infantry, then as an instructor at West Point, before joining the *503rd Parachute Infantry Battalion* in September 1941. He entered staff college in February 1942 and six months later took over command of the *505th Parachute Infantry Regiment*. In February 1944, he became the division's second-in-command and commanding officer in August 1944, replacing *Major General* Ridgway, making him, at 38, the youngest two-star *general* in the United States Army.

7. Emblem of 507th PIR.

8. The staff of *507th PIR* prior to D-day. Left to right and from bottom to top: LtC Kuhn, Chaplain Hennon, Chaplain Verret, Major Smith, Maj. Pearson, Major Volman, Capt. Dicks, Maj. Johnston, LtC Ostberg, Maj. Fagan, LtC Maloney, LtC Timmes. (D. François coll.)

9. Major Gordon Smith (left) of *507th PIR* freshly kitted out with the new M 42 jump jacket. (D. François coll.)

49

2. *508th PIR* commander Colonel Roy Lindquist (left), and Major Thomas Shanley, who commanded the regiment's *3rd Battalion*. Shanley fought outstandingly well on Hill 30 at Picauville. (Photo D. François coll.)

3. Lieutenant Malcolm Brannen (508th PIR), at Nottingham, shortly before D-day. He killed General Falley at Picauville. (D.F.)

1. Captain Roy Creek, of *507th PIR*, was to capture the bridge at Chef-du-Pont.

4. *Captain* Robert Rae (507th PIR), with some of his NCOs on a training jump. (D.F.)

5

5 and 6. Paratroopers of 508th Parachute Infantry Regiment boarded planes at Salby and Folkingham airfields in southern England. (Photos courtesy D. François.)

6

51

1

2

The **101st Airborne Division** was raised on 16 August 1941, under its commanding officer Brigadier General William C. Lee, who came to be known as "the father of the American airborne arm". In his very first talk, he told his men : "the 101st has no history but it has an appointment with destiny". The first part of this sentence was not quite true, as the division took over the tradition of an American Civil War unit, the Iron Brigade. The division's black insignia recalls that brigade's colors; it also bears an eagle's head; this bird was the Iron Brigade's mascot, named Old Abe in honor of Abraham Lincoln. The eagle's head shoulder flash earned the division its nickname the Screaming Eagles. Thus the 101st became the 101st Airborne Division, with four infantry regiments each with three battalions. Three of these were parachute regiments: - the **501st Parachute Infantry Regiment** commanded by Colonel Howard Johnson; - the **502nd PIR** commanded by Colonel George Moseley; - the **506th PIR** commanded by Colonel Robert Sink. A fourth regiment was brought across in gliders: the **327th Glider Infantry Regiment**, whose 1st Battalion was the 1st Battalion of the 401st G.I.R. which was attached to it. This airborne infantry did not enjoy the same prestige or the same pay as the paratroopers but nevertheless played a major role by arriving in greater numbers at their objectives while running easily the same risks, for a glider is a fragile thing and many crashed into hedges, with high casualties as may well be imagined. The division had four artillery battalions in support: the **377th Parachute Field Artillery Battalion**, the **321st Glider Field Artillery Battalion**, the **907th G.F.A.B.** and the **81st Airborne Antiaircraft Battalion**.

The 101st did not have the experience of the 82nd which had already seen action, as noted above. And it soon lost its commander, General Lee, who suffered a heart attack and was replaced in March 1944 by Major General Maxwell D. **Taylor**. Taylor was born in 1901. He became a career soldier, graduating from West Point in 1922 to join the engineers and later the artillery. He followed intensive training during the interwar period. He was appointed chief-of-staff of the 82nd Airborne Division in July 1942; he helped Matthew B. Ridgway turn the unit into an airborne division, which it had not been until then. He was promoted to brigadier general and put in charge of the division's artillery, in which capacity he fought in the North Africa and Sicily campaigns. He even made a mission behind the enemy lines to look into the possibility of an airborne operation near Rome; his report was negative. Eisenhower said of him: "The risks he took were greater than any I ever asked of any agent or emissary in the entire war." Thus he succeeded General Lee in March 1944 as CO of thte 101st Airborne Division and rose to the rank of major general, a deserved promotion for this outstanding officer.

The division's deputy commander was Brigadier General Donald F. **Pratt**. Among the top officers in the division were Colonel Howard **Johson**, another strong personality, commanding the 501st Parachute Infantry Regiment. With his light blond hair, suntanned face and his way of looking you straight in the eye, he looked like something out of an American action movie. But he was first and foremost an extraordinarily energetic leader who would not tolerate unpunctuality or any other human weakness. In choosing the men to lead his unit, he focussed on just one crucial quality: aggressiveness. These were the questions he asked himself before keeping the men submitted to him : are they physically capable, are they mentally agile, are they aggressive, can they kill? According to Captain Laurence Critchell (1) : *"Johnson wanted killers; he wanted to fight a bigger*

Major General Maxwell D. Taylor, commander of *101st Airborne Division.* (Photo courtesy West Point.)

force; he wanted a regiment that could be forged into a single weapon". His deputy, Lieutenant-Colonel Harry Kinvard, was altogether a very different kind of person, a small man known for his kindness, with great patience and even great humility, and yet an extremely able tactician. And the 501st turned out to be the crack regiment Colonel Johnson was looking for.

The gliders

So these two divisions were to drop six parachute regiments over the Cotentin peninsula, but they also

(1) L. Critchell, *Four Stars of Hell*, Battery Press.

Brigadier General Donald F. Pratt, the division's second-in-command.

Colonel Howard Johnson.

1. A party of Medics of *507th PIR* ready to make the big jump. (F.D. coll.)

2. The "pushman", the last man in the stick, who sometimes had to push the last ones out. (F.D. coll.)

3. Paratroopers aboard a C-47. (Heimdal.)

1. . Glider pilot's badge. (Ph. Esvelin coll.)

2. *Army Air Forces* cloth patch. (Ph. Esvelin coll.)

3. Helmet with an ace of clubs *stencilled on it, for the 327th Glider Infantry Regiment* (attached to the *101st Airborne Division*. (Photo courtesy Heimdal.)

1

2

3

4

had the use of a new weapon, the glider. Two infantry regiments and equipment were brought in close to their objectives by glider.

The American glider construction effort early in the war is one of the little-known feats of the American war machine. It all started in February 1941 when Army Air Corps chief, General Henry Arnold, (the *US Air Force* had not yet been created) requested a study into the creation of a military glider. By the end of 1946, when the production lines finally stopped, over 16 000 gliders had been built. The *Waco Aircraft Company* won the contract. It was to be the Waco *CG-4*, a glider capable of transporting fifteen infantrymen or a jeep and its crew. It was capable of carrying a heavier load than its own weight. Made of a metal tubular frame and wood and stretched canvas elements, it was extremely lightweight. There were two ways in, either through the nose, which opened upwards to let in and out any bulky loads, or through a side door for personnel. The wings and tail fins were made of plywood as was the floor, while the fuselage was made of plastic-coated canvas. The CG-4A cost somewhere between $15 000 and $25 000 to build, depending which company was used. Over 70 000 parts went into one of these gliders. Like the Horsa, the CG-4A was designed to

take two pilots with dual controls; the early models only had single controls.

The C-47 was the aircraft used to tow the CG-4A, with no problem even when the glider was carrying a jeep. It even occasionally towed two at a time with a double towrope. The CG-4A was designed to fly at a speed of 220 km/h (140 mph), which was exactly compatible with the speed of the C-47. Linked with a rope from the aircraft's tail and the glider's nose, the glider pilots were in radio communication with the C-47 pilot's cabin through a cable twinned with the towrope. Early in 1944, in England, among the troops ready to invade the continent were the glidermen, pilots and airborne infantry. The camps and airfields were selected in southern England. Every day gliders arrived in crates and were assembled at the airfields before being parked in rows along the taxiways. In the operations that followed, despite flak, the worst threat to the glider was the obstacles at the landing zones (LZ), not just "Rommel's asparagus" but primarily natural obstacles like hedges, streams, houses etc. On top of these obstacles, most of the pilots had not had adequate training, especially the copilots, who seldom had any flight experience. The experts expected 70% casualties among the glidermen on D-day and 50% for the paratroopers …

5

4. Final briefing session for the glider pilots on 5 June 1944 at Uppottery from Lieutenant-Colonel Charles H. Young of 439th TCG. (National Archives/Tariel coll.

5. The glider pilots listen carefully to his last-minute recommendations. (National Archives -Tariel coll.)

1. The Waco CG-4A glider came in for all kinds of trials in the United States. Here we see the unloading of a jeep of the 320th Field Artillery Battalion, 82nd Airborne Division. (Photo courtesy National Archives.)

3

2

2. This photo shows a pilot hooking up his glider tow rope to a C-47. Notice the wireless cable coming from his glider. (NA.)

3. A Waco CG-4A landing or training; it is not clear from this photo whether the bulldozer has just been driven out of the glider or if it is just there to move it. (NA/ F.D. coll.)

4

4. The Waco CG-4A was used throughout the Normandy campaign. (NA/ F.D. coll.)

5. Inside view of the front cell of the Waco. (Photo courtesy Philippe Esvelin.)

5

1. La Heguerie at Audouville-la-Hubert, the Birette family farm in 1944. The lefthand section of the main building was occupied by the Germans and Georgians. (Heimdal.)

2. The crossroads with the statue of the Virgin Mary. On the evening of 5 June, the Germans removed the fuses from the electricity posts. (Heimdal.)

3. The square in the center of Sainte-Mère-Eglise. (Heimdal.)

4. This aerial photo gives a good picture of the locality. Notice highway N13 passing through. Carentan and the south are off the top of the picture, Cherbourg and the north off the bottom. (US Air Force.)

1

2

On that Monday 5 June 1944, between Sainte-Mère-Eglise and the sea, in the village of **Audouville-la-Hubert**, Bernardin Birette was 20 years old, and his parents were farmers. Their farm was at La Heguerie, midway between Sainte-Mère-Eglise and the sea, on the D 67 road near the crossroads with the statue of the Virgin. The farmhouse was an imposing building typical of the Cotentin, the left half of which was occupied by the German army behind the window with medieval mullions. There were some thirty men, mostly the Georgians of *Ost-Bataillon 795* taking orders from a German warrant officer in his forties who hailed from Aachen and was a restaurant-owner in peacetime. The battalion duties mostly involved coordinating civilians requisitioned for the defensive works – digging trenches and planting stakes, "Rommel's asparagus". It was also responsible for bringing up in horsedrawn vehicles the munitions needed at the coastal battery at nearby Saint-Martin-de-Varreville. The shells came from the station at Chef-du-Pont.

At around 8 that evening, Bernardin Birette was with Edouard Pergeaux near the crossroads of the Virgin. Two "*flaks*" (German AA soldiers) cycled up and stopped by the electricity transformer across the road from the statue. One of them climbed up, cut off the current and removed two fuses which he passed down on the end of a rope to his colleague, then climbed back down and remounted his bike. Strange, thought Bernardin Birette and he asked the German what was going on. He answered over his shoulder: "*Monzieur fini electrik!*" "But whatever for?" the young Norman insisted. As he disappeared, the German

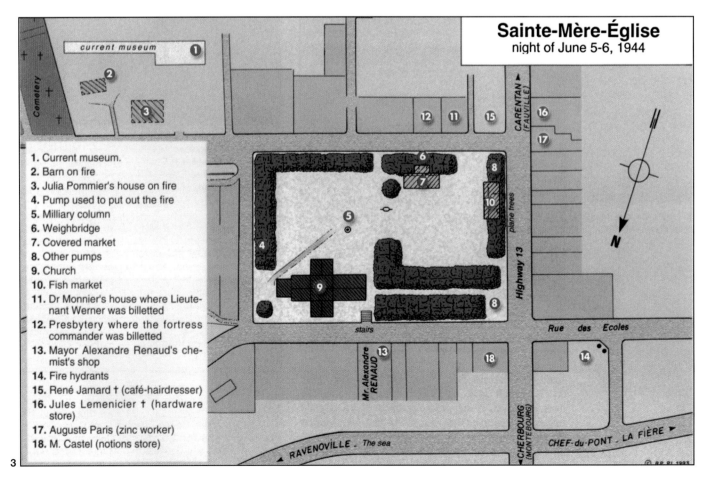

Sainte-Mère-Église
night of June 5-6, 1944

1. Current museum.
2. Barn on fire
3. Julia Pommier's house on fire
4. Pump used to put out the fire
5. Milliary column
6. Weighbridge
7. Covered market
8. Other pumps
9. Church
10. Fish market
11. Dr Monnier's house where Lieutenant Werner was billetted
12. Presbytery where the fortress commander was billetted
13. Mayor Alexandre Renaud's chemist's shop
14. Fire hydrants
15. René Jamard † (café-hairdresser)
16. Jules Lemenicier † (hardware store)
17. Auguste Paris (zinc worker)
18. M. Castel (notions store)

3

5

5. The Roman milepost converted into a war memorial, in the church square at Sainte-Mère. (Heimdal.)

6. The presbytery in the square at Sainte-Mère where the German commander stayedg. (Heimdal.)

7. Here the firefighting equipment was stored, in the Rue des Ecoles at Sainte-Mère-Eglise. (Heimdal.)

4

6

7

Sainte-Mère-Eglise at the turn of the 20th century

1. The church.

2. The crossroads on the north side of the square with the Rue de la Mer (now Rue Cap de Laine) opposite. North is to the left and south to the right.

3. The same crossroads, looking in the oposite direction, with the Rue de la Gare opposite, i.e. the Chef-du-Pont road. (D. François coll.)

retorted: "Tonight, maybe big trouble!" Bernardin then recalled the RAF attack on the Saint-Martin-de-Varreville battery the week before and just then, the fading daylight was disturbed by the hedgehopping passage of four British fighters and the sound of machine-gun fire a few minutes later coming from the Chef-du-Pont direction.

At the same moment, at **Sainte-Mère-Eglise**, a small town lying along the highway that passes through it, centered around a large treelined square on which the church stood, with another square used as a cattle market — stockfarming being the main activity in the area — life went on peacefully enough.

Monsieur Leroux was the local mayor until he died in the spring of 1944, to be replaced by his first deputy, Alexandre Renaud, who ran the chemist's shop on the square. After the chemist's, a row of houses and stores led up to the main street and M. Endelin's cycle and gun store (no guns though since the Germans arrived), Lecœur the pork butcher's, M. Leboucher's café and barber's shop, with Castel's notions store on the corner. Across the square, on the south side, from east to west were Madame Julia Pommier's home with a wooden barn used by Marcel Marie (cartwright and carpenter cum firefighter) for his wood stock, the former notary's office, Doctor Pelletier's house, an alley leading to a house used by the Germans, the late mayor M. Leroux's grocery store, the presbytery where the German commander of the place was billetted, Doctor Monnier the veterinary surgeon's house, where Lieutenant Werner, a German officer just back from the Russian front, was billetted, another alley, and on the corner, René Jamard's café and barber's shop. Almost straight opposite, in the main street, stood Jules Lemenicier's hardware store and the house of zinc worker Auguste Paris. To the north-west of the square, in the Rue des Ecoles, was the place where firefighting equipment was stored, two ancient pumps with canvas buckets; the fire chief, M. Feuillie, had had a vote passed in favor of purchasing some modern equipment, including a Lafly centrifugal motor pump, but it had not yet arrived on this evening of 5 June.

Elements of *GR 1058* were stationed in the town. At around nine that evening, German soldiers were enjoying themselves beating the lap record round the church on their bicycles. There was Sergeant Rudi **Escher** and his group of six men. They belonged to the regimental HQ company based at Château de Fauville, a kilometer south of the town. Sergeant Escher (aged 24) was called up in October 1939. He came from the *Luftwaffe* and spent some time with a training unit before joining his new regiment seven weeks earlier, like most of the men in his battalion. One of them, *Obergefreite* (acting corporal) Rudolf **May** (aged 22) had fought in Russia for two years. Throughout May, Rudi Escher and his men, who bicycled everywhere, bivouacked near Sainte-Mère-Eglise. Since 2 June, they had been assigned to monitor the sky for spies and paratroops. They did so from the church belltower. They got up from inside the church. A concealed door behind the wooden altarpiece of the altar dedicated to St Méen accessed a stone spiral staircase up to the loft over the church's south transept lit by a rectangular window opening onto the gable overlooking the square. This room between the roof and the church vaults was used as a barracks by the men on observation duty; they rested there during the day and slept there at night. From it, a steeply angled, rickety old ladder led up to the belltower. The bell room was no use as there was not a good view over the square on account of the louver boards, and it was uncomfor-

Sergeant Ruchi Escher.

Pfc Heinz Strangfeld was a member of Sergeant Escher's group.

5

4

tably close to the bells anyway. There was a ladder here right up to the top of the tower. Observation was carried out from a narrow passage behind a stone Gothic balustrade from the square side (the south side) and on the north side from another identical one, which was harder to get to.

It was now **23.00 hours**, the cycles were parked in a shed opposite the church door. Corporal Rudolf May climbed up into the belltower with a young 18-year-old soldier. They settled behind the south balustrade on their lookout watch, while Rudi Escher and four other men – Alfons Jakel was one of them – stayed downstairs at the foot of the church. It was a quiet, balmy evening.

6

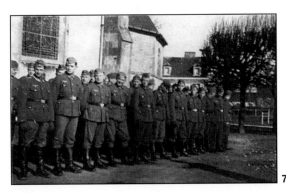

7

8

4. Inside the church, St Méen's altar conceals the stairs up to the bell-tower that became a part of history on D-day. (Heimdal.)

5. The side door through to the stairs at the foot of the altarpiece. (Heimdal.)

6. Rare items belonging to Sergeant Escher's group, including a plaque bearing the name of Grenadier Alfons Jakl (who was killed during the night of 5 June 1944) found in the church attic in 1993. (Photo Heimdal.)

7. German soldiers in front of the church at Sainte-Mère. (H.J. Renaud coll.)

8. The La Fière bridge was a crucial D-day objective. (D. François.)

The night of the paratroopers

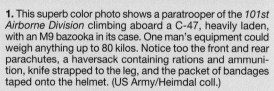

1. This superb color photo shows a paratrooper of the *101st Airborne Division* climbing aboard a C-47, heavily laden, with an M9 bazooka in its case. One man's equipment could weigh anything up to 80 kilos. Notice too the front and rear parachutes, a haversack containing rations and ammunition, knife strapped to the leg, and the packet of bandages taped onto the helmet. (US Army/Heimdal coll.)

2. This US propaganda picture shows a group of paratroopers marching to victory. (Heimdal coll.)

3. Paratrooper Clarence C. Wave gives the final touch to paratrooper Charles R. Plando's "Indian" camouflage shortly before boarding. Plando is holding a Thompson submachine-gun. (US Army.)

4. Exploded view of a C-47; each plane could carry a stick of 18 paratroopers. (Painting by Jean-François Cornu.)

5. Objective of the two American airborne divisions for 6 June: the *82nd Airborne Division* was to drop its three parachute regiments - *505th PIR, 507th PIR, 508th PIR* – northwest of the zone, over Sainte-Mère-Eglise and on either bank of the Merderet, around La Fière. The *101st Airborne Division* was to jump in the southeast of the zone with *501st PIR, 502nd PIR* and *506th PIR*. These plans went awry when the drops were badly scattered. (US Army map.)

5 June 1944, after the operation was postponed, starting orders finally came through to the airfields of England. The American paratroops mustered, checked their equipment one last time, blackened their faces and drank a last cup of coffee, as it was going to be a long night. Worried about what his paratroops were in for, the supreme commander, Eisenhower, visited a regiment of the 101st Airborne Division before boarding. The heavily loaded men climbed aboard the C-47s. They were preceded by teams of Pathfinders who were to mark out the terrain with as yet secret equipment. The big jump was to take place over the harrowing, inextricable hedgerow country and over some dangerous inundated zones.

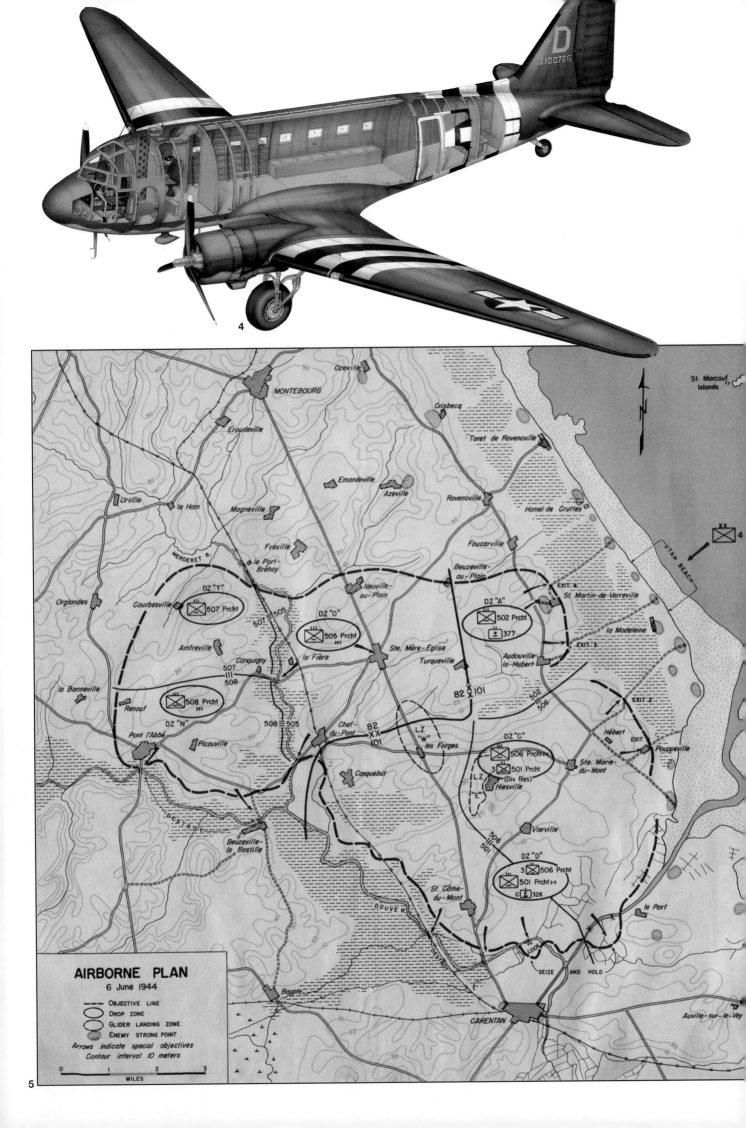

The Pathfinders

1. Pathfinder team of 1st Battalion 508th PIR (aircraft n° 16). Men of the 504th accompany the Pathfinders of 508th PIR. The soldier lying stretched out is unidentified. Front row, left to right: Pfc Nicholas Trevino (wounded, evacuated) unidentified (504th), Pfc Cipriano Gomez (Bronze Star), unidentified, Pfc Demciak, Pfc Donald E. Krause (wounded, Bronze Star), Pfc Wilburn L. Stutler (Bronze Star), Pfc J.T. Barkley (Bronze Star), unidentified, Pvt James H. Weinerth (Bronze Star). Standing : Gilliam (crew), Wilger (co-pilot), unidentified, (504th), Cpl R.J. Smith (Bronze Star), Herro (navigator), unidentified (crew), Miles (pilot), 2nd Lt Weaver (killed), soldier in the doorway unidentified (crew).

2. Pathfinder team of 2nd Battalion 508th PIR (aircraft n° 17). Front row, left to right: 2nd Lt Perez (crew), 2nd Lt Vohs (crew), 2nd Lt E.F. Hamilton (would be killed,

The Pathfinders

In January 1944, a contingent of pathfinders was assigned to mark out the drop zones in Normandy. The 82nd and 101st Airborne Divisions sent some 300 of their paratroops on a training course at *IX Troop Carrier Command Pathfinder School.* Most of the men were designated, with only a few volunteering. At this time, the pathfinders had not yet acquired their reputation as crack troops, which accounts for the small numbers coming forward for the speciality. Some came on the course just to have a speciality entitling them to promotion, other were transferred for disciplinary reasons.

In May, the *pathfinder unit comprised* 18 teams, three per drop zone (each regiment had its own drop zone designated by a letter, T,N,O…). The number of teams per drop zone was enough to accomplish the mission; even if two teams out of three on the ground were put out of action, the third could always get on with the job of marking out and welcoming the airborne regiments.

Each team was commanded by a lieutenant and comprised four operators for two Eureka radio beacons and four men responsible for protecting the operators and securing the drop zone. The chain of command included a captain for each divisional contingent and a lieutenant for each regimental team.

The first *Pathfinders* touched Norman soil at **00.16** on 6 June 1944. This was a team of *502nd PIR*, made up of 19 men including Captain **Frank Lillyman** and three members of the intelligence battalion, whose assignment involved identifying the St-Martin-de-Varreville batteries for the *101st Airborne Div.*, who hoped they had landed on DZ "A".

Bronze Star), 1st Lt Gaudion (pilot), 2nd Lt Polette Jr (killed, Silver Star), unidentified (crew), unidentified (crew). 2nd row : Sgt Katsanis (504th), Pvt Howard Jessup, Pvt R.L. Seale (Bronze Star), Cpl Ernest King (killed), Pvt Frederik J. Infanger. (CoE, Bronze Star), Pfc Murray E. Daly, (Co.D, killed, Bronze Star), Pvt John P. Perdue (Co.D, killed), Pfc Carl W. Jones (killed). Standing : Pvt Mesenbrink (Bronze Star), Pvt Robert A. Andreas (Co. E, Bronze Star), Pvt John G. Gerar (Bronze Star), Pfc Beverly J. Moss (Bronze Star), Pvt Norman C. Willis (Co.E Bronze Star), Pvt Forkapa (504th), unidentified (504th), unidentified (504th). The soldier in the doorway is 2nd Lt Murphy (504th).

3. Pathfinder team of 3rd Battalion 508th PIR (aircraft n° 18).

4. A Pathfinder with his radio beacon equipment. Notice the Eureka beacon hanging down his leg. Information on the use of this pathfinder equipment is given on pages 70 and 71.

(Photos D. François.)

The Pathfinders of *505th PIR*.

1st stick.

2nd stick.

3rd stick.
(Photos D. François coll.)

The Pathfinders of *507th PIR*.

1st stick.

2nd stick.

3rd stick.
(Photos D. François coll.)

67

1

1. These two paratroopers of *D Company, 508th PIR* are waiting to board on the edge of the taxiway. (D. François coll.)

2. and **3.** Ike meeting paratroops of *502nd PIR (101st Airborne Division)*. He insisted on seeing them before the big jump and feared very heavy casualties for the airborne troops, 50% killed and wounded for the paratroops, 70% for the glider-borne infantry. (Photo courtesy NA/D.F)

2

4

3

4. The M42 jump jacket reserved for US Army paratroops, easily recognizable with its slanting pockets. This one belonged to Clarence Hughart of *H Company, 507th PIR*. (D. François coll.)

5. Shoulder flashes and cap badges worn by the paratroopers of the two divisions' six regiments. (Heimdal.)

6. These paratroopers of *508th Parachute Infantry Regiment (82nd Airborne Division)* have a coffee and a donut as they wait to board. (D. François coll.)

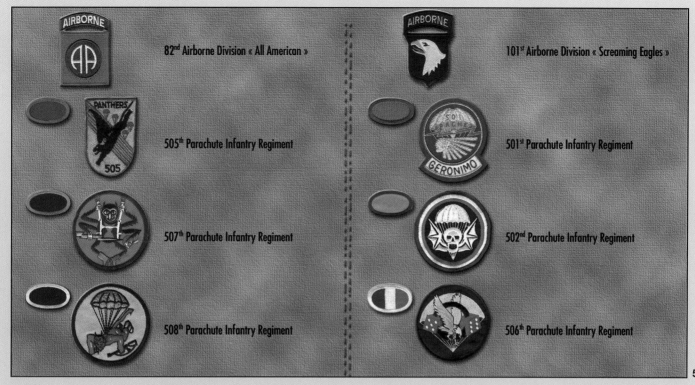

82nd Airborne Division « All American »

101st Airborne Division « Screaming Eagles »

505th Parachute Infantry Regiment

501st Parachute Infantry Regiment

507th Parachute Infantry Regiment

502nd Parachute Infantry Regiment

508th Parachute Infantry Regiment

506th Parachute Infantry Regiment

1

2

3

4

1. These paratroopers of the *82nd Airborne Division* have just received their ammunition and are about to board their plane for Normandy.

2. Last-minute checks for these paratroopers of 508th PIR before the big jump.

3. *Captain* Robert Rae of *507th PIR* soon to become one of the heroes at La Fière.

4. Sergeant Frank Stapples of *D Company*, *508th PIR* ready to jump.

(Photos D. François coll.)

« REBECCA »
transceiver

Sending interrogating waves
to a distance of c. 2.4 km

Beacon reply pulse

« EUREKA »
radar beacon

Created and designed by the British and manufactured specially for D-day by the *US Army*, this equipment had been kept secret until now. It operated on the basis of an exchange of radio frequency pulses between the aircraft, carrying the Rebecca interrogator unit and the Eureka response unit which guided the aircraft with great precision into the desired landing zone. The signals were only triggered if the aircraft the interrogator pulses using a secret code to which it alone held the key.

Once over the area, the Eureka responder was used as an ordinary sound transceiver, between the crew and the team on the ground, for the exchange of short messages, also in morse.

The 3.5 meter antenna was set up with masts, stays and stakes. According to the American instructions, the beacon weighed a total 12.5 kg with bag and harness. The equipment is shown below and on the opposite page.

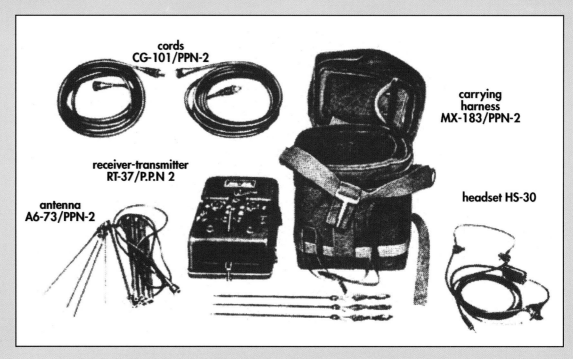

cords
CG-101/PPN-2

carrying
harness
MX-183/PPN-2

receiver-transmitter
RT-37/P.P.N 2

antenna
A6-73/PPN-2

headset HS-30

A few minutes later, the other teams of the 82nd and 101st Airborne Divisions jumped out of their planes on a mission for which they had been preparing for months. However luck was not on their side. Clouds and ground fog prevented the pilots of *IX Troop Carrier Command* from finding their way, for all their training and determination. Owing to flak, the drops were made at altitudes that were either too high or too low and at higher speed than planned during training, which led to the teams being scattered over a wide area and equipment being lost on being dropped out of the aircraft.

The most accurate parachute drop was made by a team of *506th PIR/101st Airborne Div.* which landed on DZ "C", and another which landed within a short walk of Hiesville, while the third landed literally in the sea.

Captain Lillyman had his three teams together in the same sector less than 2 kilometers north of DZ "A" at Saint Germain de Varreville. These teams were able to set up their Eureka beacons and holophane lamps quickly.

On DZ "D", the *Pathfinders* of *501st PIR* landed on enemy positions and were forced to engage the enemy before they had had time to take off their parachutes.

As for the *82nd Division*, all teams of *505th PIR* reached their mark, DZ "O" near Sainte-Mère-Eglise.

The *Pathfinders* of *507th PIR* landed on DZ "T", only to discover a heavy concentration of Germans patrolling the sector (Château Gris at Amfreville). Only one team, that of Lt. Charles Ames of the *507th's* 2nd Battalion, was able to set up its equipment.

Meanwhile the *508th*, in the Gueutteville village sector on the Sainte-Mère-Eglise-Pont L'Abbé road, had no better luck. Lt. Gene Williams and one of his men landed in a sector close to their objective and set up what little equipment they had, one Eureka beacon and two holophane lamps.

Being so scattered, many *Pathfinder teams* did not know whether or not they had landed on target. The lucky ones still could not set up their material, as sometimes it had been damaged on the way down, or else owing to the presence of the enemy.

The plan had failed and it was chaos at all the drop zones.

Carriers and jumps

Shortly after the *Pathfinders took off*, 13 000 paratroopers of the two US airborne divisions headed

This superb photo shows a paratrooper, with his front parachute and BC-611 walkie-talkie, in front of the fuselage of a C-47. (NA/Heimdal.)

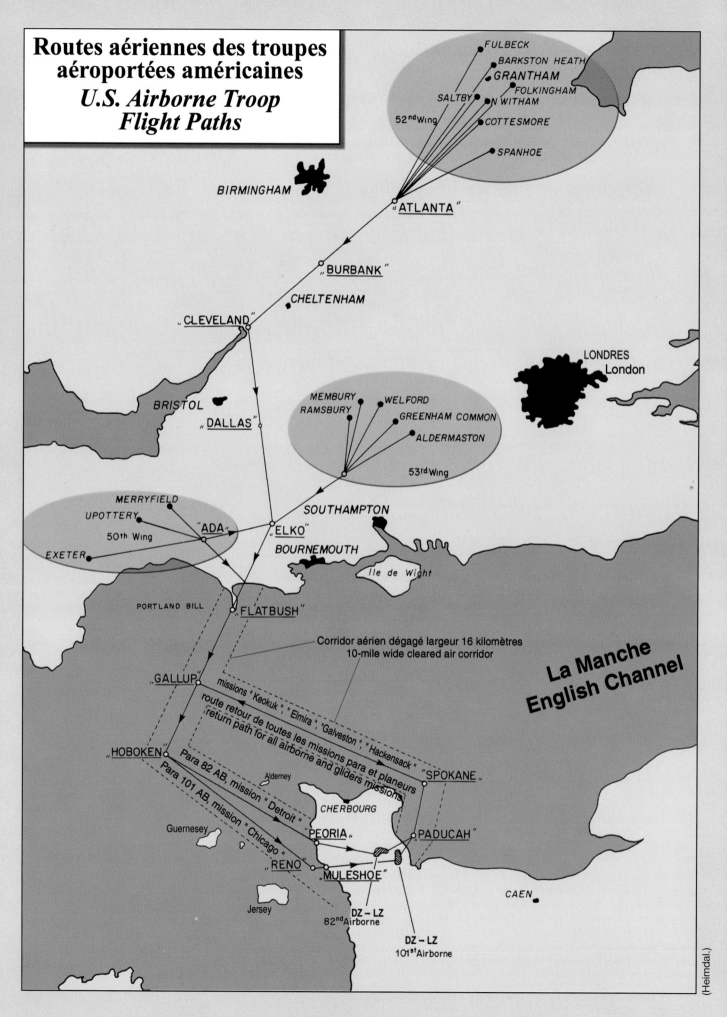

Routes aériennes des troupes aéroportées américaines
U.S. Airborne Troop Flight Paths

FULBECK
BARKSTON HEATH
GRANTHAM
SALTBY
FOLKINGHAM
N WITHAM
COTTESMORE
SPANHOE
52nd Wing

BIRMINGHAM

"ATLANTA"

"BURBANK"

CHELTENHAM

"CLEVELAND"

LONDRES
London

BRISTOL

"DALLAS"

MEMBURY
RAMSBURY
WELFORD
GREENHAM COMMON
ALDERMASTON
53rd Wing

MERRYFIELD
UPOTTERY
"ADA"
50th Wing
EXETER

SOUTHAMPTON

"ELKO"

BOURNEMOUTH

Ile de Wight

PORTLAND BILL

"FLATBUSH"

Corridor aérien dégagé largeur 16 kilomètres
10-mile wide cleared air corridor

La Manche
English Channel

"GALLUP"

missions "Keokuk" "Elmira" "Galveston" "Hackensack"
route retour de toutes les missions para et planeurs
return path for all airborne and gliders missions

"HOBOKEN"
Para 82 AB, mission "Detroit"
Para 101 AB, mission "Chicago"

Alderney

"SPOKANE"

CHERBOURG

Guernesey

"PEORIA"

"PADUCAH"

"RENO"

"MULESHOE"

CAEN

Jersey

DZ – LZ
82nd Airborne

DZ – LZ
101st Airborne

(Heimdal.)

74

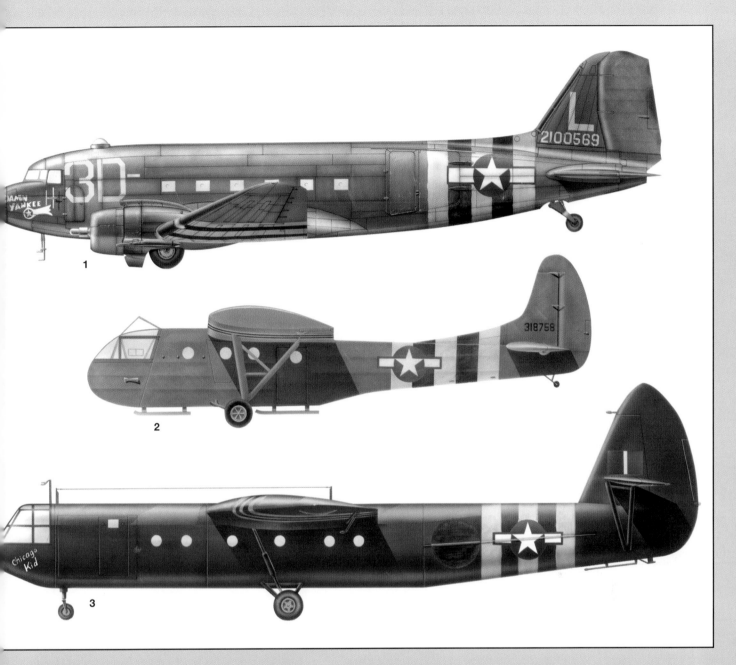

off to Normandy. Among them, *Major* Gordon Smith, Captain Paul Smith, Captain Roy Creek and Sergeant George Leidenheimer of the *507th*, Marcus Heim of the *505th* and O.B. Hill and Jack Schlegel of the *508th* witnessed the greatest airborne operation ever undertaken. Little did they know just how hard the battle would be, but of one thing they were sure: they were about to write themselves into the history books.

Mission Albany

The transport and dropping of the **101st Airborne Division** was codenamed *Albany*. The USAAF troop carriers came from the *50th* and *56th Troop Carrier Wings*, headquartered at Exeter in Devonshire and at Greenham Common in Berkshire, in the UK.

For Albany, 432 aircraft were requisitioned to take off half an hour after the *pathfinders.*

It took 9 C-47s to carry a company, as each plane carried 16 or 17 paratroopers, and 36 aircraft per airborne regiment battalion. A whole regiment mobilized 117 aircraft. For Operation *Neptune,* the squa-

drons of *IX TCC* were reinforced with 18 aircraft each, for a total 72 per group. Two groups were needed to transport a regiment.

The 101st started out from airfields in Wessex (*50th TCW* : *439th TC Group,* at Upottery; *440th TCG,* at Exeter; *441st TCG* at Merryfield, and *442nd TCG* at Fulbeck) and west of Reading (*53rd TCW*: *434th TCG,* at Aldermaston, *435th TCG* at Weldon Park, *436th TCG* at Membury, *437th TCG* at Ramsbury and *438th TCG* at Greenham Common).

DZ "A", located between Turqueville and *Exits N° 3* and 4, was the objective of the ***502nd PIR*** and the *377th Parachute Field Artillery Battalion* (PFAB), flying out from Greenham Common and Membury.

Sadly, 2 510 paratroops jumped well away from the DZ, only the *2nd Battalion* was concentrated to any degree.

DZ "C", near Sainte-Marie-du-Mont, was the objective of the **506th PIR** (minus its 3rd *Battalion* and plus **3rd Bat/501**). 15 sticks landed on the DZ, 38 close by. The rest of the 1st *Battalion, 506th* landed on the other side of the village of Sainte-Marie-du-Mont (near Exits n° 1 and 2), but the 2nd *Battalion* was

1. The US Army Air Forces placed mass orders late in 1941 for the C-47 after tests starting in December 1935.

2. The Waco CG-4, of which 13,909 were built, was used massively by the two airborne divisions.

3. The Airspeed Horsa AS 51 could transport a lot more men and equipment than the Waco, which is why the Americans used it as well.

(Profiles courtesy V. Dhorne/Heimdal.)

The US airborne assault on Normandy as depicted at the West Point museum. The east coast of the Cotentin can be seen in the background with Utah Beach and the inundated zones behind the sand dunes. On the right, the inundated zones of the Merderet marshes can be seen on either side of La Fière. The landscape is represented fairly accurately. (Airborne Museum coll., Sainte-Mère-Eglise.)

scattered over a broad area miles further north, most of its sticks landing near Sainte-Mère-Eglise. Some paratroops of *3rd Bat/501* found themselves at Sainte-Marie-du-Mont, near the Commander of 101st ABN, General Taylor and his staff.

After taking off from Merryfield and Exeter airfields, the Force jumping over **DZ "D"** had one of the most concentrated drops of the 101st, despite heavy enemy antiaircraft defenses as they arrived over the Normandy coast. Some 2 148 paratroops jumped, in relative concentration, only 18 aircraft out of 45 carrying the 1st Battalion of **501st** found their jump zone, with nine dropping their sticks over Carentan. The 2nd Battalion fared better and was able to muster 250 men quickly and head off towards their objective: St-Côme-du-Mont on the Carentan road.

The 3rd Battalion had no better luck, with eight sticks landing on the drop zone and 26 less than a mile away. But the area was heavily booby-trapped and defended by the enemy. The survivors able to struggle free of their parachutes had to withdraw fighting.

Mission Boston

Boston was the codename for the transport and dropping of the **82nd Airborne Division**. *Boston* began 10 minutes after Albany. The troop carriers were provided by the *52nd Troop Carrier Wing* from Cottesmore (*61st TCG* à Barkston, *313th TCG*, at Folkingham, *314th TCG* at Salby, *315th TCG* at Spanhoe and *316th TCG* at Cottesmore), and took off from their bases in Lincolnshire.

The operation got off to a bad start, a Gammon grenade carried by a paratrooper of 1/505 exploded inside an aircraft of *315th TCG*, killing three paratroopers and making the plane unusable.

The first formation to take off was the *316th Group* carrying the 2nd and 3rd Battalions of **505th PIR** with 2 howitzers and *456th PFAB (Parachute Field Artillery Battalion)*. Then came the rest of *505th* along with *307th Engineers*, and Divisional HQ, commanded by General Matthew Ridgway was carried over by *315th TCG.*, making a total of 2 120 paratroops on their way to **DZ "O"**.

Unlike Albany, the teams carrying 505th decided to fly over the cloud mass, which kept them clear of

some of the flak. On **DZ "O"**, the *Pathfinders* were ready waiting for their unit, with their Eureka beacon and red lights. The only problem was approaching the drop zone from high altitude, as the pilots did not have time to make out the red lights. They had to circle before dropping over the target. Of the 118 sticks dropped, 31 landed on or near the drop zone and 29 within a kilometer. 20 sticks came within 3 kilometers and another 20 landed further afield.

The **508th PIR** was brought over in the planes of the *313th* and *314th TCG* heading for their drop zone, **DZ "N"**, right in the middle of the sector of *91. Infanterie-Division*, headquartered at Picauville. The 2 188 paratroops got little help from the pathfinders landing around their drop zone. 17 sticks out of 132 landed on or near the DZ, and another 16 within a kilometer of it.

The last regiment of the 82nd Airborne Division was the **507th PIR** which took off from Barkston for its objective, **DZ "T"** (Amfreville), making the poorest approach of all.

Here unlike the others, the drop zone was not recognizable on the ground from landmarks such as a river or village. Flak was heaviest here and caused the formations to scatter. Out of the 2 000 "spiders"

(as the paratroops of the *507th were nicknamed*), just 2 or 3 sticks landed on or near the drop zone. 50 were within a kilometer and 22 over 3 kilometers away. Some sticks were dropped over 20 kilometers off target, including 180 paratroops dropped over Graignes.

The scattering of all the US airborne troops may have seemed a terrible setback in the early hours of the D-day landings, but in the days that followed it proved a huge advantage on the ground. It led the German troops to overestimate the enemy forces, and they were unable to organize effective counter-measures against the scattered airborne troops, being unable to identify where and how far they had penetrated, and wipe them out. The bottom line for the Americans was that no regrouping was possible, and for the Germans it spelt total confusion.

508th PIR HQ Company helmet. (Photo courtesy B.F.)

Panic at Sainte-Mère-Eglise

The pump used to put out the fire is still there in front of the church. (Heimdal.)

On that 5 June 1944, the last gleam of sunlight disappeared at 22.48. Some people slept with their window open, and a few minutes later, at **23.00** (local time), shouts were heard in the gathering gloom. A fire had broken out at Madame Pommier's. It was first discovered by a German sentry patrolling near a flak gun position near the house. The soldier raised the alarm. Auguste Paris quickly donned his fireman's helmet and was joined by his son Raymond and Messrs Blandin and Mauduit. After getting the "small" high pressure pump out of the fire pump room, coupled to the vehicle loaded with canvas buckets, the four men raced to the church square, stopping for a moment on a level with Dr Monnier's house. At that moment, the leading aircraft formation flew over the town. Instinctively they raised their shoulders up around their ears bracing themselves for the bombs about to fall. Nothing happened! So they started running again and set up the pump by the fire. The two rapid alternating tones of the alarm bell warned the neighbors who converged on the light given off by the blaze, some of them carrying buckets of their own. Most of these people were women. Soon a human chain was formed to bring water from the hand pump in all kinds of pails to build up pressure in the fire hose operated by the firemen. The mayor, Alexandre Renaud, busied himself at both ends of this human chain as German soldiers supervised this group of about sixty people breaking curfew.

Rudolf May, photo taken before his death.

Then, all of a sudden, while this emergency service was in full swing, a second formation of Allied aircraft flew over the town. They seemed to be flying low, they were lit up by the glow of the blaze and taken to task by flak converging on the white stripes painted on their sides and wings.

From the top of the steeple, Private **Rudolf May** observed this abrupt intrusion in a mild, calm night barely ruffled by the disturbance over the fire. At around **midnight**, the sky was filled with the drone of planes flying overhead. Rudolf May saw "things" falling out of the sky – containers. He also saw local people trying to put out the fire as it spread to a small nearby barn. While to this day nobody quite knows how the blaze was started, there has been talk of incendiary bombs, and claims that it was set off by the Pathfinders as a landmark for the C-47s.

By now it was one in the morning, French time. The fire at Julia Pommier's house had spread to the shed where Marcel Marie kept his woodpile. Meanwhile, Bob McInnes, navigator aboard a C-47 with 81st TCS, lost his way in thick cloud and arrived almost over Cherbourg amid heavy flak. He then turned back southwards, following Highway 13. Spotting the fire at Sainte-Mère, he dropped his paratroopers of the 101st Airborne Division well away from the planned zone. They were joined by elements of the 82nd Airborne Division who landed close to their objectives. Over Sainte-Mère, after dropping the Pathfinders and containers, a third wave of aircraft arrived. The drone of their engines became louder and louder, drowning the sound of the alarm bell. The planes were flying very low, with white marks standing out on their fuselages and drawing German fire. The civilians began to panic, made worse by women screaming, and the group broke up. However, it was not bombs falling from the sky but multicolored corollas drawing German light arm tracer fire. The cry rang out: "Paratroops! Paratroops!". It was **00.15** (Allied time) when two sticks of the 506th PIR jumped over the town. At least four of these men were killed by the Germans. The local population was terrified, with more planes coming over the square in a fearsome dance.

John Steele, photo taken on 6 June 1964. (Photo courtesy H.J. Renaud.)

Kenneth E. Russell, photo taken when he visited the museum. (Airborne Museum coll.)

The first US paratroops landed and the Germans in the square began picking off the troopers caught in the trees. Mayor Alexandre Renaud exhorted his people to go back to their homes. As they did so, Auguste and Raymond Paris saw the body of a paratrooper in front of René Jamard's store and hastily wrapped it in his parachute.

Twenty minutes later, a stick of F Company, *505th PIR*, was dropped over the town. Six or seven paratroopers were killled as they came down amid the Germans firing from the square. Sergeant **Ray** was the only one to land among the Germans. He crumpled up hit by a burst of machine-gun fire, but before he died he managed to kill his enemy. Private **Blankenship** disappeared into the blazing house ; he was identified that afternoon by Lieutenant J.P. Carroll of *F Company*. According to John Steele, another paratrooper named White also fell into the flames, but no paratrooper of that name is listed among those of the 505th killed in Normandy. Another was heading for the inferno but escaped with severe burns when he was caught up in a rising current of warm air. Hanging from a horse-chestnut tree with bullets flying all around him, **R. Blanchard** pulled out his knife and cut his harness, and in his hurry the end of his thumb as well, and then stole off into the night. Private **A. Maughn** hit the ground in the garden of Dr. Monnier's house opposite the church and was captured immediately by Lieutenant Werner. Private **John Steele** came down towards the square when a piece of flak hit him in the left foot. He then drifted towards the bell-tower and his parachute became snarled on it. Private **Russell** also hit the church and caught his parachute on the lower part of the roof. On being spotted by a German, he thought his time had come until Sergeant **Ray** landed just in front of him and killed the German before dying himself. The German may have been **Alfons Jakl** (see below). Russell lost no time in releasing his harness and getting out of town.

While the local people were fighting the fire, in one of the C-47s carrying a stick of *A Company, 505th PIR*, **Howard Manoian**, a young paratrooper was checking his equipment to which he had added. He had two bandoleers (broad cartridge belts with more pouches) for extra ammunition for his Garand rifle. He carried eight grenades instead of the standard issue of four. In addition to the regulation M3 knife attached to his right leg, he attached to his left leg a knife given to him by a friend with the *29th Infantry Division*. Also, on embarking, he had an antitank mine placed on his lap-pack parachute. His pockets were bursting with rations and Camel cigarettes. And his last line of protection was a holy picture in his shirt pocket. This strapping brown-haired lad from Massachusetts was 19 years old and bracing for his very first operational jump. They had an uneventful crossing. Sainte-Mère-Eglise was now the objective of the men of the *505th Parachute Infantry Regiment*. We have just followed the dramatic arrival of one stick of that regiment's *F Company* over the church square. We now follow this paratrooper of *A Company*. The time by their watches was **01.15**. The 18 men of the stick got up. The red light turned to green. Suddenly, the flak began to burst out to welcome them. The drop was swift and Howard Manoian was relieved to see his parachute open. The ground came up to him, ten yards from a low wall by a hedge; around him came gunfire and explosions. He quickly got rid of his harness, gas mask and the mine and jumped over the protective obstacle. *"Shit! A cemetery!"* There he was among the graves, south-east of the church square. He sped away into a small garden, taking his bearings from the burning house.

In another C-47 bringing over a stick of I Company, 505th PIR, was 20-year-old Pfc **William Tucker**, who hailed from the east coast of the US. Suddenly he and his comrades heard the order to go. Before he had time to realize, they were out of the plane, and their parachutes opened. They were not high up and William Tucker watched the tracer pass them by. Then he heard **Ray Krupinski**, who had been behind him in the plane, shouting *"Sonofabitch, I've been hit again!"* He landed by a tree in the La Haule park (not far from the house on fire, see map on page 58). The whole stick came down near the cemetery, in the far south-east of the town. He and one or two comrades landed in the town center near the house on fire. He slipped off his harness and then stiffened as someone came up towards him. He shouted the password, ready to open fire. It was a paratrooper in this company, Pfc **Everett Gilliland**. All around them came the snapping of the metal crickets they had been issued, and gunshots that were hard to place. But what most impressed him was the C-47s passing very low overhead. Around their small party of three or four men the crickets were clicking away and gunshots rang out under the infernal thunder of the C-47s. William Tucker hurried away from the town.

Sergeant **Robinson** now took charge of the stick of William Tucker's plane. They were now rather surprised by the tall, dense hedgerows looming up in the night – rather offputting with their *"five to seven feet high covered from top to bottom with a jungle of bushes and rows of trees"*. The sergeant mustered his men on the outskirts of the town before sending them onto the attack towards the town center which was not far, at the end of an endless narrow lane between two terrifying hedgerows. The American paratroopers had just had their introduction to the "green hell" of the Cotentin for which they were not prepared. They then stopped for an hour or so and opened a can of K rations. All the while came heavy gunfire. Suddenly, a machine-gun opened up to their left. William Tucker said to **Larry Leonard**, who had sat beside him in the plane, *"We're going to blow it to pieces!"* But while they prepared to pass through the hedge, a stream of tracer bullets clipped the branches over their heads, inciting them to greater caution. The group was reinforced and Lieutenant **Walter Kroener** took over command. The paratroopers encountered a Norman and the lieutenant told Bob Tucker to ask him if this terrifying lane led to the town center. *"Où est centre de citie?"* The local pointed the way and disappeared.

We come back to the town center, and the home of the veterinary surgeon, Dr. Monnier. His large house gave onto the south side of the square and a German officer, Lieutenant **Werner**, was billetted there. On hearing the drone of the first aircraft, Dr. Monnier had opened the windows to prevent the panes from being smashed and gone back up to his bedroom. But, gathering from Lieutenant Werner's feverish attitude that the situation was serious, the Monnier family repaired to their shelter in the south-east corner of the garden. It was then that paratrooper Maughn landed on Dr. Monnier's shoulders. But the German officer was in the garden and promptly came up with a pistol to disarm the trooper. A little while afterwards, however, Lieutenant Werner was forced to surrender to his prisoner (1)…

During these dramatic events, **Rudolf May** and his young comrade were still atop the church steeple, while Sergeant **Rudi Escher** and the other four men in his party were down below with the other German soldiers. The light from the blaze had shown the lookouts the sheer scale of the parachute drop. Two

paratroopers were hooked onto the church. Kenneth E. Russell pulled himself clear as we have seen, but **John Steele** was still hanging to the bell-tower by his suspending ropes. He looked to be dead, but in fact had no more than an injured left foot. Rudolf May and his comrade just saw a passing shadow. But after a while they heard the paratrooper talking. The young grenadier thought he would make an easy target. But Rudolf May told him to be careful. *"Are you crazy? If you fire, they'll know where we are!"* Rudolf May saw the whole scene when a German soldier fired on a paratrooper, Sergeant Ryan, with his MP 40 to be killed in his turn by the American. Grabbing his pocket knife, he set about cutting the suspending ropes in order to get rid of his unwanted guest, letting him slip away to his fate. This saved John Steele's life! After hanging for nearly 45 minutes from the steeple with the bell ringing away full blast, John Steele was picked up by the Germans, and escaped a few days later. As for Rudolf May, fearing the paratroopers got inside the church and discovered them, he threw a grenade up at the church door. But the Americans could not get up to the bell-tower, as access to it was through a well concealed side door.

Soon a second blaze lit up the town. A C-47 crashed on the southern route out of town (where the "Sainte-Mère" hotel-restaurant now stands). Seeing the paratroops endlessly raining down and the circling planes, the Germans realized that this was a large-scale operation. After the initial confusion, the square was now deserted and the house fire burned itself out. In Sergeant Escher's squad, one man had been killed, Private **Alfons Jakl** (he is buried in the Orglandes cemetery). The Germans mustered in good order in three lines on the south side of the square, still in control of this sector until they pulled back from the town center, uncertain of the situation and risking encirclement before dawn. The Sainte-Mère-Eglise garrison took advantage of a lull of sorts and the depth of night to head off out of town southward down the main street. Rudi Escher's squad mustered. The six men fetched their cycles out of the shed and set off due south to their company command post a kilometer away at Château de Fauville. Tense, their guns at the ready, they went down the main street, but joined their unit at Fauville without coming under fire.

More elements of the **505th Parachute Infantry Regiment** would now converge on their objectives. The leading paratroopers of the 2nd Battalion (2/505) landed in Normandy at **00.51**. Their commander, Lieutenant-Colonel **Vandervoort**, had injured his left ankle and began to muster his men propped up against his rifle. Then a folding munitions trailer was found for him and his party of 400 men (by D-day evening the number had risen to 575 out of the battalion's original 630) set off again towards its objective: the Neuville-au-Plain area. This village lay two kilometers north of Sainte-Mère and was to provide protection on the north side of the town. Once again, the sticks were scattered and it took about three hours for the battalion to muster!

The troopers of the 3rd Battalion (**3/505**) hit their DZ just west of Sainte-Mère at **02.03**. By around 3, the battalion commander, Lieutenant-Colonel **Krause**, had managed to muster 158 men (roughly the strength of a company). Heading this small force alongside Captain De Long, he entered Sainte-Mère from the north when the Germans had abandoned the place. As they came to the first houses, he ordered

(1) Full story in *Sainte-Mère-Eglise, les paras du 6 juin*, by Philip Jutras, Editions Heimdal.

Howard Manoian in 1944 and in 1993; he came to settle near Sainte-Mère. (Heimdal coll.)

William Tucker in 1944 and in 1993. (Heimdal coll.)

Henri-Jean Renaud when the crashed C-47's tail fin was unearthed. (H.J. Renaud coll.)

six groups to set up roadblocks around the town, with bazookas, "Gammon" antitank grenades and minefields. Once in the town, Krause cut the Paris-Cherbourg cable. Less than an hour later, Sainte-Mère fell into the troopers' hands without a fight, as, according to Rudi Escher, the Germans had fallen back at about 4 in the morning (3 o'clock for the Americans).

With the "Screaming Eagles"

To the south, the paratroopers of the **101st Airborne Division** were just as badly scattered. General **Taylor** and the troopers of the *501st PIR* were somewhere between Sainte-Marie-du-Mont and Vierville. They then linked up with some more men and with Lieutenant-Colonel **Ewell**, who had mustered 90 men. He commanded *3/501,* the reserve battalion, but he found himself in the *506th PIR's* drop zone. Near Hiesville (west of Sainte-Marie-du-Mont) there were 150 paratroopers who would defend the command post. General Taylor decided to march on one of the beach exits, choosing *Exit 1* (near Pouppeville), and a tactical grouping was formed with Lieutenant-Colonel Ewell in command of 60 troopers and 25 members of the divisional staff (a tiny fraction of his battalion strength of 706 men!) There were generals there as well and lieutenants were used as pathfinders, hence General Taylor's remark, *"Never have so few been commanded by so many [officers]".* This column first saw action passing near Sainte-Marie-du-Mont where, to their surprise, a German sentry shouted and seven soldiers appeared out of their trench. Corporal Virgil E. Danforth killed four of them, another trooper killed two more Germans and the other two got away.

General Taylor, who spoke fluent French, met a civilian and asked the name of the closest locality, which was Pouppeville. On its way, Ewell's formation picked up a few stragglers and was now 150-strong. It was marching on that small village when shots rang out from the outskirts. *Major* Larry Legere (the G-3) was hit, and a G.I. was killed, he was 101st's first

fatal casualty. One prisoner was taken: a Polish deserter. Soon a column arrived at Pouppeville and Exit 1 in reinforcement, numbering just 50 men commanded by Colonel **Turner**.

In the south, the paratroopers of Colonel **Johnson**'s *501st PIR* landed at DZ D. At least the 1st Battalion under Lieutenant-Colonel Ballard did, arriving south of Angoville to attack due west at Les Droueries. A little further south came the 2nd Battalion with *Major* Allen, attacking Basse-Addeville, again due west. Still further south, Colonel Johnson marched on La Barquette to take the crossing over the Douve River.

To the north, the *502nd PIR jumped on DZ A near* *the* Saint-Martin-de-Varreville battery. Its commander, Colonel **Van Horn Moseley Jr**, sustained a fractured leg in the jump. The *2/502* commander, Lieutenant-Colonel **Steve A. Chappuis**, also broke a leg, but not so badly. Lieutenant-Colonel **Cassidy** *(1/502)* marched up to the battery, having been assigned to destroy it; he encountered the *Pathfinder commander,* Captain Lillyman. Together they came to the battery position to discover that it had been completely knocked out, so they headed off north, arriving at Foucarville where Cassidy set up roadblocks to cover the northern front of the paratroops' sector before turning back south, leaving Lieutenant **Swanson** behind. At 08.15 hours, he sent a radio message reporting that the Saint-Martin-de-Varreville had been destroyed and was no longer a threat. Meanwhile, Lieutenant-Colonel **Robert G. Cole** (*3/502 commander*), whose assignment involved moving on Exit 3 to clear and hold it, had come down too far west, near Sainte-Mère-Eglise. He set out towards the battery initially with a force of nearly 80 men. But there was an encounter with some Germans in which Major Vaughn (Reg. S-4) was killed. He too found that his battery had been abandoned and so he reached Exit 3 very quickly, at 07.30. Captain Robert L. Clemens reached Exit 4, a little further north.

But further on, events were taking a dramatic turn. A German general was killed, an American general died when his glider crash-landed, and paratroopers were drowning in the marshes. It was to be a long and terrible night, with the outcome hanging in the balance...

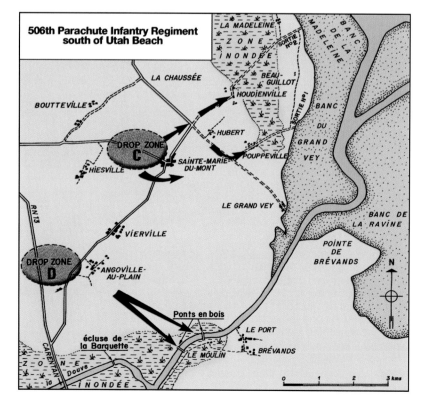

Representation of the airborne assault on Sainte-Mère-Eglise by a German painter. (Airborne Museum.)

The airborne bridgehead

This extremely rare color shot was taken at *Utah Beach* (notice the bay of Saint-Vaast-la-Hougue in the distance). The soldier in jump boots on the right is wearing the shoulder flash of the Engineers' special brigades, here *1st ESB*. The man behind him is wearing a helmet marked with the blue arc indicating an unidentifed component of that brigade. Photo taken by the Signal Corps, Miller and Steve Stevens. (US Army.)

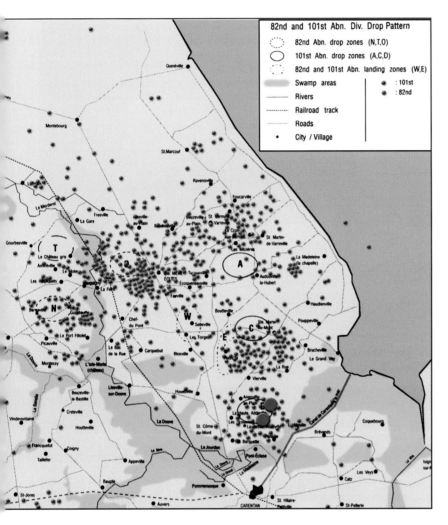

82nd and 101st Abn. Div. Drop Pattern	
⬭	82nd Abn. drop zones (N,T,O)
◯	101st Abn. drop zones (A,C,D)
⬭	82nd and 101st Abn. landing zones (W,E)
	Swamp areas
	Rivers
	Railroad track
	Roads
•	City / Village

: 101st   : 82nd

This map shows just how scattered the paratroop sticks became during the night of 5-6 June 1944. (US Army.)

During the night of 5 to 6 June 1944, 13 000 US para-troops landed on the soil of Normandy, in the Cotentin. The *Pathfinders* had marked out the drop zones just hours before the paratroops of the *82nd* and *101st Airborne Divisions* landed in an unhospitable area geographically more suited to the enemy, with its dense hedgerows facilitating the German defenses, and reduced visibility for bringing units together, and also inundated zones in which many paratroopers landed and drowned. Also, weather conditions and enemy AA guns scattered the troop carrier formations which were obliged to drop their sticks in very poor conditions, at low altitude, with high dropping speeds, and most of all often miles away from the planned dropping zones.

All the American troops had landed on Norman soil, but this in itself accomplished nothing for the Allies.

However, there was no less confusion on the German side, as it became difficult to counterattack when the enemy was so scattered. As for assessing the scale of the American forces, they was no way of telling whether they were embarking in isolated com-

mando operations or launching an offensive on altogether a larger scale.

It was a night of tragedy for many men when destiny caught up with them. They included two general officers, an American and a German.

The troops are scattered

On the ground, the initial phase of the airborne ope-ration in Normandy soon degenerated from divisio-nal level to battalion level. Even the word "battalion" seems inappropriate. Most units trying to muster had about a hundred paratroops under a field officer. But for many, the early hours of the battle in Normandy were spent on their own, lost and out of touch with their regiment. And to make communications bet-ween units even worse, very few wireless sets were in working order.

Albert Hassenzahl *(506th PIR/101st Abn.Div)*

On the night of 5 June 1944, General Dwight D. Eisen-hower visited the paratroopers of *101st Airborne* prior to the drop over Normandy. Estimated casualty fore-casts for the operation were 75 per cent, the highest percentage for any of the forces committed on D-day. Albert Hassenzahl was one of the wounded who survived the landings, and he was a changed man for the rest of his life.

"The evening before we went into Normandy we were visited by General Eisenhower, Winston Churchill, and a whole load of staff from both sides. We were in an airfield marshaling area preparing to head to Normandy that night. They just happened to hit our battalion. I was in the front row. I'll never forget one personal experience when Ike, General Eisenhower, just happened, for whatever reasons, to stop in front of me. He came up to me and looked right into my eyes and in a very soft voice said, 'Good luck, sol-dier.' That always stayed with me. I guess it did bring me good luck, because I survived.

As we boarded the planes, we were weighted with the reserve parachute, weapons stuck everywhere, your pockets bulging with ammunition, knives, or what they called 'leg bags' ; they were canvas bags that had straps with a short line that wrapped around your leg with a quick release. We never jumped with them before.

On top of that, my job when the green light went on... was to lead my people out of the airplane [...] We didn't jump very high; it seemed as though I had two oscillations and hit the ground. When I hit the ground: completely black outside, I saw nothing. The Ger-mans hit a couple of my men within a few minutes of following me out of the door.

Shortly after landing, all I can tell you is it was a run-ning firefight between a couple of hedgerows. It was near either Ste. Mère-Eglise or Ste. Marie-du-Mont. That was the general area I dropped into.

During the day we contacted some Krauts. I had this burning sensation in my right chest, and my legs went out from under me [...] I was conscious, and I remem-

ber my friend and my sergeant, Joseph Zettwich, known as Punchy, come out under risk of his own life, and he pulled me himself back behind a hedge-row under cover. My jacket was saturated with blood and I had a gaping chest wound. We all carried a large compress; each man had one. He took my com-press; I still recall his comment, something to the effect: 'Jesus Christ! I don't know what I can do, but I'll do the best I can.' He did. He patched me up as best he could.

I was in and out of consciousness [...] I was getting hauled back (I don't remember how) to the aid sta-tion. The battalion aid station was close to the figh-ting [...] This station was an old château that the Ger-mans must have known was an aid station. They were throwing mortars at it. They [...] hit some of the guys that were lying there.

The next thing I remember was taking a jeep ride down to the beach on a stretcher for evacuation to the LSTs to go back to England or wherever they were going to take you. I was laying on this beach – this was off of Utah Beach."

Captain Roy Creek
(E Co, 507th PIR, 82nd Abn. Div.)

03.30. As the last paratroopers of the 82nd and 101st Airborne Divisions had just landed small groups of men attempted to muster in the Normandy Bocage that seemed to them so hostile. Despite the moon-light, visibility was poor owing to the hedgerows, of which there were so many in this sector, enabling the defenders to engage in devastating ambush attacks on the troops that had just landed. One of these men was Captain Roy Creek who was drop-ped along with 2 004 paratroops of the *507th PIR*. He made desperate attempts to muster the men of this company, *Easy Coy*, but soon discovered that his men had been scattered over a wide area; he found out later that of the six paratroop regiments dropped that night the 507th was the regiment whose drop had gone least well.

"Through the hedgerows we could hear voices. I couldn't tell if they were German or American voices. 'Flash' had been designated as our password. From behind a tree came a challenge - Flash! The imme-diate reply was 'Flash', Hell! This is Col. Maloney the Executive Officer of the Regiment' (author's note: the expected answer was 'Thunder'). "Instantly we knew we were among friends."

Troopers kept drifting in and our force was growing. Men came from all units of the 82nd Airborne Divi-sion and some from the 101st Airborne [whose DZs were in the Carentan area].

A "cricket" used by the paratroopers of the *101st Airborne* to identify themselves to each other in the dark. (D. François coll.)

Above : Colonel Louis G. Mendez Jr. (Photo courtesy D. François.)

Opposite : aerial photo (taken in March 1944) showing part of communes of Hiesville and Vierville : **1.** Franqueville ; **2.** Calaville ; **3.** Limarais ; **4.** Colombières ; **5.** General Pratt's glider.

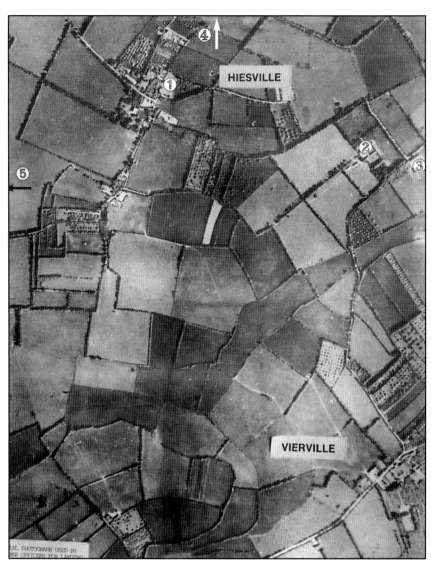

Below : at Franqueville Farm (Hiesville). Jean Lecaudey helped a pathfinder place a Eureka beacon on the farmhouse roof. (Lecaudey coll.)

Just before daybreak, the first gliders began to come in. One landed in a flooded area about 150 yards from where we had our perimeter set up. As the men started to come out of the glider, enemy machine gun-fire opened up from the hedgerow on the other side. Men coming out of the glider were being hit."

Colonel Louis Mendez *(508th PIR, 82nd Airborne Division) describes it somewhat as follows:*

"I was in command of the 3rd Battalion, which I only found five days later. We were in trouble as soon as we landed. The flak was terrible. We jumped with our whole formation at around 2000 feet, which was too high. Later when I checked my back pack, I found three bullets had passed through it during the long drop. I landed at about 02.30 a.m., and for five days I saw no-one, except for my messenger…

The Germans had a gift for communications. We felt we had groups of about sixty paratroopers coming after us all the time, they seemed to be waiting for us. Later I found three men, an officer in addition to my messenger. The most extraordinary thing I learned during those days of wandering was the Germans' intelligence capability. They were able to use our first and second names to deceive our company commanders. One of my commanders told me he had received a message with my name and nickname!..."

Hiesville

West of Sainte-Marie-du-Mont lies the village of Hiesville, which extends northwards with the manor-farm of Colombières. This was where the *101st Airborne Division* and *506th PIR* set up their command posts. Between that village and Sainte-Marie stood the hamlet of Le Holdy where the Germans had a battery *(2./243)*. Between the center of Hiesville and Colombières was Franqueville Farm where **Madame Lecaudey** (widowed in May 1944) lived with her son Jean (21) and daughter Marguerite (20). They heard planes flying over from 22.30, then Jean Lecaudey noticed a parachute in a tree and was suddenly surprised to see one of the *pathfinders* who had come to mark out DZ C. The paratrooper had slightly injured his foot. He was weighed down with his Eureka beacon and asked Jean to give him a hand. Together they set up the beacon on the farmhouse roof. The the exhausted paratrooper lay down in one of the bedrooms. The paratroops came down all around this DZ. Then two Germans aged about fifty turned up in the farmyard coming to surrender to Jean Lecaudey. More paratroops arrived, including a Canadian. Jean Lecaudey wanted to hand over his prisoners to them: *"You take care of them!"* The other replied: *"What do you want us to do with them?"* And he explained that they did not have the resources to take prisoners (instructions had been issued to that effect for the first 72 hours) (1). Jean Lecaudey pleaded for them to be spared. And they were locked up at Calaville Farm where more prisoners later joined them. A few days later, Jean Lecaudey saw the column of prisoners passing and the two Germans waved to him and thanked him. A little further southeast, towards Le Holdy, was Limarais Farm. **Louise James** and her aunt spent the night in their trench and heard the sound of snappers all around them. Louise James was 23 years old, she was a junior school teacher at Carentan and this was where she lived.

... and at Vierville

Here is a personal account by the mayor of Vierville, Léon Lenoël: *"There are no more Germans in Vierville right now, the last ones moved out early in May, but there are Germans nearby, at Basse-Addeville, Saint-Côme and La Fisée. Already you can hear sten guns in the marshes, the paratroopers are surely coming under attack by the Germans. Planes continue to fly over for the rest of the night but there must be no more bombers. At around **4 a.m.** we are confronted with the first paratroopers, they are Americans who have mostly had a hard time with a rough landing in our flooded marshes. They strike us as being very alert, always on the lookout, and fiercely determined to hold out. [...] In our fields, another sight awaits us, a number of large aircraft have landed during the night, gliders. In some of them there were about thirty men, in others small cannons or cars known as jeeps. A few local people helped the Americans to pull one of these jeeps out of a glider."* This is indeed what happened before daybreak, with gliders bringing in men and most of all equipment for the *paratroops.* The landing of gliders in the dark was a major first.

The death of General Pratt

Brigadier General Don Pratt, assistant commander of the *101st Airborne Division*, also came over by glider. His aircraft carried the marking *The Fighting Falcon.* Piloting this glider was an officer, Lieutenant-Colonel Mike Murphy. Hailing from Findley Ohio, he was 34 years old; in civilian life he was a test pilot in the aeronautical industry. It was for such outstanding ability as a pilot that he was chosen to pilot

(1) See testimony in The Devils Have Landed by Lewis Millkovics.

1. *Brig. Gen.* Don Pratt, deputy commander of the *101st Airborne Division*, in front of his maps. (Private coll.)

2. 25 May 1944 in England. Left to right : *1st Lt.* John L. May (General Pratt's aide de camp), *Brig. Gen.* Donald F. Pratt, Lt. col. Mike Murphy (pilot), *Lt* John M. Butler (co-pilot) in front of Brig. Gen. Don Pratt's glider, *The Fighting Falcon.* Only Murphy and May survived the crash. (Private coll.)

3. Site of the *Fighting Falcon* crash and memorial to *Brigadier General* Don Pratt. (E. Groult/Heimdal.)

4. Captain Charles O. Van Gorder in front of the wreckage of the glider carrying Don Pratt. Note on the right a long wooden stake used by the paratroopers to lever the glider out after it had crashed into the hedge. (Milton Dank.)

5. *Brigadier General* Don Pratt's grave at the Arlington National Cemetery in Washington D.C. (Photo courtesy Philippe Esvelin.)

General Pratt. He was followed in by another glider piloted by Lieutenant Victor Warringer, which also carried part of the medical team *(326th Medical Company)* of 101st Airborne including Captain Charles O. Van Gorder. The two gliders were making their approach over Hiesville and LZE. There was a strong 18 to 20 knot side wind. Mike Murphy landed in a field covered with heavy morning dew and the gliders started aquaplaning. The *Fighting Falcon* and the other glider both crashed into a hedge and a line of trees 250 meters from the D.329 road southwest of Hiesville. General Pratt and Lieutenant Butler were killed instantly. Lieutenant-Colonel Murphy broke his right thigh. This happened at **04.08.**

The Holdy battery

Day breaking at Limarais found Louise James in her trench with her aunt. One of the latter's farm laborers loked over the hedge and said *"The English!"*. There weere soldiers walking quietly along the road,

their faces blackened and they asked: *"Germans?"* Louise James answered *"No"*. So they asked *"French?"*. Louise James was so filled with emotion that she answered *"ja!"*. But for the Americans, this sounded more familiar than a proper British "yes". They brought out a photograph and enquired where the Holdy battery was; they made short work of its 10.5 cm howitzers. A little later, General Pratt's orderly arrived at the farm in tears and washed the *Brigadier General's* bloodstained personal belongings.

The German command in disarray

At 23.00 hours (German time, 22.00 hours British time), when the bombs again rained down on the Saint-Martin-de-Varreville battery *(1./1261)* — the final bombardment completely ploughing up the site — marked the end of the alert for the German commander of the coastal defenses, Lieutenant-Colonel Keil. He went to bed and was later woken by his warrant officer, Lieutenant Saul, announcing parachute drops over the regimental CP. Keil immediately committed his Engineers section under its CO *Leutnant* Wappaens to a counterattack, placing his regiment's sector *on Alarmstufe III* (maximum alert). However he was unable to transmit the order as his telephone line to the 1st Battalion had been cut! All he could do was to dispatch riders on motorcycles to pass on the alert. A beaming *Leutnant* Wappaens brought back his first prisoners but was killed soon afterwards with a bullet in the heart. These prisoners declined

to supply any information but their maps indicated that they were supposed to drop over Sainte-Mère-Eglise. Meanwhile, Colonel Tripel had no contact with his 1st Battalion's CP (with *I./919's* CP at Foucarville). The liaison officer dispatched by Günther Keil came back having failed to fulfil his mission after coming under fire and forced back by paratroopers. Lieutenant-Colonel Keil had no idea what had become of his units and so could not issue orders. He was reduced to commanding just his HQ company (Captain Simoneit) at Montebourg, with fifty-six men and six customs officials, reinforced by the *Divisions-Kampfschule* (divisional training school commanded by *Oberleutnant* Wendorf) with a strength of ninety men armed with eight Bren guns.

The "Screaming Eagles" at Sainte-Marie-du-Mont

Around Sainte-Marie-du-Mont, the three regiments of the *101st Airborne Division* advanced towards their objectives despite the fact that the paratroops had been scattered over a wide area and so only under-strength battalions had mustered, reinforced with various other elements who had also come down far from their planned drop zones. In the south, starting with **Drop Zone D** (see page 80), we left the 1st Battalion, **501st PIR**, commanding officer Lieutenant-Colonel Ballard, heading towards their *objective*s south of Angoville-au-Plain. *2/501* (*Major* Allen) was advancing due west on Basse-Addeville, while the regimental commander, the formidable Colonel Johnson, had set off to force a way over the Douve river at La Barquette, on the way to Carentan. This regiment was to cover the southern flank of the airborne bridgehead and march on the town, but it was to come up against a redoubtable enemy: the German paratroops of *Major* von der Heydte's *Fallschirmjäger-Regiment 6*, the Green Devils.

From **506th PIR's DZ C,** General Taylor reached *Exit n° 1 with the* Ewell column, and other elements arrived towards La Vienville and Houdienville (see below, chapter 6), for two regiments of the *101st Airborne Division,* 502d and 506th, were detailed to clear the beach exits.

Further north, starting out from **DZ A**, **502d PIR** set off on its assignments. With Captain Lillyman, Lieutenant-Colonel Cassidy *(1/502)* reported the total destruction of the Saint-Martin-de-Varreville battery following massive shelling. They then carried on north to set up roadblocks in the Foucarville area and cover the northern flank of the airborne bridgehead against possible German counterattacks; a mission accomplished at dawn (see page 80). Meanwhile, after a skirmish, Colonel Cole *(3/502) reached Exit n° 3* (la Vienville/Houdienville) and Captain Clemens *reached Exit n° 4*. Thus by dawn, beach exits 1, 2, 3 and 4 were in the hands of the paratroops, ready to welcome the infantry as they landed.

Fighting also took place at **Sainte-Marie-du-Mont**, the main locality in the sector and a major crossroads at Beach Exit n° 2. Jean Lelarge was 13 at the time and lived across the road from the boys' school (see map), he came into contact with the Germans living in the school. During the night he saw the paratroops arriving: *"I had the impression the planes were flying very low. A group of men jumped, their parachutes opened, they floated around a little and then hit the ground; no doubt to avoid becoming a target if they stayed up in the air too long. I can see that for this to be visible in the pitch dark meant that the sky was lit up by flares also coming down by parachute."* A little later, there was

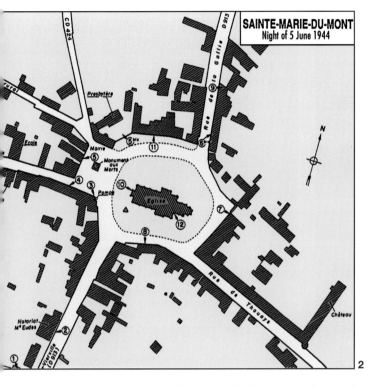

SAINTE-MARIE-DU-MONT
Night of 5 June 1944

1. The Holdy battery's 10.5 cm howitzers; the battery was destroyed by the paratroopers on 6 June. (NA.)

2. Map of Sainte-Marie-du-Mont indicating signs relating to battle actions during the night of 5-6 June. (Map by Heimdal.)

3. Aerial view of Sainte-Marie-du-Mont **(1)** huddled up against the church, the emplacement of the four 8.8 mm guns alongside Brécourt Farm **(2)**, the line of advance of Lieutenant-Colonel Strayer (2/506) **(3)**, the road to La Vienville and to Exit n° 2 (towards W5) **(4)**, the Manor Farm **(5)** on the edge of the marshes and the farms at La Houssaye **(6)**, La Vienville **(7)** then the direction **(8)** of the 76.2 mm gun battery. (US Air Force.)

4. Advance of the 1st and 3rd Battalions, 502d PIR with arrival times over their objectives during the night and morning of 6 June. (US Army.)

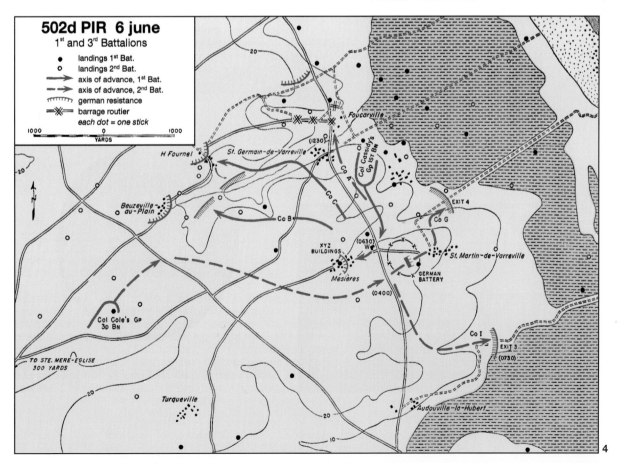

502d PIR 6 june
1st and 3rd Battalions

- ● landings 1st Bat.
- ○ landings 2nd Bat.
- → axis of advance, 1st Bat.
- ⇢ axis of advance, 2nd Bat.
- � german resistance
- ⬛ barrage routier
- *each dot = one stick*

1000 0 1000
YARDS

Photo taken from the top of the church at Sainte-Marie-du-Mont showing the bocage country as far at the lowlying areas and the coast. One spring day in 1944, two German officers were there with an ordnance survey map which was blown out of their hands by a gust of wind and landed in the square where the local painter picked it up before the officers could get to it... The church changed hands several times over during the night of 5 - 6 June 1944 ; the Germans had been using it as a lookout post. (Photo courtesy Heimdal.)

Sign n° 11 was placed to one side of the medieval porch leading to the old château belonging to the Aux Epaules, lords of Sainte-Marie-du-Mont until the early 17th century. The house on which this signboard was placed was used as a garrison office. The civilian population had to go there for any business it had with the garrison, and lists of men requisitioned for labor and fatigue duty such as Rommel's asparagus were drawn up here. (Photo courtesy Heimdal.)

a knock at the door and his father found himself facing two men with blackened faces; the men went upstairs with a map and were pleased to discover that they were at Sainte-Marie-du-Mont. Signs placed all around the square mark the main events of the night. The garrison's deputy commander Lieutenant Lid, opened fire on the paratroops falling out of the sky; he was in position near the notary's office (marked 2 on the map). Further on (8), paratrooper Ambrose Lie landed on a house overlooking the square. Unhurt, he undid his harness and slid down the drainpipe where he was picked up by some Germans who took aim. But then there was a burst of gunfire from the church; the Germans scattered, and some were wounded. This spared Ambrose Lie an awkward predicament. Nearby, (3), a spare, stocky paratrooper, recognizable from his bow legs, lay in ambush behind the pump and fired at the panic-stricken Germans, his M1 rifle in the bend of his arm. He is thought to have shot about ten Germans in this way. Two German soldiers were on guard in front of the church (10). After firing at the paratroops with their MP 40s, they disappeared, probably into the church, where they lay low until first light. Almost straight opposite (5), near the war memorial, under the white shutters of the saddler's house, a paratrooper and a German soldier spotted each other at the last moment and fired at each other. The paratrooper, wearing peccary-skin gloves, was killed instantly. The badly wounded German was taken to the butcher's, where a US doctor looked after him.

Picauville, the death of General Falley

In these early hours of 6 June 1944, as the first paratroopers of the US 82nd and 101st Airborne Divisions were landing in the Normandy Bocage, General Wilhelm Falley, commander of *91. (Luftlande) Infanterie-Division* headquartered at the Château de

Bernaville near Picauville, was taking part in a *Kriegspiel* at Rennes, along with other staff officers. On being alerted to what was going on in his sector Falley hurried away in his car with his aide-de-camp *Major* Bartuzat and his driver.

Unbeknownst to General Falley at the time, his headquarters was just a few hundred yards from the *508th PIR* drop zone, and since 02.15 that morning, groups of paratroopers were attempting to muster in the sector.

Among them were two men; one was Lieutenant **Malcolm Brannen of** HQ&HQ Company, 3rd Battalion (3/508), who had gathered up a few men of his regiment together with two artificers of the *307th Airborne Engineer Battalion*. The other was Corporal Jack Schlegel of the same company, who had mustered another ten men. The two groups were advancing in the same sector, a few hedges apart, without linking up.

Fearing the château might be bombed, General Falley had transferred his HQ to a caravan concealed on a back lane behind the château.

Early that morning, the powerful limousine turned into the road round the château, on its way to its meeting with fate.

But to tell the story from Malcolm Brannen's viewpoint:

After I landed, I met a corporal of 2d Bn who was acting as a pathfinder and a soldier from that same company who followed me, along with two artificers of 307th Airborne Engineers *which formed our rearguard, one of them was a sergeant. We came to a*

The notary's office with signboard n° 2 recalling 2nd Lieutenant Lid, from Hamburg, the German garrison's second-in-command (1./919). During the night of 5 - 6 June 1944, he was close by, in front of the studfarm, and shot at the paratroopers with a submachine-gun that fell from the sky into a meadow just opposite. (Photo courtesy Heimdal.)

508th Parachute Infantry Regiment cap patch. (D. François coll.)

On a visit to Normandy, via Caen and Saint-Sauveur-le-Vicomte, Feldmarschall Rommel stopped off at Picauville and was welcomed by Generalleutnant Falley at his command post at Château de Bernaville. Here we see Rommel on the huge flight of steps up to the château as he prepares to take leave of his host. (BA.)

1. Today at the same spot, the shutters are closed. (E. Groult/Heimdal.)

Lieutenant Malcolm Brannen at Camp Mackall in 1943. (D. François coll.)

2. A paratrooper of the *508th PIR* armed with a bazooka rests for a while. Lieutenant Brannen and his men had found a bazooka with a dozen rockets in a container. (Photo courtesy D. François.)

3. Paratrooper Robert White examines a German sniper he has just shot, after nearly getting killed himself. Notice the bullet hole the sniper made in his righthand jacket sleeve. (Photo courtesy D. François.)

4. Map of the sector where the skirmish and killing of *General* Falley took place. (Map by B. Paich.)

Sergeant Jack Schlegel in 1942 ; he has just earned his spurs as a paratrooper. (D. François coll.)

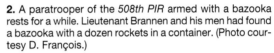

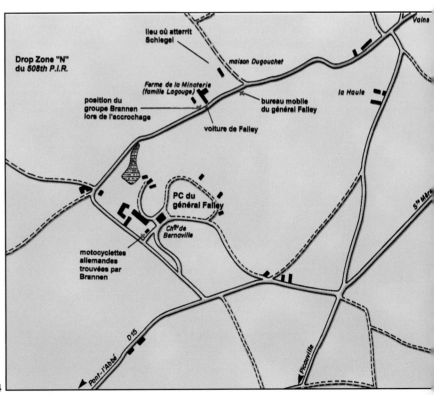

Above : postcard dating from the turn of the 20th century showing the Bernaville flour mill when it was still in operation. (DR.)

Below : the Minoterie (flour mill) farm nowadays. Falley's car crashed into the front wall. (Photo courtesy E. Groult/Heimdal.)

Opposite : in 1943, Jack Schlegel belonged to Airborne Command at Fort Benning. (D. François coll.)

Above : the Dugouchet home behind which Sergeant Schlegel landed on 6 June 1944. (Photo courtesy E. Groult/Heimdal.)

road in a line north-south, but not daring to stay on it, we crossed over quickly.

Later we found wires along a road, which my engineers recognized to be phone wires. I cut them in several places and took a few yards of them which I concealed.

After walking along the hedges northeastwards for a while, we headed du north. We saw C-47s releasing their gliders, then a C-47 disappearing behind a hill where it crashed. As we advanced, we came across some equipment containers that had been dropped earlier. Some had been opened, others not. In one of them we found a bazooka with a dozen rockets. We exchanged it for an M1 rifle which had had its butt broken during the jump.

A few hedges further on, we were still heading north, we found two tents and two motor-cycles. We searched the area very carefully, because they might have been boobytrapped. There was nobody around. It must have been some German officer's escort. We punctured the tires on the two motor-cycles, to render them useless.

Later we found Lt. Harold V. Richard of A Co, 508th and his wireless operator Sgt. Hall. We decided to ask our way at a farm located 50 yards from our position. There were about twelve of us by now and we were able to surround the farm. Lt. Richard, one of the men and myself knocked at the farmhouse door. A few minutes later, a Frenchman arrived very excitedly. Others were looking through the the upstairs windows. In the house, the children admired our American uniforms which were so different from the ones theye were used to.

Then we heard the sound of a car speeding up to us. Lt. Richard came out quickly and stood in front of the house. The French people went back inside and closed the doors. A few paratroopers come up to the house. As soon as the door was closed, I went onto the road. I raised my hand and shouted 'Stop!' but the car just accelerated. As it passed me, I ran to the other side. We opened fire simultaneously, scoring at least a dozen hits on the car. The car was badly damaged when it crashed into the farmhouse wall. The driver was thrown out of the car onto a stone wall near the farm, before the car had stopped. It was riddled with bulletholes from all over. The driver, a corporal, tried to get away by slipping through a barn window.

One of the car's passengers was crawling up the middle of the road towards a Lüger pistol which had been ejected from its holster in the accident. The third passenger was not visible at this precise moment. The car was a Dusenberg or a Mercedes. (I heard later that Lt. Bush, G2 of the 82nd Division, had been using it again to get around in).

The corporal was still trying to get into the barn. I fired at him but he was protected by the doorway. He was later hit by one of my bullets, in the top of the left shoulder. The Major, the man in the car, was killed. The third man crawling towards his Lüger looked at me as I walked along the embankment to get an overview of the *situation.* He complained in German and shouted to me in English 'Don't kill! Don't kill!'. At that moment, I told myself I am not a cold-blooded killer, I am a human being, but if he reaches his gun, it will be him or me, or one of my men. So I fired! He was hit in the forehead. He did not feel a thing, the blood came spurting out of his forehead like water from a spring. On examining his personal belongings, we discovered that we had killed a major and a major-general, and captured a *corporal.* We made him carry two small cases we found in the car containing numerous papers and maps. As we left the ambush sec-

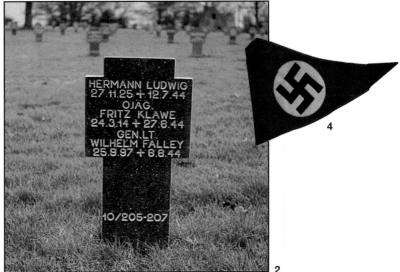

tor, I looked at the general's cap to identify him or his unit. All I found was a name: Falley.

Meanwhile, the **Schlegel group** a few hundred yards from the Brannen group, decided to knock at the door of a house (Dugouchet-Lecomte Farm).

"Je suis Américain!" announced Corporal Schlegel in schoolboy French to some frightened civilians after banging on the door of their house. He and his party of paratroopers were invited inside. Using sign language, French, German and American English, we troopers learned we were near Picauville and our hosts were Monsieur and Madame Le Comte. The Le Comtes served bread and wine to the paratroopers as we sat round the dining table and planned our route. As a parting gesture I gave my paratrooper wings to Madame Le Comte as a remembrance.

Later Schlegel's men met other members of their company and their battalion. At dawn, the group came to a bullet-riddled German car rammed up against a wall, with two dead Germans lying on the road. These were *Generalleutnant* Wilhelm Falley and his aide-de-camp, *Major* Bartuzat.

Looking over the car, Schlegel found a package containing a large swastika banner, General Falley's command flag, and a few pennons. A few moments later, they heard footsteps. The men hid behind a stone wall and waited. It was another party of paratroopers who joined up with them.

Later on, the group came to a barn and went in through the only door to discover two Germans trying to escape through the same door. They were soon captured. While the prisoners were guarded in a small room, Schlegel "slipped away alone to another part of the barn. I pulled up a loose board, stuffed my package of loot containing the German flag.

With our prisoners as insurance, we troopers left the barn safely. After travelling a few hundred yards, we came face to face with a German tank, which fired

1. *Generalleutnant* Wilhelm Falley. (Photo Charita/Heimdal coll.)

2. *Generalleutnant* Wilhelm Falley's grave in the German cemetery at Orglandes, block 10/grave 267. (Photo courtesy B. Paich.)

3. *Oberstleutnant* Joachim Bartuzat's grave is just beside it, block 209. (Photo courtesy B. Paich.)

4 and **5.** The pennon and a piece of flag recovered by Schlegel from Falley's car. (Photos courtesy E. Groult/Heimdal.)

6. In 1969, at the top of the steps up to Château de Bernaville, Jack Schlegel presents General Falley's flag to the press. He later donated it to the Sainte-Mère-Eglise museum. (D. François coll.)

Jack Schlegel in 1969, in front of the door of the Minoterie farm, where Brannen knocked to make enquiries. (D. François coll.)

its big gun. A shell exploded just behind the group, wounding many. One of the prisoners, although bleeding from his wounds, jumped up and waved ceasefire gestures to the tank commander. The insurance paid off. The tank commander decided to take prisoners rather than finish off the Americans. After capture, I recall walking several miles to a château where there were about 250 prisoners, Americans, British and Canadians. *"The next day, we were loaded on about ten unmarked German trucks with canvas covers and moved in convoy toward St Lô. About noon, Allied planes strafed the convoy and I estimate that 30 or 40 of our men were killed (many from the 508th). Over 80 were wounded. I remember moving three from my own company with the dead and placing Lt. Bodack with the wounded. He was hit with a large-caliber shell in the spine and never walked again."* (Author's note : but he survived the war). Among the survivors was 507th PIR commander, Col. Millett, the highest ranking prisoner. The Germans put him in charge of the prisoners."

Opposite : Jack Schlegel with the Picauville parish priest and M. and Mme Lecomte. (D. François coll.)

Above : on 6 June 1995, the Rue de Picauville, where the incident with *Generalleutnant* Falley occurred, was officially renamed "Chemin Jack Schlegel". Here we see him with Tom Porcella (red cap) of H Coy, *508th PIR* and O.B. Hill (white cap) of 1st Bn *508th PIR*. (Photo courtesy D. François.)

Prisoner Lieutenant Bodack, wounded during the strafing; he would never walk again. (D. François coll.)

Above and below : American prisoners, here paratroopers of the *101st Airborne Division*, are brought together by the Germans and taken to a transit camp at Saint-Lô studfarm before being transferred to Rennes and on to POW camps in Germany. (ECPA.)

Sergeant Schlegel in 1945, after his escape. Notice his British paratrooper's certificate obtained in 1944 and sewn onto the bottom of his right sleeve. (D. François coll.)

Saint-Marcouf, 6 June 1944.

A stick of *508th PIR,* comprising elements of the Headquarters Company, with Captains Abraham and Johnson, and *Tech 5* McCloud, was dropped by mistake nine kilometers south of Cherbourg, miles from their DZ *(DZ A)*. They had to walk south to join up with their unit.

1 and **2.** They enter Saint-Marcouf, a village just a short distance from the battery (3./1261) of the same name (the Americans called it the "Crisbecq battery"). But there were too few of them to attack the position whose guns continued to strafe Utah Beach until 9 June. The US censors have masked the signpost naming the locality as Saint Marcouf. The presentday view shows how one country aspect of the place has changed with rhe laying of sidewalks. (D.F and E.G./Heimdal.)

3 and **4.** Then the paratroopers entered the village and patrolled along the cemetery with the church towering over it. The place has changed little. (D.F. and E.G./Heimdal.)

5. The church's imposing saddle-back belltower dominates the village of Saint-Marcouf. (E.G./Heimdal.)

6 and **7.** The paratroopers are now resting at the foot of the church. For a long time this reportage used to be dated 8 June. However recent identifications have now dated it to D-day, which is confirmed by the fact that the men in this photo still have their faces blackened with the greasepaint they put on before leaving on the evening of 5 June. On the presentday photo, notice how the steps leading to the cemetery have been modified. (D.F. and E.G./Heimdal.)

8. A paratrooper and some small children at Saint-Marcouf. (D.F./Heimdal.)

From Saint-Marcouf to Ravenoville.

1 and **2.** Shortly afterwards, the group of *508th PIR* paratroopers who had lost their way under Captain Johnson (seen here on the right with the field glasses) continued to fall back southwards, stopping for a while in the village of Ravenoville, a further three kilometers after leaving Saint-Marcouf. The wall has been cemented and the village is almost intact. (Heimdal/ E.G. coll.)

3. The Americans left some equipment at the entrance to Saint-Marcouf in 1944, and it has been there ever since. (E.G./ Heimdal.)

4, 5 and **6.** The paratroopers advance cautiously, questioning civilians as they go. (D.F./ Heimdal.)

5

6

Ravenoville, 6 June 1944.

Instead of finding themselves near Sainte-Marie-du-Mont in DZ "C", about thirty paratroopers of *E Company, 506th PIR (101st Airborne Division)* were some ten kilometers north of their objective. They then had to pass through some tightly-knit hedgerow country to get to their sector. On the way they met another party commanded by Major John P. Stoplea *(502d PIR)*, made up of paratroopers from various units (including members of the *377th Parachute Field Artillery Battalion* or the *82d ABN Div.*). Together these men captured a farm near a farm near a crossroads controlling access to the beach at Ravenoville.

3

1

2

1. Marmion Farm south of Ravenoville facing the D15 road from Sainte-Mère. In his book Point of No Return, Michel De Trez shows paratroopers preparing to take the farm, then held by a group of German soldiers, from this sector. (E.G./Heimdal.)

2. A few plants identical to the ones seen in that photo... (E.G./Heimdal.)

3. Under their commander, *Major* Stopka, the paratroopers have taken the farm, captured some German soldiers and a precious tracked vehicle with a trailer. The victors show off their trophies. The paratrooper holding the flag is James W. Flanagan of *C Coy*, 502d PIR. (D.F./Heimdal.)

4. Here we see Marmion Farm, a huge farmhouse flanked by farm buildings on either side. (E.G./Heimdal.)

5. Thee paratroopers have formed a group in front of the buildings on the right. The censors have masked their divisional insignia. In the foreground is a French-made Renault UE tracked vehicle, recovered and used by the Germans and now by the paratroopers. In another photo published by Michel De Trez (*op. cit.*, p. 58), we see the tracked vehicle with its trailer loaded with US supplies, including a bazooka and a machine-gun. Throughout D-day, these paratroopers held off German counterattacks. (D.F./Heimdal.)

6. The same spot today, the junction between the two buildings is clearly recognizable. (E.G./Heimdal.)

7. The same wing taken from further back showing where it stands, to the right of the farm, near the porch. (E.G./Heimdal.)

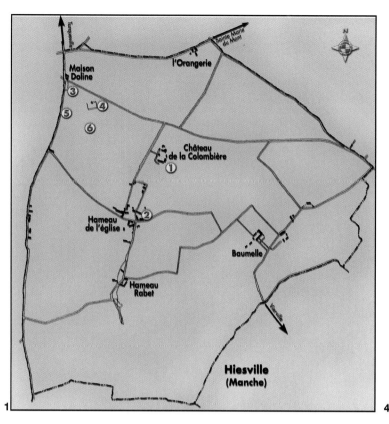

1

4

Hiesville.

1. The first hospital in Normandy was operational at the Château de la Colombière **(1)** as early as 8 in the morning on 6 June 1944. A little further on, *101st Airborne Division* set up its first HQ at Lecaudey Farm **(2)**. Dr Crandall performed his first operation near **(3)** where the gliders crashed. The bend taken by Mike Murphy's glider **(4)**. The site of General Pratt's glider crash **(5)**. Glider of the Mike Murphy group **(6)**. (Heimdal.)

2. Aerial view of the same sector, see also page 84. (US Air Force.)

3

2

5

6

3. Plaque placed at then entrance to Lecaudey Farm recalling the presence here of *101st Airborne Division HQ*.

4 and **5.** In Lecaudey farmyard, paratroopers of the *801st Ordnance Company* distribute C rations to civilians. (D.F./Heimdal.)

6. *Major General* Taylor at the wheel of his jeep in the farmyard. (US Army.)

8

The Château de Colombières

7. The *101st Airborne Division* divisional hospital was set up at the Château de Colombières early in the morning of 6 June 1944, near the divisional HQ, as commemorated by this monument. (E.G./Heimdal.)

8. The Château de Colombières was rebuilt in 1597. Here we see it in the early 20th century, as it still looked when the Americans arrived. (D.F.)

9. *Major* Crandall's medical staff settled in straightaway on 6 June. (D.F./Heimdal.)

10. This rare color photo was taken sometime beetween 6 and 7 June 1944 by glider pilot F. Robert Winer. Notice the *326th Airborne Medical Company* tents near the gatehouse. (Private coll.)

9

10

Major Albert J. Crandall, who commanded the *326th Airborne Medical Company*, the *101st Airborne Division's medical company*, set up the first Allied military hospital in Normandy at Colombières. (M.S.M.E. coll.)

1

2

3

5

4

6

7

8

9

The Château de Colombières, *101st Airborne Division's* hospital.

Under its commander Major Albert J. Crandall, the *326th Airborne Medical Company* left Aldermaston airfield in England, at 01.19 on 6 June 1944, carried by glider. The leading glider, piloted by Lieutenant-Colonel Mike Murphy and carrying *Brigadier-General* Don Pratt, tragically crashed. An advanced element of the medical company followed behind in another glider.

This medical company comprised Major Albert J. Crandall, Captain Charles O. Van Gorder, Captain John S. Rodda, Captain Saul Dworkin, Sgt. Allen E. Ray, Sgt. Emil K. Natalle, *Sgt.* Francis J. Muska, Sgt. Ernest Burges. The surgical team was also accompanied by Captains Charles Margulies and Curtis Yearry. A single glider brought over the surgical team, with the bulk of the company coming by sea. On D-day the gliders arrived at around H-4 (02.30). Brig. Gen. Pratt was killed when his glider crashed, he was the first US general killed in Normandy. Three members of the team stayed on the spot where the accident happened while the other two went by jeep to Château de Colombières, which they reached at around 7 that morning. The paratroops who came with them neutralized the Germans they found there, and also found the Cotelle family living in. With the help of the Cotelles, paratroopers and glider pilots, the first Allied military hospital in Normandy was operational before 9 and immediately the wounded began flooding in. The other members of the surgical team arrived shortly afterwards. They used recovered parachutes as sheets for the wounded. At around 21.00 hours, another glider brought in more elements of the company. Those arriving by sea made their way to join their unit in the course of D-day. Five operating tables were then being used. Wounds to the head, thorax, abdomen and extremities were operated as a priority on those who could not be evacuated. All this went on for two days amid the insecurity of skirmishes with the Germans. A small German medical unit was captured and given the byres in which to work and take care of the German wounded. On D + 3, the fourth day of operations, the *42d Hospital* was set up nearby with its personnel.

But at around 23.45 on 9 June, a German bomber flew over the hospital and dropped two bombs. The first hit the west wing of the château, which was very badly damaged. The second went through the gable to complete the destruction. There were over twenty killed and about sixty wounded. However, company members sustained only slight casualties and were able to carry on their assignment.

1. One of the exceptional color photos taken by F. Robert Winer on 6 and 7 June 1944. It shows the Château de Colombières converted into a hospital with a quarter-ton trailer in the foreground. (Private coll.)

2. Here another color photo showing the round tower flanked by its stairs. (Private coll.)

3. View of the outbuildings in ruins after the bombing raid. (Private coll.)

4. The restored outbuildings as they look today. (E.G./Heimdal.)

5. The ruined gatehouse; it was later demolished. (M.S.M.E.)

6. The château was gutted in the bombing. Notice on the upstairs floor the fine 16th c. fireplace which was later dismantled and saved. (Private coll.)

7. The château ravaged by the bombs; sadly, it was later demolished. (M.S.M.E.)

8. The house that replaced the château. (E.G./Heimdal.)

9. The fireplace salvaged from the ruins. (Heimdal.)

10. Captain Charles O. Van Gorder, one of the surgeons of the *326th Airborne Medical Company* in 1943.

11. Captain Van Gorder in 1986.

12. His helmet. (Private coll.)

13. First aid was administered in the open air. Here we see, on the right, a *101st Airborne Division* medic wearing a German belt. Notice the marking on the helmet and armband. (NA/Heimdal.)

6 Utah Beach

1. At dawn the shipping making up Force U approached *Utah Beach*. Naval guns opened fire, pounding the German positions. (Musée d'Utah Beach coll.)

2. Rear-admiral Moon commanded Force U. (Musée d'Utah Beach.)

3. Map showing the approach channels and fire support zones opposite *Utah Beach*. (Map by B. Paich/Heimdal.)

Force U at Utah Beach

While the gliders brought in the paratroopers' first supplies as they made their way through the maze of Cotentin hedgerows, a small force prepared to take the first obstacle forward of **Utah Beach**: the **Saint-Marcouf islands**.

This tiny archipelago has two main islands. The western island is a kind of large reef. On the eastern island stands an imposing fort with an access gate, built to Napoleon's instructions but never used. The Allies thought that this archipelago might house a German garrison or at the very least a place for exploding minefields by remote control. Elements of the 2nd and *4th Cavalry Squadrons*, commanded by Lieutenant-Colonel E.C. Dunn, were detailed to capture these islands. Two hours before H-Hour, at **04.30**, four men armed with nothing but knives swam up to the creeks planned for the landing, only to discover that the islands were deserted, having been abandoned by the Germans. The main force landed an hour later, sustaining some losses to mines, nineteen men altogether by D-Day's end.

A quarter of an hour after this initial conquest, at **05.45** (H-45 min), the landing fleet approached the coast. This **Force U** for Utah Beach was under the command of Rear-Admiral D.P. Moon (U.S. Navy), on board the *U.S.S. Bayfield*, which sailed from Plymouth at H-20 hrs. He had at his disposal the tremendous firepower of Task Force 125: *U.S.S. Nevada, Erebus Tuscaloosa* and *Quincy, H.M.S. Hawkins, Enterprise, Black Prince* (1), based at Belfast in Northern Ireland, and which had sailed forty-four hours before H-Hour, at 10.30 on 3 June (2). *U.S.S. Nevada* opened fire on the Azeville battery (2./1261), *U.S.S. Erebus* on the two La Pernelle batteries (9./1261 and 10./1261), *U.S.S. Tuscaloosa* and *U.S.S. Quincy* on the Mont Coquerel battery (4./1261) and Saint-Marcouf/Crisbecq battery (3./1261), *H.M.S. Hawkins* on the one at Saint-Martin-de-Varreville (1./1261 already destroyed), *H.M.S. Black Prince* on the one at Morsalines (6./1261) and *H.M.S. Enterprise* on the *Utah Beach* landing zone (3). The Dutch gunboat Soemba concentrated its attack more specifically on the beach defense positions. The supporting force also included eight destroyers [the *U.S.S. Forest (Relief Flagship), Hobson, Shubrick, Cory, Herndon, Fitch, Butler* and *Gherardi*] and L.C.T. (r) rocket launchers to pound the coastal positions. Also, a few minutes later, 276 *B-26 Marauder* bombers of the *9th U.S. Air Force* dropped 4 404 tons of 250 pound bombs on seven targets, from Beauguillot beach (*W3*) to Les Dunes de Varreville (*W 10*).

On the ground, the results were devastating. At first light, Lieutenant Rohweder, at Pouppeville, saw Allied shipping off *W2a* and *W3*. Then the bombers came in several waves, "covering the sky", and dropping bombs on *W3*, *W4*, *W5* and *W7*. *Leutnant* Ritter (commander of *W3*), there were only himself, an NCO and one man, armed with a Bren gun, a Sten gun and a 98 K rifle! The position was more or less wiped out, but Rohweder ordered him to hold out and told him support was on the way. However, this was a promise he could not keep on account of gliders landing between *W2a* and *W3*. Also, while Colonel Keil had lost contact with his *Infanterie-Regiment 919*

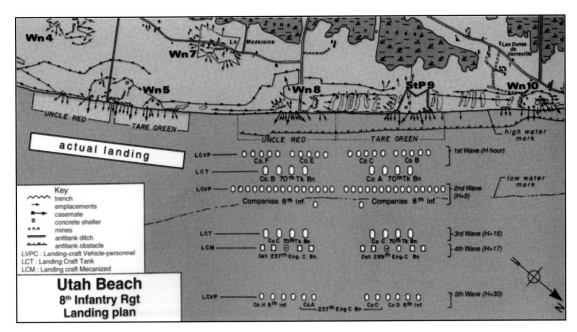

Theoretical plan of attack at Utah Beach. It ended up taking place opposite W5 (left) in a more favorable spot. (Map by Heimdal.)

battalions defending the entire sector, the same was true between units. The Post Office Resistance workers had done a great job; communications had broken down the German units and the whole chain of command was in tatters. These units were left alone to their own devices. Lieutenant Rohweder lost contact with Captain Fink at 1st Battaliion headquarters. During the night, he did make contact, through *W1*, with *W99* east of the Baie des Veys. From there, he managed to link up with the army corps at Saint-Lô. At *W5*, commanded by Lieutenant Jahnke, the situation was just as dramatic as at *Leutnant* Ritter's position.

But the waves of the amphibious assault force failed to come ashore at the appointed spot. Owing to the peculiar currents off the east coast of the Cotentin, an "alternative tide", the landing craft were carried off course southwards on the rising tide, when the undertow was much stronger and shorter than when the tide was going out. Instead of arriving before *W8* and *StP 9*, the landing ships came in front of Lieutenant Jahnke's *W5*, or what was left of it.

This navigational error proved a blessing in disguise. The landing took place a little over a mile (1 800 meters) to the south and was thus less exposed to shellfire from the Azeville and Saint-Marcouf batteries, which were almost out of range. From **06.20** to **06.40**, Thunderbolt P-47s carried out a rocket attack on the coastal positions to finish them off.

Out at sea, the assault waves of *8th R.C.T., 4th Infantry Division* moved in towards the beach with twenty LCVPs bringing in four companies of the 8th Regiment. On the left (to the south), facing **Uncle Red** beach, came ten LCVPs carrying **F** and **E** Companies (2nd Battalion). On the right (to the north), facing Tare Green beach, came ten LCVPs carrying **C** and **B** Companies (1st Battalion). These four infantry companies formed **the first wave** for H-Hour, with two DD tank companies of the **70th Tank Battalion** coming in just behind them in support on LCTs. These were **B** Company on the left and **A** Company on the right.

The second wave was planned for five minutes later, at H + 05. It was made up of another four infantry companies of the 8th RCT, **H** and **G** (2/8) Compa-

nies on the left and **D** and **A** (1/8) Companies on the right. Accompanied by special obstacle demolition elements: C Company of the 237th Engineer Battalion and four NCDUs (4) on the left and A Company of the *237th Engineer Battalion* and another four NCDUs on the right.

The third wave was scheduled for H + 15, when eight LCTs brought in the tanks of **C** Company of the 70th Tank Battalion, followed two minutes later (H + 17) by a **fourth wave** with more Engineer elements, a further three NCDUs, and some BODPs (5).

By now the beach was in sight. It was a low-lying coast, with very few landmarks and the confusion caused by drifting off-course might have ended in chaos. As it turned out, three guiding patrol craft were to mark out each of the two beach sectors: PC 1261, LCC-80 and 90 on *Uncle Red*, PC 1176, LCC-60 and 70 on Tare Green. The two patrol craft were to mark the start line for the assault waves, one of the LCCs guiding them in to the beach while the other remained in the troop transport anchoring zone. However, there were a number of hitches. PC 1261 sank first thing in the morning, LCC-80 could not make the crossing owing to a jammed propeller, so there was no patrol boat for *Uncle Red*, and radio silence meant that LCC-90 knew nothing of these mishaps. But LCC-60, with naval officers Sims Gauthier and Howard Van der Beek, was able to mark out the other objective accurately with its radar equipment (6). In fact, owing to a very strong swell, the amphibious DD tanks could not be launched as planned and the LCTs brought them in close to shore behind schedule and in disarray. More than drifting currents, it seemed that the presence of the LCTs was the real cause of the chaos that pushed the landings further south. This incident delayed the launch of the first assault waves and the landing craft, LCVPs, are thought to have veered to the left to avoid the LCTs.

Thus, at c. **06.40**, ten LCVPs brought **E** and **F** Companies of the *8th Infantry Regiment* onto *Uncle Red* beach, south of *W5* which had been shelled to pieces. Some 300 meters from the beach, the leading company commanders fired special smoke shells to request that the fleet lengthen its range. *Brigadier General* Theodore Roosevelt came ashore with the first wave. Ten minutes later, **B** and **C** (1/8) Compa-

Notes 1 to 11 : see page 126.

nies in turn came ashore on the right flank, at *Tare Green*, opposite *W5*. They were soon followed by the DD tanks of A and B Companies of the *70th Tank Battalion*. This staggering of the landing was soon noticed.

W5 was taken practically without putting up any resistance. Roosevelt then quickly organized a party to reconnoiter inland. It located the causeway to be used to move off the beach. This was *Exit 2* towards Sainte-Marie-du-Mont instead of *Exit n° 3* to Audouville-la-Hubert and Turqueville. Teddy Roosevelt then came back to the beach to confer with his *8th Infantry Regiment* battalion commanders, Lieutenant-Colonel Conrad C. Simmons (1st Battalion) and Lieutenant-Colonel Carlton O. MacNeely (2nd Battalion) over the decision to continue the landings on this beach sector which was not according to plan; in view of the good early results and the more favorable situation, it was finally decided to carry on. As Roosevelt famously put it: *"We'll start the war from here"*.

Once the beach had been taken, passages needed to be cleared to let through reinforcements and equipment, the Gap Teams gathered into the BODP (see note 5) under the command of *Major* Hershel Linn, CO of the *237th Engineer Combat Battalion*. This unit's personnel was taken from that battalion and from B Company of the *299th Engineer Combat Battalion*. His Tankdozer teams were taken from the *612th Engineer Light Equipment Company*. Unfortunately, *Major* Linn's landing craft was hit and sunk near the shore; the officer was picked up but did not come ashore until the following day. However, only six sappers were killed off Utah Beach, when their landing craft was shelled. However the first engineers to land were those of Lieutenant Commander Herbert Peterson's NCDUs. Five minutes after the first wave came in, eight of the eleven NCDUs landed to open up five 45 meter-wide passages on either of the two beaches. Immediately, Gap Assault Teams were sent in to assist the infantry in reducing the German defensive positions, which proved unnecessa-

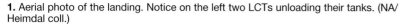

1. Aerial photo of the landing. Notice on the left two LCTs unloading their tanks. (NA/Heimdal coll.)

2. On this other aerial view of Utah Beach, the coast can be seen distinctly to bend round in the distance (to the south) towards the Baie des Veys. (US Air Force.)

3. *Brigadier General* Theodore Roosevelt Jr. was President Theodore Roosevelt's son. On 6 June 1944, he was second-in-command of the *4th Infantry Division* and landed with the first wave. (Heimdal coll.)

ry owing to the damage already sustained by *W5* in the shelling. To paraphrase *Leutnant* Jahnke in Paul Carell's book (7): *"Everything that took months of careful preparation was smashed like a child's toy after a hurricane. The 7.5 antitank gun was reduced to scrap metal. The 8.8 gun was also hit. Two ammunitions bunkers exploded, and all the rifle pits were flattened. Fortunately losses in men were only light as the attack caught the gun servers in their shelters. And they put up a fight, even against the direct hits. Then at 04.00 the P-47s launched a fresh attack (8): they only attacked the two corner turrets housing the 5cm antitank guns. The rockets rained down in the bunkers, bursting against the embrasures and aiming slits".* The two concrete tobruks were destroyed (see map on p. 15). Corporal Friedrich's Renault tank turret mowed down some *Engineers* with its heavy machine-gun but it received a direct hit from a tank in the second wave (9).

By **08.00**, i.e. 1 hour 25 minutes after the first demolition team came ashore, more than 600 meters of beach had been cleared, and it had been totally cleared by around 09.30. According to a report drawn up on 26 June 1944 by *Lieutenant Commander* Peterson, the beach obstacles on *Utah Beach* were slightly different from the ones on Omaha Beach. First there were wooden ramps, then Element C obstacles (2.5 meters high by 2.5 meters wide), reinforced concrete stakes (1.5 meters high) and concrete tetrahedra. The demolition teams used C-2 or Tetrytol-based charges. In view of all the destruction, no mines were found on the beach. A Company, *237th Combat Eng. Bn.* Opened up two breaches in the concrete antitank wall on Uncle Red and blew up two Belgian gates at the entrance to *Exit n° 2*. A few tankdozers reached the shore, and cleared the debris. The NCDUs came under sporadic fire and lost 4 killed and 11 wounded, the Engineers 6 killed and 39 wounded.

Thus at **08.00**, Colonel Van Fleet's *8th Infantry Regiment* was at full strength. It was joined at 07.45 by the 3rd Battalion, *22d Infantry Regiment*. The rest of this regiment was ashore by 10.00. And while the Engineers were busy clearing the beaches, Colonel Van Fleet's regiment started to move inland. **1/8** advanced on the right towards La Madeleine and *W7*. It had to move a little to the north on the cau-

seway from Exit n° 3 leading to Audouville-la-Hubert. One company was enough to reduce this rather weak resistance nest. Along the coast, demoralized elements put up very little resistance. The other two battalions advanced in a different direction.

The third **(3/8)** advanced straight on Exit n° 2, at **La Vienville**. Approaching this exit, near the hamlet, it came up against two antitank guns blocking the road, and a little further on four guns belonging to 13./919 (*Oberleutnant* Schön). These Russian-built 76.2 mm infantry guns were covering the coast and were in position south of the road while their ammunition had been stored in a small house on the north side. The Germans had planned on blowing up the bridge ahead of this position. To the north of the road, edging the inundated area, stood a few farms that might hold pockets of resistance: the Manoir, la Houssaye, La Vienville (manor-farm) and Haudienville. At La Vienville Manor, Robert Laisney and his family heard shell and machine-

Appearance of the wooden ramps placed in front of the beach in the *Utah Beach* sector. (US Army.)

(cont'd from page 120)

This Sherman, washed up on *Utah Beach*, is not a DD tank but a standard Sherman fitted with a hood over the engine grilles to facilitate getting it ashore off the LCTs amid the waves coming into the beach. It bears the name Cannonball on the bodywork. A tank like this belonged to a C Coy. The only one committed on D-Day at *Utah Beach* was a unit of the *70th Tank Battalion, C/70th*. The figure 2 on the bodywork is indeed in line with those seen on that unit's vehicles. (US Army.)

1

At dawn on D-day, the biggest armada ever was on its way to the Normandy coast. Soldiers and sailors were tightly squeezed in the ships, and sometimes had been so for several days. Some units, like *U.S.S. Nevada*, *Erebus*, *Tuscaloosa* and *Quincy*, *H.M.S. Hawkins*, *Enterprise* and *Black Prince*, based in Northern Ireland, had sailed from Belfast at 10.30 on 3 June.

2

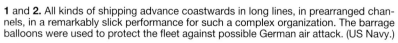

1 and **2.** All kinds of shipping advance coastwards in long lines, in prearranged channels, in a remarkably slick performance for such a complex organization. The barrage balloons were used to protect the fleet against possible German air attack. (US Navy.)

3. These ships brought over the *8th Infantry Regiment, 4th Infantry Division.* Its two leading battalions came in with the first wave. (D.F./Heimdal.)

4. 4 308 ships of all kinds were mobilized for Operation Overlord. On approaching the shore, the LSI, APA and AKA type troop transport ships transferred the men into LCVPs (Landing Craft, Vehicle Personnel). This type of landing craft (there were 839 of them for Overlord) could carry 36 men and 3 tons of equipment ; it was 12 meters long, weighed 18 tons, and had a speed of 9 knots and a crew of three. (US Navy.)

3

5. Each loaded with 36 infantrymen, the LCs are launched towards Utah Beach as part of Force U. (NA/Heimdal.)

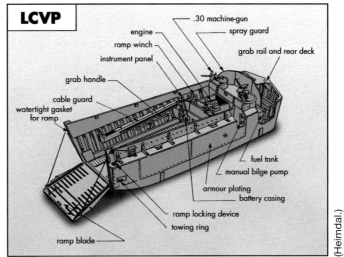

LCVP

.30 machine-gun
engine
spray guard
ramp winch
instrument panel
grab rail and rear deck
grab handle
cable guard
watertight gasket for ramp
fuel tank
manual bilge pump
armour plating
battery casing
ramp locking device
towing ring
ramp blade

(Heimdal.)

4

5

6. The LCs then had to circle until H Hour came (this photo was taken during training). The men were often seasick as they bobbed up and down among the waves. (US Navy.)

Utah Beach.

1. Twenty LCVPs bring in the leading elements of the first wave, with E and F Companies on the left and C and B Companies on the right. However the landing troops sustained relatively light casualties. W5, which was supposed to take on this landing force, had been smashed in the bombardment. (US Navy.)

2 and **3.** The *4th Division* was substantially reinforced for the landing with other units, including the tanks of the *70th Tank Battalion* (in the first wave), the tank destroyers of the *801st TD Battalion* (SP) (from 9 to 13 June), the artillery batteries of the *13th FA Obsn Bn*, Battery B of the *980th FA Bn* (155 mm guns), Battery B of the *65th Armored Field Artillery Battalion*, the *915th FA Bn* (105 mm guns – a unit detached from the *90th Division* – all its artillery units were attached to the *4th Division* from 6 to 8 June). Anti-aircraft units were also attached to the *4th Division*: the *377th AAA AW Bn* as of 14 June and Battery B, *453d AAA Aw Bn*. Here we see medics belonging to a medical company coming ashore. (DAVA/Heimdal.)

4 and **5.** Medics treating the wounded on the beach. Out of 197 casualties, the 4th Division had only 12 killed for the *8th IR* and *22d IR*. One of the 4th Division medics (notice his divisional insignia on his sleeve), in Photo 4, was wounded as well and laid out on a stretcher. (NA/Heimdal.)

6. The troops are now landing unopposed. Notice the "Chalet Rouge" on the left. (NA.)

1 and 2. As infantrymen clamber over the dunes on their way inland, others shelter behind the antitank wall awaiting orders to do likewise. This wall is still standing in 2004. (NA and E.G./Heimdal.)

"Hutte à Biches".
In La Brèche de Sainte-Marie-du-Mont, a book by François Lemonnier-Gruhier containing numerous eyewitness accounts gathered shortly after the battle (the book was published in 1948), the author tells the story of how the civilians first came into contact with the landing troops. At Saint-Martin-de-Varreville, the young villagers gathered together near the church on 7 June, after the fighting in this sector located to the north of the beachhead. They were told *"Well, gentlemen, we're taking you off to Utah Beach where some officers will be interrogating you."* The young men of Varreville looked at each other. One asked his neighbor : — *What's that he said?* — *He's going to take us to the the deer hut* (hutte à biches, sounds like Utah Beach).

3. The units continue organizing themselves at the foot of the antitank wall where the wounded are brought. (NA.)

4. This was no idle precaution. The artillery guns of the Azeville and Saint-Marcouf/Crisbecq batteries kept harassing the troops once ashore with their fire. Here we see a shell exploding. (D.F./Heimdal.)

5. The medics continue treating the wounded on the beach. In the background, infantrymen can be seen in foxholes they have dug in the sand. (D.F./Heimdal.)

6. This photo shows one side to the effects of the bombardments. A German soldier has been "buried" in the sand dune and is struggling to pull free. (D.F./Heimdal.)

1. In this photo, taken in the sand dunes at *Utah Beach*, we see the *4th Division* commanders in discussion: *Brigadier General* Roosevelt, without his helmet (as seen by Sergeant Liska), and *Major General* Barton. Brig. Gen. Roosevelt came ashore with *E Company* in the first wave. (Heimdal.)

2. Sherman tanks of the *C/70th Tank Battalion*, with their hoods protecting their engine grilles against the sea, lend support to the landing troops. (NA/Heimdal.)

3

3. These vehicles have just landed from an LCT (Landing Craft Tank). The "Chalet Rouge" house, a useful landmark, can be seen again here. It stood north of W5, on Uncle Red. (D.F./Heimdal.)

4. Here is the Hurricane tank, a standard Sherman with protective hoods. This one belongs to the *746th Tank Battalion*, a unit sent in to support the landing troops and which set up its command post at Audouville-la-Hubert on D-day evening. (D.F./Heimdal.)

4

1 and **2**. North of W5, the "Chalet Rouge" was a landmark visible from a long way off. *4th Division* infantrymen advance close by before heading off inland. The man in front, with a scaling rope round his neck, has put on impregnated gas protection drill. Many soldiers feared a combat gas attack on Utah Beach, as did Sergeant Liska. This group is followed by an amphibious DD tank, with its skirts lowered. On the right we can see Engineers pushing back barbed wire and, on the left, Medics with their distinctive armbands. Today the "Chalet Rouge" is still standing, albeit slightly modified. (NA/Heimdal.)

3 and **4**. A little further on, to the northwest, stood the chapel of La Madelaine (W4). This photo was taken a few days after D-day and shows sappers of the 1st ESB (*Engineers Special Brigade*) leaving the chapel after a service. The unit's mark, a white arc, can be seen painted on their helmets. This fine chapel, typical of the first half of the 17th century, was restored after bomb damage and continues to be a landmark near *Utah Beach*. (NA and E.G./Heimdal.)

5 and **6**. Two stained-glass windows placed in the chapel. One depicts a companion of Duke Rollo, Vieul "Aux Epaules", who had vowed to become a Christian in 900; he was a Viking and the founder of the dynasty of lords of Sainte-Marie-du-Mont. The second recalls the participation of the Free French Forces in the D-day landings. (Photos courtesy E.G./ Heimdal.)

7. An *8th Infantry Regiment* support squad leaves the sand dunes of *Utah Beach* for one of the causeways through the inundated zone. The soldier on the left is carrying the tripod of an M1917 A1 heavy machine-gun. The weapon itself is being carried by a man to the right, not shown in this picture of Shelton's. Medics advance in the rear. (NA/Heimdal.)

8. More men photographed in the same sector by war correspondent Shelton. On the right, a soldier using a walkie-talkie. (NA/Heimdal.)

9. A long column of men and vehicles heading towards Sainte-Marie-du-Mont, the objective of the 3rd Battalion, 8th Infantry Regiment. As a landmark, the "Chalet Rouge" can be seen in the distance. White tape marks out sectors cleared of mines. (D.F./Heimdal.)

1. In this other photo by Shelton, infantrymen of the *8th Infantry Regiment* advance along the inundated causeway towards *Exit n° 2*. Heavily loaded soldiers especially had to keep to the causeway, lined with numerous ditching forming deadly traps. These men are still wearing their lifebelts round their waists, by no means a pointless precaution should they need to leave the causeway and venture into the water holes to escape enemy fire. The first in the line is carrying his gun still packed in a plastic case by a piece of string, as the shoulder strap is not free. He is also carrying a bazooka fastened to his lifebelt. (D.F./Heimdal.)

2. Once they arrived on terra firma, in the hamlets before they came to Sainte-Marie-du-Mont, the infantry began to shed whatever equipment they no longer needed. They did keep their lifebelts however. Some who got a soaking on the way in were completely kitted out again, the DD tanks had their skirts removed and the others dropped their protective hoods. Shelton took this shot after his other D-day pictures. (D.F./Heimdal.)

3

3. A little further up the causeway, near the beach exit and antitank barrier, the men advance on dry land, although the surrounding fields are partly under water. The "Chalet Rouge" can be seen in the background. The men are still heavily loaded. A German soldier has been killed, and can be seen on the left, his unhelmeted body lying on the road beside his rifle. A DD tank (recognizable from its skirt) of the *70th Tank Battalion* has skidded into the roadside ditch; the leading men can be seen behind. Another tank advances in the middle of the column. (NA/Heimdal.)

4

4. In this other photo, a DD tank, rid of its skirt, advances down the narrow streets of the Sainte-Marie-du-Mont sector, passing a German horsedrawn van loaded with prisoners. They make a striking contrast. It is followed by a standard Sherman with its hoods off. (NA.)

5. But after the dunes of *Utah Beach*, men of the *8th Chemical Battalion* used their 4.2 inch mortars to support the infantry's advance.

6. The dunes of *Utah Beach*, on W5 land, with the "Chalet Rouge" to the rear and the hill of Val de Saire, with Quettehou and Saint-Vaast in the distance. (E.G./Heimdal.)

5

6

1. At the end of the causeway from the sea *(Exit n° 2)*, the German anti-tank battery emplacement with the house that caught fire on the left. (E.G./ Heimdal.)

2. Avenue leading to the manor-farm at La Vienville, its fine 17th century porch can be seen in the background. (E.G./ Heimdal.)

1

2

Robert Laisney, here in 1940, in his senior sergeant's uniform. He was detached from his Stalag in 1942 to return to look after his stockfarm of 120 head at La Vienville. (R. Laisney coll.)

all the mined obstacles designed to blow them up as they came in on the high tide. Later on, tanks and other vehicles did arrive at high tide, brought in on landing craft that were beached, enabling them to hit the beach ready and running. While in the morning out of the window, we saw the last Germans leaving the sector, after 10 a.m. we only saw very few going down to the beach with their hands on their heads. While the first vehicles were being cleaned, the first men too were cleaning themselves as they had been kitted out to go in the water, they all had a flexible lifebelt which allowed them to advance not only through the seawater but also across the inundated marshlands. Meanwhile, along the coast, the Germans pinned down between the sea and the marshes were quickly taken prisoner. All the Americans who landed in the sea changed while cleaning up their vehicles and left their wet clothes on the spot together with the ten-liter jerrycans of gasoline used to degrease the engines. We also recovered quite a few liters of gas which proved very handy, as the electricity had been cut off on D-day morning and was not restored until 15 August 1945. After cleaning up, they would come to the farm and in particular so enjoyed the cider that my farmhand sat down at the tap on a milking stool and served everyone a glass. By way of thanks, they would leave a packet of tobacco or cigarettes on the barrel."

As for **2/8**, it marched south as far as *W2a*, then veered west along the short causeway leading to Exit n° 1, then on to Pouppeville, reached at **noon**.

The US infantry links up with the paratroops

As the leading elements approached the exits, men and equipment streamed ashore across the beach under sporadic fire from the German Azeville and Saint-Marcouf batteries. At **10.00**, the *22d Infantry Regiment* landed at full strength while the *8th Infantry Regiment* moved on inland. At **noon**, the *4th Division's* third infantry regiment, the *12th Infantry Regiment*, began to land.

Sergeant **Ted Liska** was with the *12th Infantry Regiment's D Company*. His unit landed at 10.30. Once the ramp went down, the men waded ashore. There was deep water in places, but for Sergeant Liska, at 1.85 m and 90 kilos, it only came up to his waist. The beach was littered with all kinds of debris and it was necessary to pass between the white tapes marking out sections where the mines had been cleared. Further on, Ted Liska spotted a bare-headed *Brigadier General* Roosevelt (10), walking with a stick and with his trousers legs outside his boots. But the inundated area had to be crossed, meaning more water to walk through. Then came the link-up with the paratroops. Sergeant Liska then took part in the battle for Cherbourg and many others up until the battle for Mortain on 10 August 1944, when he was wounded. Since then, he has only missed the D-day ceremonies twice: in 1951 (committed in Korea) and 1965, in Vietnam (11).

At **12.05**, the German artillery east of the Baie des Veys (*352. ID*'s sector) joined battle by opening fire on *Utah Beach* with the cannon of *I./AR 352*. But despite the harassment this caused, the landing troops were by now advancing inexorably inland. 3/8 passed through *Exit n° 2* after losing two DD tanks. It left the antitank guns behind to its left (on a level with the small house that had caught fire) then destroyed three or four of 13./919's 76.2 mm field guns. By day's end, this infantry battalion had reached Les

gunfire coming closer, starting at 7 in the morning. Shells had gutted the buildings facing the sea, with bullets smashing window panes. At around 8, the front door opened and American soldiers rushed into the passageway, while Robert Laisney was in the kitchen opening onto the passageway. The Americans asked him *"No Germans?"*. He said no. The Americans asked to look round the place and came to a small cellar with some bottles laid down. Having previously landed in Italy, they exclaimed *"vino, vino!"*. Robert Laisney opened a bottle for them and the four men had a drink. One of them was carrying a walkie-talkie and reported to his commanding officer that there were no Germans around. They left quickly, one of them leaving across the fields with a bottle in his hand. Not long afterwards, some neighbours arrived to tell Robert Laisney that some German artillerymen (6 or 7 men) had blown up one or two bridges on the causeway and set fire to the house where they had dumped their munitions. These civilians managed to put out the fire and prevent the munitions from blowing up. Robert Laisney was surprised at the size of the convoy now advancing towards Sainte-Marie-du-Mont. *"It was going to this house that we realized the scale of the operation with an unending procession of tanks, jeeps, first of all. The first ones that landed in the sea stopped in my meadows to remove their protective covers. The jeeps had their engines completely greased over with a small copper tube as an air inlet to the carburettor, another for the gas tank cap and one in reinforced rubber for the exhaust. These tubes were fixed to branches (cut in England) used to hold their ends clear of the water as they drove along. The tanks that landed in the sea (there were 29 of them) carried a waterproof canvas belt reinforced with tubing, a sheet-metal air intake over the engine cowling and a propeller to move it forward until the tracks got a proper grip. These were the vehicles that came ashore while the tide was out, contrary to what the Germans expected, and this enabled them to destroy*

1. Two columns of infantry, lines of trucks, the *4th Infantry Division* advance inland. (US Army.)

2. The uninterrupted stream of troops moving up from the coast is held up by the narrow hedge-lined lanes. (US Army.)

3. Machine-gunners draw up alongside an abandoned German horse-drawn wagon. (D.F./Heimdal.)

support, then advanced past Audouville-la-Hubert, to be held up at day's end before Turqueville, where the town and vicinity were firmly held by Captain Stiller's Georgian battalion.

Following these battalions came two other infantry regiments of the *4th Infantry Division*. The **12th Infantry Regiment** advanced to Beuzeville-au-Plain with its three battalions. The **22d Infantry Regiment** advanced with its two leading battalions up to the high ground at Saint-Germain-de-Varreville while **3/22** advanced along the dune ridge, capturing strongpoints (*W8*, *StP 9*, *W 10*) on its way to Hamel de Cruttes.

At Audouville-la-Hubert

We come back now to Bernardin Birette on the family farm (see page 58). An hour and a half after he got back to the farm, the whole countryside was shaken by a tremendous bombardment as more than 850 bombs were dropped on the village, killing three civilians and over a hundred stock. The Carrefour de la Vierge and the Birette family farm were not hit. A soldier in German uniform under arrest and locked in a small room on the farm had smashed down the door of his prison in terror. He had jumped for shelter in the trench alongside Bernardin, his parents and Monsieur Lefrançois, where they spent part of the night. Bernardin Birette couldn't help marvelling at all kinds of flares and tracers flashing across the dark sky. Then, after the bombardment was over, shadows passed through the sky. Suddenly there were guns trained on the people in the trench; Monsieur Lefrançois saw that they were not Germans and he explained to the American paratroopers what the disarmed Georgian was doing with them. The paratroopers then seized the prisoner and made off.

By now, dawn was about to break. So, for extra safety, Bernardin and his mother headed for the field across the way where they thought they would be more out of the way of unexpected visitors. They ran for shelter in the ditch by the hedge overlooking the meadow. *"Wer da!"* They froze. Eleven German guns were aimed at the ditch they were in. The Germans' faces were extremely tense. An NCO – the warrant officer - came up. He recognized Madame Birette straightaway and told his men to back off. He told them it was the owner of the "Kassel", as he called the farm. Madame Birette was Belgian-born and as such had experienced the exodus of World War I; she had kept a working knowledge of Flemish, which made it easier for her to cope with her unwelcome German "guests". Seeing that they were no safer here, Bernardin Birette and his mother went back to the farm. It was almost **6 in the morning**.

In the farmhouse, twelve silhouettes of American soldiers surrounded Monsieur Birette. German and Georgian prisoners, some of them wounded, were being held in the ditch opposite the farm. Everything was quiet, the American paratroops controlled the crossroads. Then Monsieur Birette noticed the broken kitchen window (which he had locked before the events of the previous night. He went up and saw bloodstains. Two Americans were alerted who made him open the house, then, taking Bernardin in front of them, cautiously entered the building. The bloodstains led upstairs. With a sten gun muzzle against his shoulder, young Birette went up the stairs, closely followed by the two Americans. When they came to the bedroom they found lying between the beds two Georgians bleeding profusely, their two Mausers by their sides. One of them had his thigh cut to

1. Infantrymen in two columns, lines of trucks, the *4th Infantry Division* heads inland ***s still at Camp Gordon **(2)** in 1942 then on 2 December 1942 this time **(3)** with the new US helmet, and in Normandy **(4)** in 1944 with the new uniform. (T. Liska/Heimdal coll.)

Sergeant Ted Liska, recently at the grave of one of his comrades in the US cemetery at Colleville. He still attends the D-day commemorations. (T. Liska/Heimdal.)

Forges on Highway 13.

After passing through *Exit n° 1* and Pouppeville, then Sainte-Marie-du-Mont, 2/8 also came to Les Forges and was reinforced with elements of the *70th Tank Battalion*. So that evening, the two battalions were in position at this major crossroads leading north to Sainte-Mère-Eglise, west to Chef-du-Pont, south to Carentan, and east to Sainte-Marie-du-Mont. Naturally they linked up wiith the paratroops on arriving on dry land, coming out of the flooded areas. The first to link up were the paratroops **(3/501)** with the seaborne infantry **(2/8)**. Further north, 1/8 (reinforced by A Company, *70th Tank Battalion*) came through *Exit n° 3* already held by the paratroops (Lieutenant-Colonel Cole). That battalion, with tanks in shreds, and could not stand. The other had been hit in the stomach and got up in surrender. Then, oddly, after opening his tunic, he picked open with his knife a dummy lining on his shirt and brought out a photograph he handed over imporingly. On the photograph, he could be seen as a Soviet soldier, with a red star on his cap. The paratroopers looked at it incredulously, and packed them both off to join the other prisoners. With M. Lefrançois holding him up, the Georgian with the smashed leg hobbled downstairs in excruciating pain.

Towards 11, a group of American soldiers coming up from the beaches arrived at the farm. One of them, the interpreter, asked Bernardin Birette to take them to the German command post in the village of Le Brocq near Turqueville. But first, the American placed a badge over Bernardin's left-hand breast pocket, telling him it would save him from being treated as a sniper if ever the Germans captured him. The group advanced along the hedge-lined lane. The sun was already warm. Leading the way were two civilians, Maurice Blaizot and Bernardin Birette, with the interpreter on his left. Suddenly, coming round a hedge, a grenade went off near the group. The GIs were quickly down and firing at an ash tree. The two Normans had not moved. By some miracle, no-one was hurt. At the foot of the ash tree, a German had fallen with a beltful of six grenades. He was finished off by bayonet. When they got to the house occupied by the local German staff, the house was deserted; a few US soldiers entered and ransacked the place in search of documents. Some came to the window sporting German caps abandoned there and mimicked the previous owners to their comrades who had stayed outside.

1. At Audouville-la-Hubert, the crossroads with the statue of the Virgin and La Herguerie Farm (in the background) were spared by the bombardment on the night of 6 June. (E.G./Heimdal.)

2. La Herguerie Farm, the Birette family home on 6 June 1944. The Georgian prisoners and members of the German officering were liquidated at c. 15.00 by paratroopers round the back of the farm. (E.G./Heimdal.)

3. This map shows the crossing of the inundated zones by the three battalions of the *8th Infantry Regiment*. Notice *Exit n° 2* with the destroyed bridge and the antitank battery at La Vienville. (Heimdal.)

Shortly before the party got back to the Birette's farm, an American photographer asked them to pose for the US press. Weston Haynes had come ashore that same morning at Utah Beach. He had already photographed the group earlier as it advanced. But this time, he set up his tripod and asked the two civilians to pose with the army interpreter. It seemed an eternity before he was ready to take the picture. They could be seen from the high ground at Turqueville from where there were Germans and Georgians firing in their direction, with bullets whistling past them. Weston Haynes moved his tripod forward and back again, asked Maurice Blaizot to point to where the Germans were, or Bernardin Birette to put his hand on the interpreter's shoulder. More focussing. An

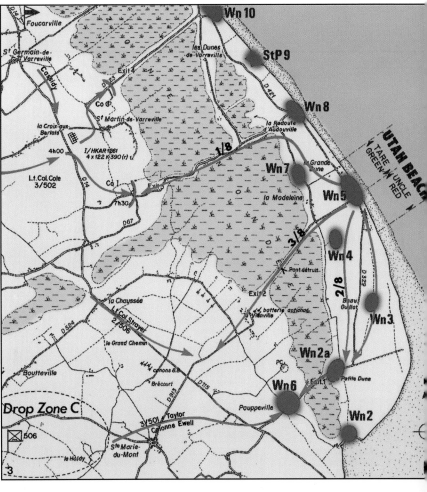

War correspondent Weston Haynes also came ashore at *Utah Beach* on 6 June 1944 when he took some now famous pictures. (Heimdal coll.)

exasperated Bernardin said to his friend: *"This American is crazy, he's going to get us killed for a photograph!"* It was finally taken. Bernardin suggested going back a different way avoiding the road the Germans could see - to no avail.

Back at the farm, Bernardin talked with the US sentry guarding the thirty Germans and Georgians held prisoner in front of it. The soldier gave him cigarettes, although he didn't smoke. He didn't dare turn them down. In fact, he felt embarrassed, a lot of these prisoners and wounded had familiar faces, from fatigue duty they had done together. Several had white faces, drained of blood They eyed him silently. It would have been different of course, had it been "Goatee", a hairy-chinned German NCO known for his persecutions. What if the Germans regained the upper hand?

At around **15.00 hours**, a tall paratrooper raced up to shake him out of this state of mind. After a brief word with the sentry, the sentry took Bernardin Birette by the arm and escorted him behind the farm wall. They were hardly out of sight of the farmyard when they heard a long burst of gunfire coming from the yard. Back on the road, Bernardin Birette found the prisoners' bodies. They were left there for a fortnight until a special fatigue party loaded them onto a truck.

As the bodies were on a busy tank passing place, the dried out bodies ended up looking like planks. The uncertain outcome of the battle and lack of manpower to cope with all the prisoners in this sensitive sector seem to have been the cause of this decision, which was not an isolated incident.

Later, at **Ecoquenéauville**, Weston Haynes continued his reportage with the American advance on Sainte-Mère. At the Lerévérend home, he caught on film Marc Lerévérend, his wife Henriette, and Marthe and Denise, their two daughters, aged 19 and 21. The father brought out some cider for the paratroopers. Marthe exchanged a few words with the shorter of the two soldiers, who was a Canadian. Marthe noticed this odd photographer soldier who wore a beard. Leaving the Lerévérends', he crossed over to take the Leroux children, Claude and his sister, with Madame Chardon and Madame Agnès. Then, turning round, he caught a picture of German (or Georgian) prisoners being escorted from Turqueville. They are passing by a wall on which a small child is sitting, in Madame Leroux's safe hands, while other children look on.

This was how Weston Haynes advanced on Sainte-Mère-Eglise with the seaborne troops to relieve the paratroops.

1. Weston Haynes followed the landing troops as they advanced. He then took this photo in which we see a group of American soldiers accompanied by two Normans: Maurice Blaizot (leading with the cap — he had joined the Birette family after his house was bombarded) guiding GIs to Le Brocq, late in the morning, and Bernardin Birette (center with the beret). This photo was published in a small American propaganda booklet intended for the French and captioned: "Our invaluable French guides enabled us to locate stores, enemy snipers, and did everything to help us." (Heimdal coll.)

2. The familiar photograph posing under German gunfire at Le Brot. (Heimdal coll.)

3. Bernardin Birette in April 1993, nothing has changed. (Heimdal.)

At Sainte-Marie-du-Mont

At **Sainte-Marie-du-Mont**, the troops linked up sometime around midday. Late that morning, a small German (salvaged French-built) tracked vehicle arrived from the coast amid the retreating German troops. But the paratroops were there and a shot rang out from the belltower; the German sitting in the back slumped and was killed. The driver called out *"Bernhardt, Bernhardt?"*. He got out of his seat and was also hit; he died a slow death ("6bis" on the map). At **13.10**, the cannon thundered ten times over, hitting the church's Renaissance belltower. The clock stopped at 1.10, marking the exact time. The parapets on the upper walkway collapsed, smashing into the roof. Then the infantry and tanks arrived down the Rue de la Gallie (D913). Jean Lelarge saw them coming: *"I saw a huge vehicle starting to come down the street, a tank. It passed in front of the house, its turret reached up to my window. It was full of sand, with bows and tarpaulins round it, the exhaust came out of a kind of funnel. It was the sign that the landing had taken place, there were not just the paratroops, the equipment was following. Then it was an endless stream of traffic, one-way of course, the first*

Carrefour de la Vierge at Audouville-la-Hubert. (E.G./Heimdal.)

1. Weston Haynes continues his reportage. We have now come to Ecoquenéauville, the village closest to Sainte-Mère-Eglise, west of Turqueville where the Georgians have dug in. The Lerévérend family are in front of their house, with the paratroops. The smaller of the two paratroopers of the *101st Airborne Division* talking with Marc Lerévérend is a Canadian. Marthe Lerévérend is with her sister by the chair. (Heimdal coll.)

2. The same spot today. (Heimdal.)

3. Marthe Lerévérend in 1993. (Heimdal.)

4. Weston Haynes took another photo at Ecoquenéauville. A GI is greeting some civilians. They include two children, Claude Leroux and his sister. (Heimdal coll.)

5. Claude Leroux in 1993.

6. Weston Haynes turned round to take the other side of the street, photographing this group of prisoners, probably Georgians, being led off by GIs, past a farm. (Heimdal coll.)

7. The same spot today. (Heimdal.)

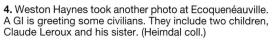

days, but day and night, without stopping, tanks, GMCs, jeeps, and, this surprised me, men on foot, in two columns, one on each sidewalk, again an endless stream."

Thus the *Utah Beach* landing was a success. It took place in good conditions with relatively few losses

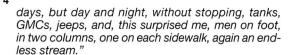

against defenses that had been crushed in their positions. Total casualties for the *4th Division* came to 197 men, roughly equivalent to one company. The *8th* and *12th R.C.T.* lost just 118 men that day, and only 12 killed. These were losses on nothing like the scale seen at Omaha Beach where the *116th R.C.T., 29th Division* alone lost 608 men including 341 killed and 26 missing, and where the *16th R.C.T., 1st Division* suffered 962 losses. Also the troops had linked up with the paratroopers and Highway 13 had been reached. Mission accomplished. But there were still German pockets of resistance, notably at Les Forges, on Highway 13 and in the Turqueville sector.

(1) The initials *U.S.S.* were used for United States Ships in the war navy, the initials *H.M.S.* (His Majesty's Ship) designated *Royal Navy* vessels.

(2) Only *H.M.S. Erebus* sailed from Weymouth at 17.30 on 5 June.

(3) *U.S.S. Nevada* had ten 14 inch (355 mm) guns and sixteen six inch (152 mm) guns, *U.S.S. Tuscaloosa* and *U.S.S. Quincy* nine 8 inch (203 mm) guns and eight 5 inch (127 mm) guns, *H.M.S. Hawkins* seven 7.5 inch (190 mm) guns, *H.M.S. Enterprise* six 6 inch (152 mm) guns, *H.M.S. Black Prince* eight 5.25 inch (133 mm) guns and the *Soemba* three 5.9 inch (150 mm) guns.

(4) *Naval Combat Demolition Units*. The eleven NCDUs assigned to *Utah Beach* were commanded by *Lt.* Herbert Peterson. Each comprised one officer, five navy sappers, five army sappers and three seamen.

(5) Abbreviation for *Beach Obstacle Demolition Party*. These units were equipped with heavy vehicles such as tankdozers, i.e. tanks with a bulldozer blade on the front.

(6) These details are taken from the accounts of these two naval officers on board LCC-60 as reported by Jonathan Gawne in *Spearheading D-Day: American Special Units of the Normandy Invasion*, Histoire et Collections, 1999.

(7) In « *Ils arrivent !* », Robert Laffont, 1961, pp. 73 and 74.

(8) *Op. cit.*, p. 75.

(9) *Op. cit.*, pp. 82 and 83.

(10) As seen indeed in a photo taken on the beach on 6 June.

(11) Account published in *Veteran recall*, by Hilary Kaiser, Editions Heimdal, 2004.

1 and **2.** These two famous photos, taken at Turqueville on 6 June, show a paratrooper of the *101st Airborne Division*, Wilbur Shanklin of *HQ Coy*, *506th PIR*. Carrying an M1 gun with bayonet, he also has a machete, and US and German grenades. A cricket is fastened to his left epaulet with a piece of string. His name Shanklin is marked on the sheath of his M3 knife. Notice also, on his right epaulet, a gas detector armband and a .45 Colt wrist strap. He has added a German water bottle over his chest. A fully kitted out paratrooper! The "German" soldier surrendering is in fact a Georgian. This is Turqueville where the Georgians of *Ost-Battalion 795* put up some stout resistance until 7 June. He is poorly equipped, with a salvaged belt, and worn old drill trousers. (US Army.)

3 and **4.** Two US paratroop knives, the M3 on the left and another less standard model, against American parachute canvas. (D. François coll.)

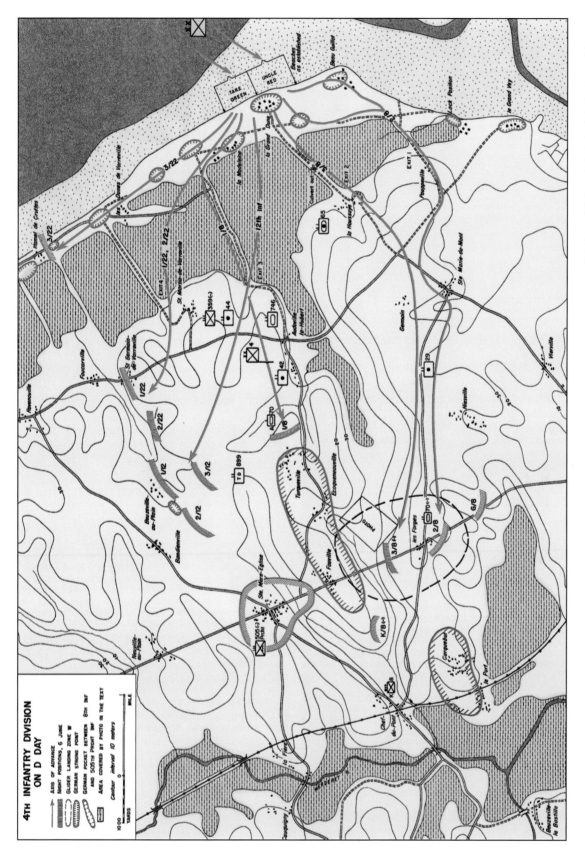

On this second map, we see the *4th Infantry Division's* D-day advance to the hamlet Les Forges, on Highway 13 which 2/8 reached, with the *70th Tank Battalion's* tanks in support. Notice the sector still held by the Georgian battalion around Fauville and Turqueville. But as we have seen, US troops had reached Ecoqueneauville. Not also the position of Audouville-la-Hubert at a crossroads. The linkup was achieved at Sainte-Marie-du-Mont. The *505th PIR* on the other hand was still cut off at Sainte-Mère-Eglise.

4TH INFANTRY DIVISION
ON D DAY

AXIS OF ADVANCE
NIGHT POSITIONS, 6 JUNE
GLIDER LANDING ZONE W
GERMAN STRONG POINT
GERMAN POCKET BETWEEN 8TH INF
AND 505TH FIGHT INF
AREA COVERED BY PHOTO IN THE TEXT

Contour interval 10 meters

MILE
YARDS

Sainte-Marie-du-Mont.

1, 2, 3 and **4.** These two photos **(1** and **3)** were taken by war correspondent Kaye and together form a panoramic view of the church square. From left to right we see: the town hall, the presbytery (behind the gate and the trees), several houses, then the road leading off to Utah Beach (Rue de la Gallie, see map on page 87), invisible here, and the square surrounded by lime-trees overlooked by the church. The pump is behind the photographer. The small tracked vehicle is a Weasel issued to the landing troops. The vehicle was designed on the basis of a programme for a light transport vehicle with low bearing soil pressure, for use on soft snow. Constructed by Studebaker, the Weasel M 29 had a 65 horsepower 3,600 rpm engine with a row of 6 cylinders placed on the front right-hand side. Designed to run on snow, this small tracked truck was also ideal in the sand dunes of *Utah Beach*. The photo on the left is

thought to have been taken on D + 1 (and not as has sometimes been written on D + 2 – it is dated 7 June by Kaye). It would seem to show 3/502 of the 101st heading off towards Blosville-Houesville, and more specifically H Coy with Tech. 5 Robert Marois facing the camera. The presentday photos **(2** and **4)** show how the place has remained as it was. (D.F. and E.G./Heimdal.)

5. This other vertical photo by Kaye shows the Gothic church bell-tower, topped by a Renaissance dome. Notice the clock has stopped at 1.10. (DAVA/Heimdal.)

6. This fourth photo of Kaye's shows a group of paratroopers of the *101st Airborne Division* meeting civilians by the water pump. (DAVA/Heimdal.)

7. War correspondent Montgomery pictured the same place from a little farther back, again on 7 June. (DAVA/Heimdal.)

8. Today, nothing has changed. (Heimdal.)

9. In the spring of 1944, German soldiers came to fetch water from this same pump using A. Brohier of Sainte-Mère-Eglise's tank. (ECPA.)

10, 11, 12, 13, 14, 15. A few pictures taken at the same spot on 7 June 1944. (US Army.)

129

1. Near Sainte-Marie-du-Mont, this paratrooper lies in a ditch after falling in action. Another Montgomery picture taken on 7 June. (D.F./Heimdal.)

2. This other photo shows a more peaceful scene, with MPs and paratroopers meeting the population. (US Army.)

3. Towards 6 on D-day evening, German paratroopers of 1st Battalion, *Fallschirmjäger-Regiment 6*, under their commander Captain Preikschat, counterattacked the US paratroopers of the *501st PIR* at La Basse-Addeville and Vierville. The latter were forced back to Sainte-Marie-du-Mont. The Germans burst into the village and kept going towards Sainte-Marie, hoping to reach some coastal positions. A German paratrooper's belt and cartridge belts. (D. François coll.)

4. Porte cartes d'un officier de para allemand provenant du secteur. (Coll. D. François.)

5. But the German paratroops of *I./FJR6* came up against some stiff resistance on the outskirts of Sainte-Marie-du-Mont. During the night of 6 to 7 June, the battalion was encircled by the Americans. Also, the II Battalion *(II./FJR 6)*, commanded by Captain Mager, attacked northwards towards Sainte-Mère-Eglise and came up against the *505th PIR*. Attacks and counterattacks followed each throughout the day of 6 June. The "Green Devils" sustained heavy losses. Here we see some of their bodies in the Sainte-Mère sector. (D.F./Heimdal.) Death was everywhere in the bocage of the Cotentin. Many civilians too were killed in the confusion of the battle with Americans and Germans passing each other in the thick hedgerow country prior to forming a front line. Casualties of the bombardments or of artillery fire as at Sainte-Mère-Eglise (see page 144 - 147). Some fell to American bullets in the heat of the skirmishing. A few details are reported by François Lemonnier-Gruhier at *La Brèche de Sainte-Marie-du-Mont*. At Manoir de la Fisée, in the village of Le Holdy, M. de Veyrac found himself in the middle of the fighting and in the confusion he was hit in the head by an American bullet. At Manoir de Brécourt (the de Valavieille family seat), near the German battery a "nasty mistake" occurred. The paratroopers made the civilians leave the manor. Near some wounded Germans, Michel de Valavieille (one of the sons of the lord of the manor, Colonel de Valavieille) waved a handkerchief to indicate that people were injured. Did the paratroopers take him for a German? They sent him running and fired at him *"like a beast caught in full flight"*. After being very badly wounded and taken care of by American surgeons, he made a miraculous recovery and he became curator of the Utah Beach Museum after the war. At Brécourt, *"the paratroopers killed everything. They killed without stopping, without distinction, with no letup, no pardon both men … and animal teams. The bodies of machine-gunned, shot, knifed young Germans were piled up along with horses that had been shot or had their carotid cut. You had to cut across the fields; there was no way of getting through the pileup of cars, animals and dead men lying all over the place. Blood, there was blood flowing freely everywhere; you were walking in it… like at a slaughterhouse!"* (*op. cit.*, p.98).

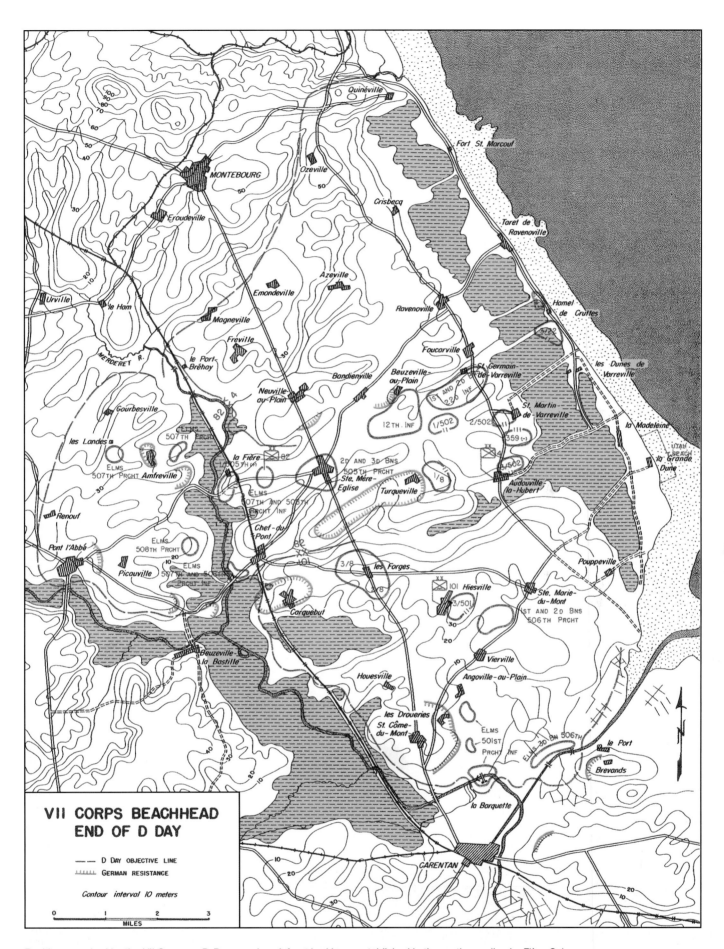

Positions reached by the *VII Corps* on D-Day evening. A front had been established in the north on a line La Fière-Sainte-Mère-Eglise-Saint-Germain-de-Vareville. In the south and west, the Merderet line was reached with elements west of the river near Amfreville on Hill 30. But there were still substantial pockets of German resistance in this American beachhead: the Georgians in the Turqueville sector, around Carquebut and Saint-Côme-du-Mont.

131

Sainte-Mère-Eglise and the Battle of the Merderet

Alexandre Renaud, mayor of Sainte-Mère-Eglise in 1944.

Henri-Jean Renaud in June 1944.

Lieutenant-Colonel Edward Krause was commander of the 3rd Battalion, 505th PIR. He landed a kilometer west of Sainte-Mère-Eglise. He sent a message from that locality at 05.00 hours on 6 June. (US Army.)

At **04.00 hours**, a convoy of 52 gliders started flying out from Ramsbury to bring succour to the defenders of Sainte-Mère-Eglise. One of them, carrying sanitary equipment, crashed into the Hospice wall, another into the schools with a 57 mm gun. They brought in Batteries A and B of the *80th Antitank Battalion, 82d Airborne Division*. They were to consolidate the roadblocks around the town. Their objective was Landing Zone "O", but only 23 gliders landed there, with 3 killed and 23 injured among these airborne elements. 82d Airborne second-in-command *Brigadier General* Gavin now had 11 of his 22 jeeps and 8 of his 16 guns. A field dressing station was immediately set up on *DZ "O"*, where a number of wounded paratroopers were recovered. Then Gavin's personal jeep was brought out, with his automatic coffee maker on the back seat.

The antitank battalion was placed under the temporary command of Captain W. Irland and Brig. Gen. Gavin wanted to be sure he was getting his guns. Commenting on his men's action after they had hit the hedges with their gliders following a difficult Channel crossing, Irland had this to say: *"These guys don't get paid enough!"*

And soon, after daybreak and while it was still quiet, in Sainte-Mère *"a few inhabitants began to come out onto their doorsteps and in low voices exchange their first impressions of the exceptional events of the previous night"*. The Mayor's son, Henri-Jean Renaud, recalls these unforgettable moments:

"Making the most of this lull, my father was keen to go back to where he saw the first paratroopers land at his feet and witnessed the first murderous exchanges during the night. My elder brother and I so pleaded with him to take us along that he finally gave in. Usually so quiet and orderly, the square hardly looked the same at all. Apart from soldiers coming and going all over the place, there were lots of parachutes lying on the ground or hanging from trees, a few recalcitrant vehicles that had failed to start and had been left by the occupying forces, and here and there, you began to find some of those odd items you see in classic war films, whatever the war – abandoned bicycles, empty boxes, broken chairs, all kinds of debris.

It was as we were crossing this large square, heading for the Roman milestone in the middle, that I saw the first dead body in my brief existence. It was a German. He was lying there on the ground in his purplish blue Flak uniform. He had no obvious wound, there was no blood. I looked at him in surprise, without emotion, the way I looked at others a little later on. I probably didn't understand very well, but it was my first confrontation with death. My grandfather had died a few months before, but as a child I was prudishly kept from seeing anything and all I saw was the coffin carried off under the flowers. Grandfather had left us and that was all there was to it. But one thing did impress me with this corpse in uniform, it was so terribly still.

As we continued our walk, my father explained to us what he had seen during the night and showed us where he saw the fighting. The house was reduced to a pile of cinders and a few sections of wall. He took us to the right towards the Parc de la Haulle. On the gravel path a paratrooper lay on his stomach, with his face to the ground. Oddly enough, he had only his combat jacket and trousers. He had no weapon, no helmet, no harness, no boots. My father thought he had been shot down by the Germans who then stripped him of anything likely to give them information as to his nationality, unit, rank or the nature of the assignment he was on. Another ten yards further on, there was a paratrooper hanging from the end of his parachute in the top branches of a tree. His feet were just fifty centimetres off the ground. The three of us looked at him and, probably not having quite grasped the situation, I went a little closer, and with the tip of my fingers, I gave his boot a little push. The body swayed slightly, interrupting the tragic stillness. A G.I. nearby came straight up to us and told us to "get out". Just a few steps away, in the middle of a large field, in the soft grass, already quite tall in the Normandy spring, lay another paratrooper. He had a tiny hole in his temple. He probably just had time to slip off his parachute before he was shot pointblank by a German who'd seen him landing heavily. Finally, just on the corner of the destroyed house, was the body of a young American whose combat uniform was partly burnt. I can remember exactly the great burn on his back and the wisp of smoke coming from his clothing, still smoldering like the wick of a candle that has just been extinguished.

We hurried back home. The lull was soon broken with the first bullets whining through the sky and it had us dropping our heads in between our shoulders. The war was about to start up again, it was hard for civilians and fighting men alike, and everyone paid the price of freedom."

Lieutenant-Colonel Edward Krause, CO of the 3rd Battalion, *505th PIR*, landed during the night a kilometer west of Sainte-Mère-Eglise, right in the field

chosen for his stick to muster. Resistance on the ground had been nonexistent. Once they had mustered, the men in his stick were split into four groups and dispatched in opposite directions to reconnoiter, with orders to be back within forty-five minutes. The reconnaissance parties brought back a group of ninety paratroopers guided by a Norman visibly the worse for drink, who told them that the German unit garrisoned in Sainte-Mère had evacuated the place (see page 79) to join up camp with a transport and quartermaster unit.

Sainte-Mère-Eglise

Krause then quickly reorganized his unit into two companies and marched on the town behind the shelter of the hedgerows. On reaching the outskirts of Sainte-Mère-Eglise, Krause ordered six battalions to form roadblocks on the various routes into town, except for the one they intended to use themselves. When he considered these combat groups were in position, he set off with his own party towards the town center to destroy the German communications link to Cherbourg. Taking the town proved no very difficult task. Some thirty Germans were taken prisoner and another eleven were killed trying to escape.

At **05.00 hours**, Krause dispatched a runner to the regimental commander, Colonel William Ekman, with the following message: *"I am in Sainte-Mère-Eglise!"* then an hour later, a second liaison officer was dispatched with the new message: *"I have taken Sainte-Mère-Eglise!"*. But neither of the runners found Ekman. However the second man met General Ridgway and passed on the message to him. There were a lot of messages not getting through that morning. As a consequence, up until noon, Colonel Ekman, although less than a mile away, continued to entertain the mistaken belief that Sainte-Mère-Eglise was still in German hands.

The 2nd Battalion **(2/505)**, commander Lieutenant-Colonel Benjamin Vandervoort, made one of the few grouped landings (27 of its 36 sticks landed on or near the DZ). By dawn, he had mustered some 575 of the battalion's 630 paratroopers. Unfortunately, Vandervoort broke his ankle on landing and had to be carried around in a cart they found nearby. The assignment involved mopping up the northern entrance to Sainte-Mère-Eglise, on Highway 13, where a German counterattack was expected.

At **06.15**, on finally making radio contact with Ekman, he informed him that he was in position at Neuville.

For almost the next two hours, he heard no news. At **08.00**, he was issued orders, counterorders and disorders, as tends to happen during operations in enemy territory. First Ekman signalled that he had heard nothing from the 3rd Battalion. Then at **08.10**, he ordered him to do an about-turn and capture Sainte-Mère-Eglise! At **08.16**, he was told to double back to Neuville, because the 3rd Battalion was thought to be in Sainte-Mère-Eglise! At **08.17**, he was ordered to ignore the previous order and proceed to Sainte-Mère-Eglise! Vandervoort received all these contradictory messages with caution (don't forget he was hobbling around on a broken ankle) and decided to retrace his steps, but leaving a party of forty-one paratroops under Lieutenant Turner Turnbull of D Co to put up a skeleton defense at Neuville-au-Plain.

Turnbull was a "half-Cherokee", nicknamed "the Chief" by his battalion, and respected as a gifted soldier, which he again proved amply in the hours that followed.

Above: the Château de Fauville to which the German garrison at Sainte-Mère-Eglise withdrew.

Opposite: 2nd Battalion, *505th PIR* was commanded by Lieutenant-Colonel Benjamin Vandervoort. At dawn, with a broken ankle, he contrived to muster 575 paratroopers of his battalion. (D. François coll.)

Towards **09.30**, **3/505** was attacked south of Sainte-Mère-Eglise by two companies of Georgians, with three light tanks and two self-propelled guns in support. They were repulsed by the men of the 3rd Battalion. Vandervoort then came on the scene with his 2nd Battalion *(2/505)*. After talking with Krause, the new arrivals looked to defending the northern part of the locality.

Meanwhile, Turnbull's party marched athletically on Neuville and took that village in a matter of minutes. It was unoccupied and Turnbull took up position on the north side on a promontory with an overhanging hedge which provided him with a five hundred meter firing range to the north. He had ten men and a machine-gun, in an orchard edged with open land to the west of Neuville. To complete his disposition, Turnbull placed a bazooka-aimer with two infantrymen in the houses along Highway 13.

Twenty minutes later, the men stationed behind the hedge spotted a long column of German infantry singing as they went. Just then, Vandervoort turned up in a jeep that had arrived a couple of hours previously in one of the gliders transporting the division's heavy equipment. He had a 57 mm gun in tow. While the artillery were getting into position to reinforce the strongpoint, Vandervoort and Turnbull were talking together when a Frenchman rode up on a bicycle pointing his finger towards the road behind him. The two officers then saw troops on the march. The man told them they were German prisoners being escorted by paratroopers. True, there were a few men dressed as paratroopers waving

505th PIR patch.

This map shows the *505th PIR's* drop zone, mostly west of Sainte-Mère-Eglise, as planned. Each dot represents one stick dropped by a plane. Lieutenant-Colonel Krause's *3/505* headed for Sainte-Mère. Lieutenant-Colonel Vandervoort's *2/505* headed for Neuville-au-Plain, before returning to Sainte-Mère. As for *1/505*, it mustered to march on La Fière. German resistance was fiercer north of Neuville-au-Plain and south of Fauville. (US Army map/Heimdal for the coloring.)

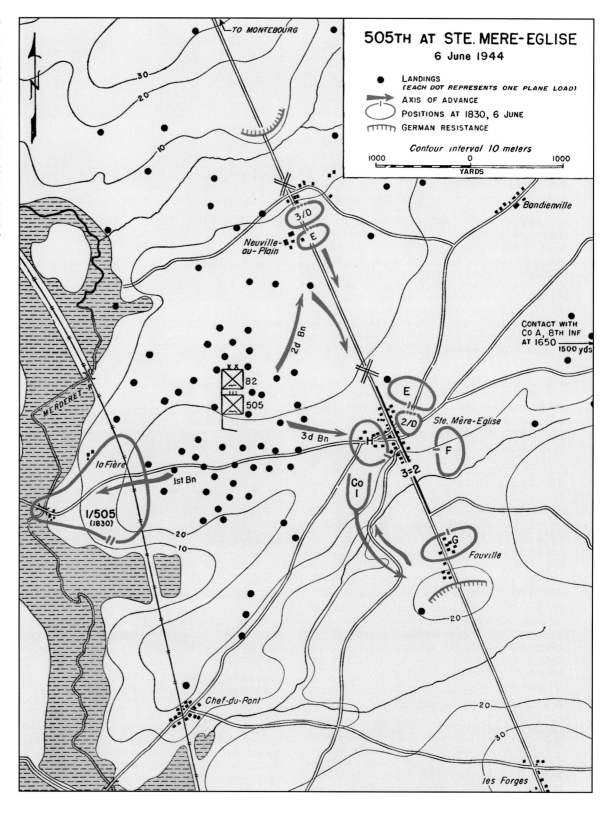

orange triangles, Vandervoort noticed, but he began to smell a rat on seeing the column marching in such perfect order. When the column came within 800 meters, Vandervoort was absolutely certain what was going on before his eyes and ordered a machine-gunner to open fire. Quick as a flash, the men opposite scattered onto either side of the road and started firing back. This was the Frenchman's cue to make himself scarce.

It was in fact a 190-strong company of *Grenadier-Regiment 1058, 91. (Luftlande) Infanterie-Division.*

The battle raged on until early afternoon. Turnbull's men, still lying behind their hedge to the west, managed to pin down the Germans along the road, but the Germans tried to outflank them.

Vandervoort dispatched a runner to ask Turnbull if everything was OK or if he needed help. He came away with the assurance that Turnbull had everything under control and not to worry about him! Vandervoort had faith in the "Chief's" reputation.

Shortly after battle commenced, a German SP gun coming from the Cherbourg direction appeared less than five hundred meters away and opened fire. Its second round killed the bazooka-aimer in the defensive position by the roadside. Its fifth round just missed the antitank gun and its servers dived into a house for cover. Then after a few minutes they came out again and returned to their gun, scoring two hits on the SP gun. Then a German assault gun arrived on the scene, a *Sturmgeschütz* which they managed to damage.

The German infantry used the cover of the Bocage to try and outflank Turnbull's positions with mortar support. By mid-afternoon eighteen Americans had been killed or wounded.

Back at his command post, Vandervoort was alerted by the bad news and dispatched Lieutenant Theodore L. Peterson and his C Co platoon to cover Turnbull's withdrawal. When Turnbull was back in the safety of the battalion's perimeter, Peterson in the rearguard was finally able to fall back with his platoon.

By holding out all day his position north of Neuville-au-Plain, Lieutenant Turner Turnbull halted the advance of *Grenadier-Regiment 1058*, and covered the northern flank of 82nd Airborne's disposition, at a cost however of twenty-five killed and wounded out of his platoon's forty-one paratroops. Turnbull himself was killed the following day by a mortar shell.

La Fière Sector

The *505th PIR*, commanded by Colonel William Ekman, was probably the luckiest of all the airborne regiments dropped on D-day. It mustered easily and was able to complete all its assignments.

The plan was for the 1st Battalion **(1/505)** to leave the drop zone and take the La Fière causeway on the Sainte-Mère-Eglise/Pont-l'Abbé road, on a level with the Merderet river. In actual fact, a single company, A Co, was detailed to this mission.

The 800-meter long "Chaussée de la Fière" had strategic importance, surrounded by marshlands and inundated areas under several meters of water, being one of very few ways across the Merderet.

Lt. John Dolan of A Co, followed by elements of C Co and a few paratroopers of the 507th, was the first to arrive in this sector with his company. Near the bridge was a manor-farm occupied by a German detachment which had fortified the barns and farmhouse. It took Dolan and his men several hours to dislodge the enemy from this entrenched camp.

A few *engineers* of the *307th Glider Engineer Battalion* then arrived with a 57 mm gun. Dolan set up his defensive perimeter around the bridge and manor, and along the river.

The Germans appeared at Cauquigny on the other side of the causeway. There were 250 of them, with artillery and large-caliber mortar support, but most of all they were following two Renault tanks, with a third bringing up the rear. There followed an intensive exchange of fire on either side of the Merderet, the causeway hotted up and both sides began to count their dead.

The tanks were destroyed by two bazooka teams placed on either side of the bridge. The Germans withdrew in disarray, but late that afternoon launched a further unsuccessful counterattack.

Major F.C. Kellan, commander of the 505th's 1st Battalion, was killed on 6 June, as was his successor, *Major* James McGinity that same day. Which left Lieutenant Dolan in command of the battalion in the La Fière sector.

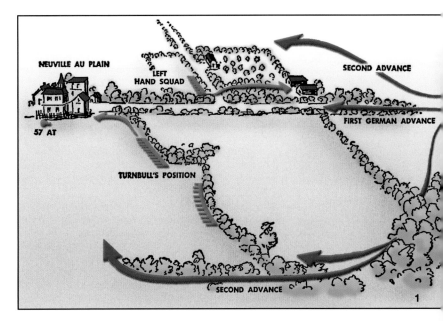

Marcus Heim (*505th PIR, 82nd Airborne Division*)

"Shortly after midnight on June 6 1944, Marcus Heim jumped out of a C-47 transport plane over Normandy. The division's objective was to control road communications around Ste Mère-Eglise and the Merderet and Douve River valleys. Heim was part of A Company, 505, their specific objective was to seize and hold the La Fiere Bridge over the Merderet River.

I landed about twenty-five feet from a road and before I could get my rifle assembled, I heard a motorcycle approaching. I remained still as I did not have time to assemble my rifle, and watched two German soldiers pass by. After they passed and I had my rifle together I found other paratroopers and our equipment bundle and set off for the bridge over the Merderet River. We were to hold the bridge until the soldiers who landed on the beach arrived later that day, but it was three days before they reached our position.

1. This sketch, after General S.L.A. Marshall's book, shows the German maneuver in two stages (*first German advance* and *second advance*) to outflank Turnbull's position and left hand squad. Notice too the position of the 57 mm antitank gun. (Heimdal after S.L.A. Marshall.)

2. Tracked vehicle used by the Germans and destroyed in the Neuville sector. There is a glider behind the hedge. (US Army/D.F.)

Pvt Marcus Heim, as a young paratrooper at Fort Benning in 1943. He has just won his paratrooper's certificate. (Photo courtesy D. François.)

As you stand at the La Fiere Bridge looking in the direction of Ste Mère-Eglise, the Manor House is on the right and was the living quarters. There were several buildings, one a large barn, which was close to the Merderet River. The Germans had occupied the Manor House and were driven out by 'A' Company, 505 [Lt. John Dolan], after heavy fighting.

When we arrived at the bridge, men were placed down the pathway to the right and to the left of the Manor House and outbuildings. The four bazooka men included: Lenold Peterson, and myself, John Bolderson and Gordon Pryne. Peterson and I took up positions on the Manor House side facing Cauquigny, below the driveway.

We knew that when the Germans started the attack with their tanks, we would have to get out of our foxhole and reveal our position to get a better view of the tanks. Bolderson and Pryne were on the right side of the road just below the pathway. I do not remember how many paratroopers were around us, all I saw was a machine gun set up in the Manor House yard. On the right side down the pathway a

few riflemen took up positions. There was a 57-millimeter cannon up the road in back of us along with another machine gun. We carried antitank mines and bazooka rockets from the landing area. These mines were placed across the causeway about 50 or 60 feet on the other side of the bridge. There was a broken down German truck by the Manor House, which we pushed and dragged across the bridge and placed it across the causeway. All that afternoon the Germans kept shelling our position, and the rumor was that the Germans were going to counter attack.

They arrived...

Around 5:00 in the afternoon the Germans started the attack. Two tanks with infantry on each side and in the rear following them was a third tank with more infantry following it. As the lead tank started around the curve in the road the tank commander stood up in the turret to take a look and from our left the machine gun let loose a burst and killed the commander. At the same time the bazookas, 57 millimeter and everything else we had were firing at the Germans and they in turn were shooting at us with cannons, mortars, machine guns and rifle fire. Lenold Peterson and I (the loader), in the forward position got out of the foxhole and stood behind the telephone pole so we could get a better shot at the tanks. We had to hold our fire until the last minute because some of the tree branches along the causeway were blocking our view. The first tank was hit and started to turn sideways and at the same time was swinging the turret around and firing at us. We had just moved forward around the cement telephone pole when a German shell hit it and we had to jump out of the way to avoid being hit as it was falling. I was hoping that Bolderson and Pryne were also firing at the tanks for with all that was happening in front of us there was not time to look around to see what others were doing. We kept firing at the first tank until it was put out of action and on fire. The second tank came up and pushed the first tank out of the way. We moved forward toward the second tank and fired at it as fast as I could load the rockets in the bazooka. We kept firing at the second tank and we hit it in the turret where it is connected to the body, also in the track and with another hit it also went up in flames. Peterson and I were almost out of rockets, and the third tank was still moving. Peterson asked me to go back across the road and see if Bolderson had any extra rockets. I ran across the road and with all the crossfire I still find it hard to believe I made it to the other side in one piece. When I got to the other side I found one dead soldier and Bolderson and Pryne were gone. Their bazooka was lying on the ground and it was damaged by what I thought were bullet holes. Not finding Bolderson or Pryne I presumed that either one or both were injured. I found the rockets they left and then had to return across the road to where I left Peterson. The Germans were still firing at us and I was lucky again, I return without being hit. Peterson and I put the new found rockets to use on the third tank. After that one was put out of action the Germans pulled back to Cauquigny and continued shelling us for the rest of the night. They also tried two other counter attacks on our position, which also failed.

After I went across the road and found more rockets for the bazooka and returned, the third tank was put out of action and the Germans retreated. When the Germans pulled back, we looked around did not see anyone, we than moved back to our foxhole. Looking back up the road toward Ste Mere-Eglise, we saw that the 57-millimeter cannon and the machine gun were destroyed. Looking down the

Above: La Fière causeway, 7 June 1944, the three Renault tanks of *Panzer-Ersatz-u.Ausb. Abteilung 100* knocked out by Heim and Peterson. (Photo courtesy D. François.)

Below: the third Renault tank, reused by the Germans Heim and destroyed by Heim and Peterson on the La Fière causeway. (Photo courtesy D. François.)

pathway across from the Manor House we could not see any of our men. We were thinking that we were all alone and that maybe we should move from here, then someone came and told us to hold our position and he would find more men to place around us for the Germans may try again to breach our lines. We found out later, of the few that were holding the bridge at this time, most were either killed or wounded."

For holding the position and repelling the Germans during the first battle of La Fière, Marcus Heim and Lenold Peterson were awarded the *Distinguished Service Cross*, the second highest US Army distinction. Those survivors who witnessed the two men's conduct during the battle said later that what they did that day should have earned them the Congressional Medal of Honor. Marcus Heim died on 26 October 2002 in his hometown of Middleburg NY, where he was a judge.

Chef-du-Pont

Captain Roy Creek (Co « E », 507th PIR, 82d Abn. Div.)

"About **09.00 hours**, Lt. Col. Ostberg, Commander 1st Battalion 507 Parachute Infantry Regiment, returned from the command post of Gen. Gavin, Assistant Division Commander, and informed us that General Gavin was moving toward La Fiere and that we were to follow. This meant fording the flooded area that we had already struggled through earlier in the day.

As we waded in water sometimes chest deep, we were fired on by snipers, who appeared to be firing

The *505th PIR's* command post set up in the bocage. (US Army.)

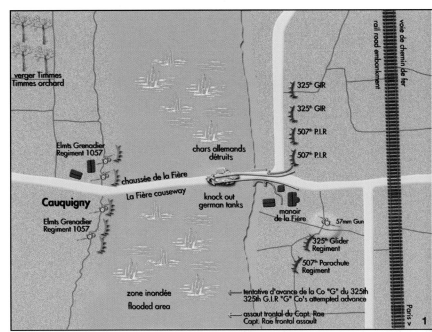

1. Sketch of the Battle of La Fière, 6 June 1944, showing the forces in presence. (Heimdal.)

2. Aerial photograph taken looking eastwards, placing the Manoire de La Fière on the east bank, in the foreground. The Germans were on the west bank, on the other side of the inundated area, marked in blue.

3. The Manoir de La Fière as it is today, viewed from the same angle. (E.G./Heimdal.)

137

1. Marcus Heim receives the *Distinguished Service Cross* from General Omar Bradley at La Haye-du-Puits in July 1944. (Ph. courtesy D. François.)

2. The DSC awarded to Marcus Heim by General Omar Bradley. (Ph. courtesy D. François.)

3. Marcus Heim by the grave of General Gavin at West Point cemetery in 1999. (Ph. courtesy D. François.)

4. Marcus Heim with his wife Gloria and his granddaughter, surrounded by local officials during the official unveiling of the "Chaussée Marcus Heim" near the Pont de La Fière. (Ph. courtesy D. François.)

5. The bloody La Fière causeway is rénamed "Chaussée Marcus Heim". (Ph. courtesy D. François.)

Lieutenant-Colonel Edwin J. Ostberg, commander of the 1st Battalion, *507th PIR*, heads for Chef-du-Pont. (Coll. D.F.)

from long range because of the inaccuracy of their fire. But one couldn't help being concerned about the shots splashing water in his face. All that could be done was to keep on walking and hoping. We made it to the other side without mishap. We marched south until we reached high ground overlooking the La Fiere Bridge. When we arrived, Gen. Gavin told us we should proceed south along the railroad to Chef-du-Pont where we were to seize the town and bridge across the Merderet west of the center of town.

A few men who had been able to get some automatic weapons from some of the bundles dropped as we jumped, were attached for this mission and under the command of Col. Ostberg, proceeded down the railroad toward Chef-du-Pont."

There were about 100 men altogether equipped only with what they could carry. Rifles, submachine guns, three machine guns and grenades of various types including the British gammon grenade which packed a terrific wallop. At about **10.00** 6 June Col. Ostberg and his force, comprised of men of all units of the 507th and some from the 508th had reached the railroad station of Chef-du-Pont without any opposition. The railroad station was in the center of town and the small but important bridge was a short distance southwest.

Holding the bridge… A squad was sent to clear the section of town northeast of the station, which they did without incident. The remainder of the force led by Col. Ostberg started to race through the part of the town leading to the bridge. This group was fired upon from several buildings simultaneously. Four of the men were hit and the remainder was forced to

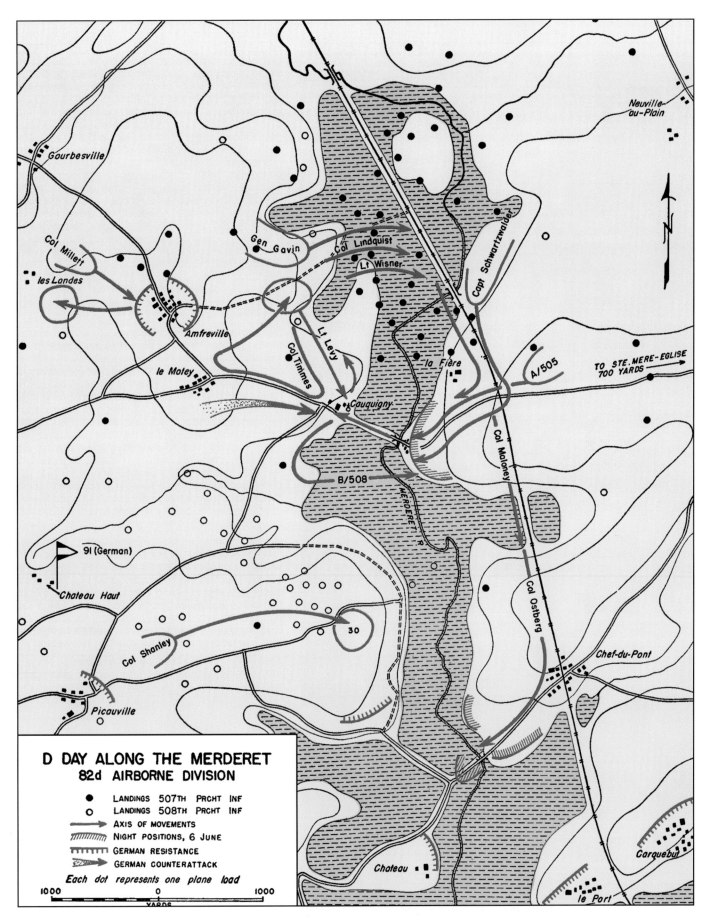

Gourbesville
Col Millett
les Landes
Amfreville
le Motey
Col Timmes
Gen Gavin
Col Lindquist
Lt Wisner
Lt Levy
Cauquigny
la Fière
Capt Schwartzwalder
A/505
TO STE. MERE - EGLISE
700 YARDS
MERDERET R.
B/508
Col Maloney
91 (German)
Chateau Haut
30
Col Shanley
Col Ostberg
Chef-du-Pont
Picauville
Neuville-
au-Plain
Chateau
Carquebut
le Port

D DAY ALONG THE MERDERET
82d AIRBORNE DIVISION

● LANDINGS 507TH PRCHT INF
○ LANDINGS 508TH PRCHT INF
→ AXIS OF MOVEMENTS
⊤⊤⊤⊤⊤⊤ NIGHT POSITIONS, 6 JUNE
⊥⊥⊥⊥⊥⊥ GERMAN RESISTANCE
⟶ GERMAN COUNTERATTACK

Each dot represents one plane load

1000   0   1000
YARDS

hold until the town could be systematically cleared. This took about two hours.

"By that time, most of the Germans had withdrawn ahead of us, apparently headed for the bridge. Speed seemed to be the answer. We knew the bridge must

This map shows the fighting for La Fière and the crossing of the Merderet with the American attack and the German counterattack. To the west of the inundated area, the Germans dug in around Amfreville while groups of paratroopers moved back onto the east bank of the Merderet, first hitting the rail causeway which took them on to dry land. Further south, we see Colonel Shanley falling back onto Hill 30. We also see Lieutenant-Colonel Ostberg's advance on Chef-du-Pont.

be taken before the Germans could organize their defense so we made a semi-organized dash for it. We were too late. Two officers reached the bridge and were both shot - one toppling off the bridge and into the water. The other officer falling on the eastern approach. The officer toppling into the river was Col. Ostberg. He was rescued shortly afterward by two soldiers of the 507 and lived to fight again. The other officer was dead. A short time later, Col. Maloney arrived with about 75 more men and we set about dislodging the stubborn enemy. The railroad split the town and the bridge lay to the south and west of the railroad station. Houses lined both sides of the road leading to the bridge. A short distance from the bridge on the left side of the road leading to the bridge was a large creamery [author's note: today Nestlé's] which was two stories high and afforded good observation from an upstairs window. South of the creamery and on three sides of the bridge, there were obstacles, flooded areas. For practical purposes, the only approach to the bridge was the one we had chosen through Chef-du-Pont.

Our own position along the edge of the road east of the bridge had become almost untenable because rifle and direct artillery fire coming from our right flank. Just as it was beginning to look as though we might have a stalemate, Col. Maloney was called back to La Fière with all men available, leaving only about 34 men at Chef-du-Pont. Concurrent with his departure three things happened: One, direct artillery fire on our positions around the creamery reduced our strength to 20 men; two, an observation point in the creamery noted what was estimated to be a company of Germans moving around to our left rear (...) three, an officer delivered a message from Gen. Gavin, 'hold at all costs.' It was pretty obvious that it couldn't cost much more, but at the same time, it was doubtful we could hold something we didn't have.

Reinforcements were requested, and as from heaven, C-47s began to appear, dropping bundles of weapons and ammunition. (...) Within 30 minutes, the officer who had previously delivered the 'hold at all costs' message returned with 100 men and a 57mm gun which was pulled into position on our side of the bridge. We started firing at the enemy field piece. I'm sure we didn't hit it, but we stopped the firing and that is what we had to do in order to survive.

At the beginning of this period of heavy shelling, I found myself exposed with no place to go. I spot-

1. A C-47 has crashed near the bridge at Chef-du-Pont, at the junction with the Prussel road. (D. F.)

2. Paratroopers of the *507th PIR* check the houses in a village. (D.F.)

3. The bridge over the Merderet at Chef-du-Pont in 1944. (D.F.)

mans made a run for it down the deathtrap causeway and were immediately shot down. That did it. The battle was over. The bridge was ours and we knew we could hold it."

That same day, Captain Roy Creek rejoined his own regiment mustering east of the Merderet in the La Fière sector, and took part in the heavy fighting that followed on 9 June.

This girl watches admiringly paratroopers of the *82d Airborne Division*. (D.F.)

ted a very small brick sentry house just short of the bridge on our side. I made a dash for it and went inside and found a still burning enemy soldier, victim of a white phosphorous grenade, which apparently had been tossed in on him during earlier fighting. The house only had room for one man standing. So it became crowded with my arrival and the other guy in there wasn't going anywhere. This coupled with the fact that the smoke and stench from the burning man caused me to make a quick decision that I would rather take my chances out in the open than risk the consequences of smoke inhalation and besides I reasoned that this lone house was surely an aiming point for the artillery. With our reinforcements, strong positions were organized to our rear and along the flooded area on either side of the road and east of the bridge. The defenses were tied in with natural obstacles on three sides of us. We opened fire with every weapon we could get into position, including our 60mm mortar. On a prearranged signal, all fires lifted and ten men and one officer stormed the bridge and went into position on the western approach to guard the causeway. Five Ger-

1. Two paratroopers of the *82d Airborne Division* in the Normandy bocage. (D. François coll.)

2. Many cattle and horses were killed by artillery fire. A paratrooper of the *507th PIR* has found the Normandy cow that has just been killed, a spot of fresh meat for his unit. (D. François coll.)

3. Captain Creek is promoted to *Major* by Colonel Edson Raff at the close of the Normandy campaign. (D. François coll.)

4. Roy Creek at the opening of the Roy Creek Bridge at Chef-du-Pont in June 2000. (Photo courtesy D. François.)

Roy Creek retired to Kansas state. (Photo courtesy D. François.)

Sainte-Mère-Eglise.

The photos presented in this two-page spread are particularly famous. They have often been published and have contributed towards the huge celebrity of the little town of Sainte-Mère-Eglise. "The Longest Day", first the Cornelius Ryan book then the movie based on it, turned this Cotentin village into one of those places found in history books. At Sainte-Mère-Eglise, as at Sainte-Marie-du-Mont, paratroopers landed among the houses during the night. Conditions at Sainte-Mère were all the more dramatic because Julia Pommier's barn was ablaze, lighting up the square as the paratroops came down, especially because the civilians who came to put out the fire saw the whole thing, with the Germans opening fire on the paratroops. But the Germans regained control of the situation. However, they evacuated the locality before dawn (see page 79) and Lieutenant-Colonel Krause's 3/505 entered the locality and settled in, facing a German counterattack from the north that afternoon; And from 11.00 in the morning, the village came under German artillery fire.

1. This famous photo shows a paratrooper rumning towards the church porch. Is it just a reconstitution for the war correspondent's camera or was it actually taken in the heat of the moment? There were indeed German soldiers in the church belltower (see page 79) and, during the night, Rudolf May threw a grenade on a level with this entrance. But all the Germans had evacuated by dawn, including those inside the belltower. This race would therefore have been a prudent step towards a by now empty church. (NA/Heimdal.)

2. The church as it is today, with the parachute and dummy caught in the belltower, recalling how John Steele was caught in this position during the night. (E.G./Heimdal.)

3. In this other photo, taken on 7 June, American infantry dislodge a German sniper from the belltower... (Heimdal coll.)

4. Here we see two soldiers searching for snipers in a store in the village's main square. It is in fact Jules Leménicier's hardware store (see map p. 58, n° 16). (NA/ Heimdal coll.)

5. This photo was recentered and published full size in a small American propaganda brochure for the French presenting pictures by Weston Haynes (see pages 138 and 139). In the brochure, this photo was published with the following caption: "The Germans had orders to behave themselves. But before leaving, they looted this store and killed the owner." In actual fact they was no act of looting by the occupying forces at Sainte-Mère-Eglise. Jules Léménicier and his family were still there at 11.00 hours on 6 June 1944, playing cards with the neighbors when the owner was harassed by some gunfire. At 11, a German shell went off in the middle of the street. Jules Leménicier died from shrapnel wounds. There are numerous shrapnel marks on the shop front. Notice the "quincaillerie" (hardware) sign and the village gas pump. (Heimdal coll.)

1

2

6 June 1944, late afternoon at Sainte-Mère-Eglise

As of 11.00 hours on this 6 June 1944, the civilian population of Sainte-Mère-Eglise found itself in a hellish situation. An explosion broke the calm of the little town. An initial shell fired from Fauville heralded a salvo of others which enfiladed the main street. The impact landed right in th the middle of the street, between Jules Leménicier's hardware store (marked "16" on the map on page 58) and René Jamard's barber's shop (marked "15" on the map). The two fronts were showered with shrapnel, which passed through doors and windows. Jules Leménicier was hit in the middle of his store. At the end of their meal, René Jamard, sitting at the end of the table and facing the street offered to play a game of cards with Auguste Dubost and Emile Brohier when suddenly he fell in a pool of blood, his face flat on the table top. A paratrooper was alerted who gave him a shot of morphine – to no avail, as he was already dead. A magnificent white parachute was used as a shroud for him. Thereafter the horrors of war fell upon the village. Two 88 mm guns rushed up by the Germans began firing on the center of Sainte-Mère from Fauville, later joined by 80 mm

3

4

1 and 2. In the main street, facing north towards Fauville, an 88 shell has ripped open the corner of a house. Medics of the 505th PIR load up an American truck with wounded Americans and civilians. The men have their backs to the Town Hall, on the left where the gr had set up the Kanton Kommandantur. On the right, wearing a dark jacket and a French helmet is a civilian medical orderly, M. Métayer. The presentday photo shows that the damaged house has been modified. (US Army and E.Groult/Heimdal.)

mortars. A young girl, 22-year-old Christiane Dorey, was killed at her window in her white nightdress. The nonstop bombardment of the center and the prospect of a siege prompted several families to flee. In so doing, at 15.00 hours, Omer Leménicier's 60-year-old grandmother, Esther Legigan, was killed and his mother had her jaw blown off. The two women were hit by an 88 mm shell fired from the north. The wounded woman received first aid at the Hospice, which had been turned into an American infirmary. The whole Leménicier family was evacuated to Lalonde Farm on 7 June.

6

5

3. Now another truck is coming to collect a load of German prisoners in front of the Hospice at Sainte-Mère, photo by Weston Haynes. (US Army.)

4 and **5.** Negotiations between a German WO (junior grade) and an American lieutenant of 505th PIR, surrounded by German and American medics. Photos by Weston Haynes. (US Army.)

6. The same spot today. (E.G./Heimdal.)

7. The negotiations are over. A 505th PIR medic offers a German NCO a cigarette. Photo by W. Haynes. (US Army.)

7

Field dressing station at the Hospice at Sainte-Mère-Eglise, 6 June 1944.

1. Another view of the Hospice, as it is today. (Heimdal.)

2 and **3.** Evacuation of a wounded German through a side door of the Hospice. The leading civilian stretcher-bearer is M. Métayer. This door was later surmounted by a concrete staircase. (US Army and Heimdal.)

4. The 505th PIR chaplain, the Rev. Wood, photographed by Bob Piper. (US Army.)

5. We see him again here in front of the side door of the Hospice with a paratrooper and an infantryman of the 4th Division. (US Army.)

6. Wounded Germans are taken care of by Medics inside the Hospice. (US Army.)

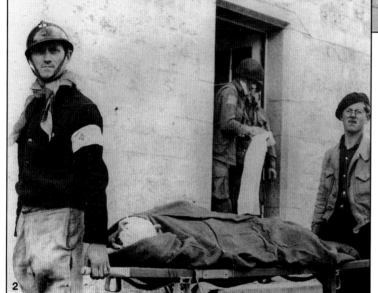

11. Monument to civilian casualties in front of the Town Hall. Notice the names of Christiane Dorey and Jules Lemé-nicier. (Heimdal.)

12. This photo taken in 1993 at 7, Rue du Général de Gaulle shows impacts still visibles on several houses. (Heimdal.)

7 and **8.** The Paris grands-parents' Rue Cap-de-Laine house damaged in June 1944, and now. (Heimdal.)

9 and **10.** The Rue de la Gare, near the crossroads, wounded civilians are loaded onto an American vehicle. (US Army and E.G./Heimdal.)

Sainte-Mère-Eglise, 7 June 1944.
On D-day + 1, the *505th PIR* rounded up horses, of which there were plenty in this sector of Normandy, mostly taken from the Germans, most of whose static units in position in the Cotentin peninsula were horsedrawn. After Sainte-Mère-Eglise was taken, these patrols would appear to have taken place on 7 June 1944. **(Photos 1, 2, 3, 4, 5)**. The place has remained intact, apart from changes in the signposting. (US Army and E.G./Heimdal.)

All these photos were taken at the same spot, in the main street looking south with the church square behind. Then came a horsedrawn cart captured from the Germans along with an ambulance and some jeeps (photos **6, 7, 8** — US Army.) Each year, the US paratroops come back to Sainte-Mère-Eglise. Here we see some young paratroopers of the 505th parading through Sainte-Mère-Eglise on 6 June 2003. (Photo 9 - G. Bernage.) The hairdresser's marked "coiffure" is recognizable on the right of photo **8**.

In photo **8,** we can see Jules Leménicier's store (he was killed on 6 June), with its gas pump.

149

7 June 1944 at Sainte-Mère-Eglise.

1 and **2.** This photo was taken from the square, looking north in the other direction, the church is on the right. Notice the shrapnel marks left by an 88 mm shell on the house on the left. Photo taken by Bob Piper. (H.J. Renaud coll.) Today this neighborhood is more or less as it was. Only the old trees have gone. The "Castel" house was already there in 1944. (Heimdal.)

3. The paratroopers of the 505th return to where their predecessors fought. This photo was taken on 6 June 2003. They are facing the church for the ceremony, with their backs turned to the houses seen on the left of photo **1.** (Photo courtesy G. Bernage.)

4 and **5.** Having passed the church square moving up northwards, this photo was taken facing south. The church square, further down on the left, can be seen amid the trees. Here we again see elements of the mounted patrol. (US Army/D.F.) Some of the frontages are still the same, although repainted. (E. Groult/Heimdal.)

6 and **7.** Close-up shot of the same spot. This picture was taken by war correspondent Shelton on the corner of the Rue Cap-de-Laine with the signpost indicating 9.7 km to the sea. (DAVA/E.G./Heimdal.)

8 and **9.** The same crossroads from the station road, looking eastwards towards the sea. The corner of the house near the road sign has been damaged by a shell. The explosion has only just taken place. (D.F. and E.G./Heimdal.)

4

5

7

6

8

9

82d Airborne Division field dressing station near Sainte-Mère-Eglise.

1. An *82d Airborne Division* field dressing station was set up at a farm not far from Sainte-Mère-Eglise by the *307th Airborne Medical Company*, whose markings appear on the Jeep fender: 82A/B-307. Notice the German prisoners in the background. (D.F./Heimdal.)

2. This Medic of the *307th Airborne Medical Company* gives first aid to a wounded German. (US Army.)

152

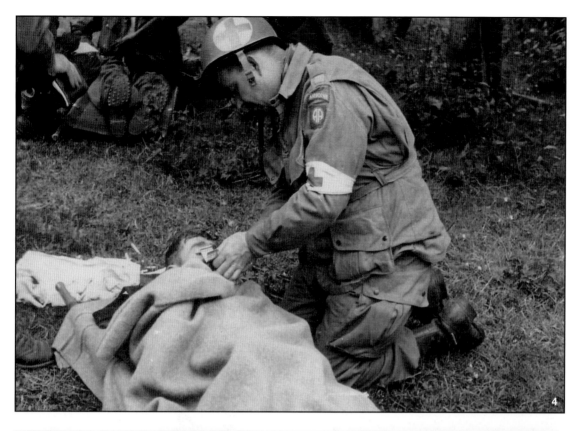

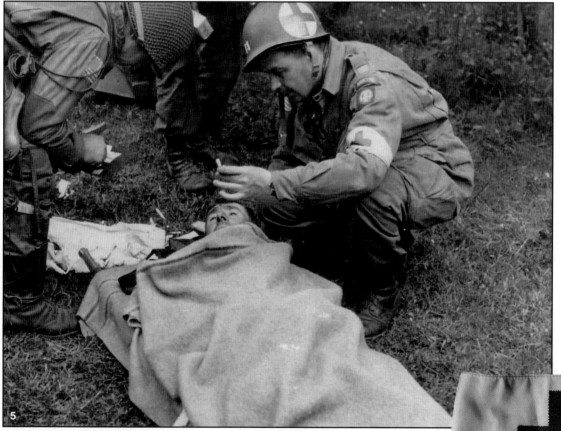

3. Another Medic gives a wounded man something to drink. (US Army.)

4 and **5.** The medical officer lights a cigarette for a wounded German. Another wounded German, recognizable from his hobnailed boots, can be seen behind on a stretcher. (D.F./Heimdal.)

Georgian prisoners of Ost-Bataillon 795.

After digging in in the Turqueville sector, this battalion, commanded by Captain Stiller, at first bravely resisted the assaults by the *8th Inf. Regt.*, *4th Infantry Division* until the morning of 7 June. They then negotiated their surrender and *1/8* took 174 prisoners, some of whom were taken off to the beach.

1. In this photo, American infantrymen gather up prisoners on a farm. They are apparently Georgian prisoners as one of them is wearing a Caucasian style smock. (US Army.)

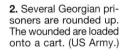

2. Several Georgian prisoners are rounded up. The wounded are loaded onto a cart. (US Army.)

3. La Herguerie Farm at Audouville-la-Hubert, where the Birette family lived in 1944. At around 3pm on 6 June 1944 some thirty Georgian and German prisoners were liquidated behind this farm. (E.G./ Heimdal.)

4. Here we see a Georgian Leutnant who is a prisoner of *4th Division Infantrymen* who came ashore with the second wave (their shoulder flashes have been partly covered over by the censor). (NARA.)

5. Earlier we saw this same Georgian officer on the staff of *Ost-Bataillon 795* (see page 30) posing proudly for photographer Zucca in the spring of 1944, in the Cotentin. (BHVP.)

6. We see him a little later on in this famous photo taken on 7 June 1944, as he informs the Americans about his battalion's positions. This photo was taken from the same angle but the officer is no longer in such high spirits and he needs a shave. (NA/Heimdal.)

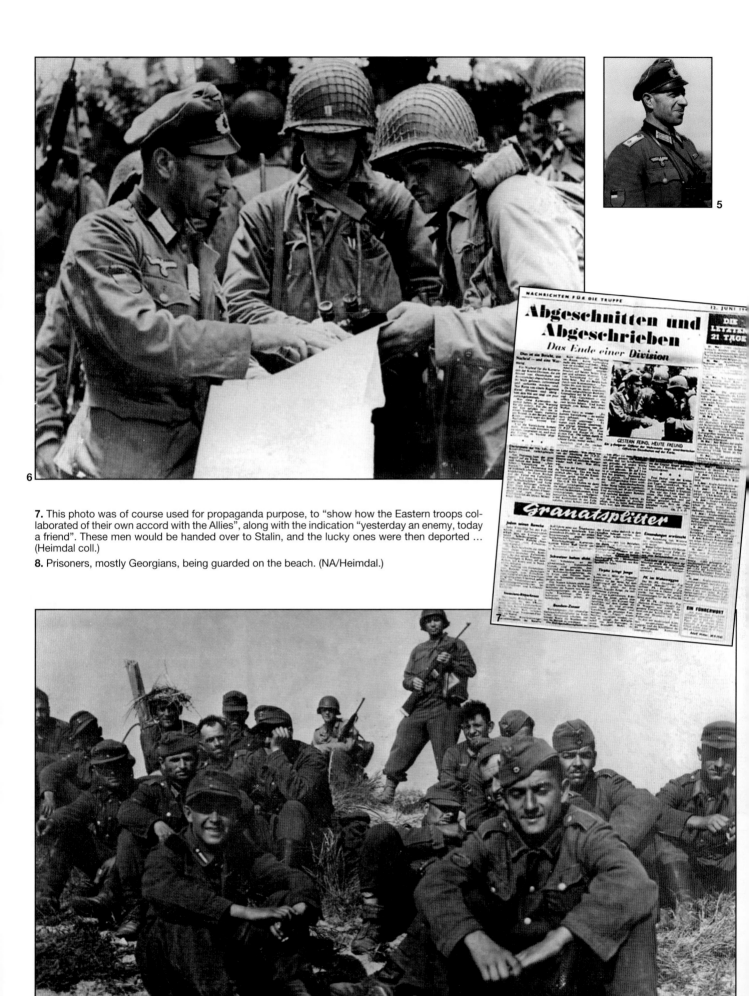

7. This photo was of course used for propaganda purpose, to "show how the Eastern troops collaborated of their own accord with the Allies", along with the indication "yesterday an enemy, today a friend". These men would be handed over to Stalin, and the lucky ones were then deported … (Heimdal coll.)

8. Prisoners, mostly Georgians, being guarded on the beach. (NA/Heimdal.)

1. This *Sturmgeschütz* of *Panzer-Jäger-Abteilung 709*, still smoking on the morning of 7 June, was destroyed by *Pvt* J. Atchley of *H/505*. This photo was taken about a hundred yards from the northern entrance to the village of Sainte-Mère-Eglise. According to the testimony of Heinz Wittmann, who took part in the German counterattack on the morning of 7 June with his two 8,8 cm Flak guns, the counterattack was directed by *Generalleutnant* Karl Willhelm von Schlieben, who was in command of 709. ID and had finally made it back from Rennes. Heinz Wittmann then went to take orders from the general who was in a sunken lane heading west from Highway 13, three or four hundred meters north of Sainte-Mère. Suddenly, von Schlieben appeared from behind a hedge; *"he was there in front of me, standing tall and broad"*. The general, finding himself in the front line like this ordered H. Wittmann to fire his two 8,8 cm guns at the village, *"the hub of all the enemy's operations"*. The crossroads then came under heavy fire from the powerful 88 guns firing twenty shells a minute. Unfortunately the range-finder broke down and the two guns were pulled back before dawn on 8 June. (D.F./Heimdal.)

2. *Generalleutnant* Karl Wilhelm von Schlieben stood *"tall and broad"*. On 6 June, he got back from Rennes. This meant that on D-day, with *Generalleutnant* Falley killed and von Schlieben late returning, there had been no German general in the sector, with units left to their own devices. On 7 June, on the other hand, von Schlieben found himself in the front line before Sainte-Mère-Eglise. (NA/Heimdal.)

The gliders bring in reinforcements

The *325th Glider Infantry Regiment*, which was attached to the *82d Airborne Division*, was brought in by glider as reinforcement. It left England under fighter-bomber escort at **04.30** on the morning of **7 June**. The 200 gliders landed at the Les Forges *LZ* in four waves, from **7 to 09.10**. There were many accidents on landing. Then, starting at **16.00 hours**, this *325th Glider Infantry Regiment* marched on Chef-du-Pont. From there, *1/325* headed off for La Fière, *2/325* for Sainte-Mère-Eglise. *3/325* (actually *2/401* Glider, a battalion attached to *325th GIR*, to replace its 3rd Battalion) was kept in reserve.

Gliders also brought in two airborne artillery groups, the *319th Glider Field Artillery Battalion* and the *320th GFAB*, with 48 tons of munitions, at the Les Forges *LZ* from 21-23.00 hours on D-day. Ten glider pilots and 29 artillerymen were killed on landing. There were 135 wounded and 64 gliders were destroyed. At **09.30** on 7 June, six of the *320th GFAB's* 105 mm guns opened up on Sainte-Mère-Eglise, soon joined by six of the *319th GFAB's* 75 mm guns, from the east of the town in support of *505th PIR's* assault.

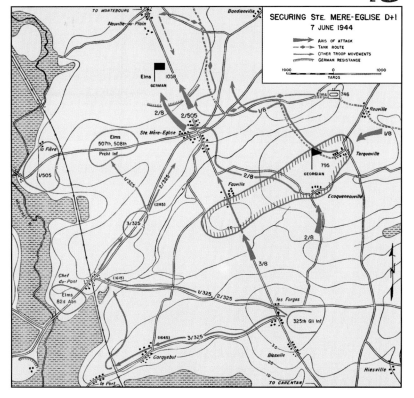

SECURING STE. MERE-EGLISE D+I
7 JUNE 1944

AXIS OF ATTACK
TANK ROUTE
OTHER TROOP MOVEMENTS
GERMAN RESISTANCE

Reinforcement of the Sainte-Mère-Eglise sector on 7 June. On the evening of 6 June, two battalions of the *8th Infantry Regiment (2/8* and *3/8)* had arrived at Les Forges on Highway 13 but had failed to make contact with the paratroops of *2/505* who were still cut off at Sainte-Mère-Eglise. The arrival of 200 gliders on the Les Forges LZ from 07.00 to 09.10 on the Wednesday 7 June enabled the *325th Glider Infantry Regiment*, brought in by these gliders, to join the front line. During the day, this regiment reinforced the paratroops at La Fière and Chef-du-Pont. It also took the strain off the *8th Infantry Regiment* whose battalions went on to tackle the German pocet of resistance in the Fauville and Turqueville sector. Also, contacts were made between *1/8* and *D/505* as of 10.00, northeast of Sainte-Mère-Eglise.

The seaborne elements arrive

The troopers had made contact with the men of the *12th Infantry Regiment* late on D-day evening, in the Beuzeville-au-Plain sector. However, at dawn on 7 June, Ridgway's *82d Airborne Division* was still cut off with practically no communications. Since 17.00, on 6 June, the *70th Tank Battalion's* tank column had been held up at Les Forges with two battalions of the *8th Infantry Regiment*. East of Turqueville, *1/8* and the *A/70th Tk Bn* were fighting the Georgians and the rest of the coastal strongpoint garrisons. Only one platoon of *K Company, 8th Inf. Regt.* had managed to make contact with the paratroopers at Chef-du-Pont.

About **09.00** a radio message informed the paratroopers holding Sainte-Mère-Eglise that the *4th Infantry Division* was just outside the town. At **10.00**, first contact was made in the sector covered by *D/505* (Captain Smith).

Shortly before, a German counterattack was stopped and a *StuG* continued burning in front of Vandervoort's CP, this assault cannon was destroyed by Private J. Atchley of H/505. Meanwhile, *2/8* was still fighting the Georgians south of Sainte-Mère. It finally cleared the Fauville-Turqueville sector, taking 300 prisoners (mostly Georgians of *Ost-Bataillon 795*) and entered Sainte-Mère at **about noon** from Les Clarons. A column of tanks of the *70th Tank Battalion* also arrived which were in reserve around Reuville and had been ordered to race to Sainte-Mère. Then when Collins met Ridgway at his HQ on the La Fière road, the troopers there knew that they were safe!

To the north-west, German elements were repulsed towards Neuville-au-Plain (Misère valley) with the arrival of *746th Tanks* on their left flank and *2/8* and the men of *2/505* in support. At **17.30**, four German tanks were destroyed and many prisoners were taken. *E/505* captured 160. 400 Germans were killed. General Gavin told Vandervoort not to kill them all but to keep a few for interrogation. The Germans then fell back to Montebourg, leaving Neuville in the hands of the Americans who promptly set about establishing a front: in the east, the *12th Inf. Regt.* was almost at Azeville and the *899th TD Battalion* stopped for the night at Baudienville. The *505th PIR* took up positions west of Highway 13 while the 1st and 2nd Battalions, *8th RCT* occupied the sector east of the highway. *3/8* was kept in reserve east of Sainte-Mère-Eglise.

Chef-du-Pont - Hill 30

On the morning of **7 June**, Lt.-Colonel Shanley of the *508th PIR* and his group of 300 paratroopers received orders by radio from Colonel Lindquist to move up to *Hill 30 overlooking the western bridge exit at* Chef-du-Pont. Shanley dispatched patrols to test the enemy defenses and pick up stray paratroopers. In the afternoon, fifty Americans settled into the farm at the crossroads at the foot of the hill (village of Caponnet) to cut off access to the bridge from the west. The officer now knew through a radio link with Lindquist that the *508*th held Chef-du-Pont.

On the hill, munitions, rations and medical supplies began to run low as the wounded increased in numbers under the rounds of German mortar fire raining down on Hill 30. Shanley and his men were completely under siege, facing two battalions of *Gren. Rgt.1057* with support from the artillery of *91. Division* headquartered at Château de Bernaville at Picauville.

Some skirmishing went on to test the defenses on the north side of Hill 30. Lt. Albright received support from the howitzers of the *319th GFA* based at Chef-du-Pont, which he directed by wireless.

At dawn on **8 June**, the Germans attacked the bottleneck at the crossroads at the foot of Hill 30 and

Early in the morning of 7 June, 200 gliders (152 Wacos and 48 Horsas) brought reinforcements over the Les Forges LZ, south of Sainte-Mère-Eglise – the men of the *325th Glider Infantry Regiment* and artillery guns as well. (NA.)

were only repelled thanks to the intervention of a section led by Shanley and Shield Warren taking them on the flank.

Amfreville

On the morning of 8 June, Lieutenant-Colonel Timmes, who had 200 men of the 507th in the Amfreville sector, which later became the famous "Timmes orchard", was worried about his group's predicament, with intermittent but persistent mortar and artillery shelling of his position leaving him no room to maneuver. Given the lack of ammunition and rations, and most of all his force's isolation, the future looked bleak. He decided to dispatch Lt. John Marr and Private Norman Carter to find a ford across the marshes and the Merderet (north of post 104) enabling the group to link up with the rest of the division. Marr and Carter had not gone far before they

Lieutenant-Colonel Shanley in 1943, when he was commander of the 2nd Battalion, *508th PIR*. (D. François coll.)

The paratroops arrive in the Amfreville sector. This man is probably an airborne soldier of the *325th Glider Infantry Regiment*. (D. François coll.)

Lieutenant-Colonel Charles G. Timmes. (D.F.)

Colonel G.V. Millett.

came to a path paved with pebbles that had been flooded over. The followed it paddling through the mud as far as the railroad embankment and joined elements of the 325th. From there they reached General Ridgway at his HQ at La Fière.

Late in the afternoon, Carter came back with some sappers marking out the route and informed Timmes that the 325th's 1st Battalion had arrived overnight.

During the night, contact was made in the north-west with 507th commander Colonel Millett, who had been going round in circles with a large group ever since landing in Normandy. They had also received orders from the Division to join Timmes, but on the way the Millett group was split up by a German attack. In the confusion, some headed off northwards, crossing the Merderet, led by Captain Paul Smith, and joined the 505th at La Fière, but Colonel Millett and his group were captured.

Captain Paul Smith (507th PIR/82d Airborne Division), paraphrased.

"I landed in a field by a road. After releasing my harness, I went up the drop line to pick up the men in my stick; at that time, I was unable to locate my position on the map. A little later, I finally found some elements of my unit commanded by Major Pearson. Not long afterwards, our little group encountered a French farmer walking along the road. He told us we were a short distance from the village of Le Ham about two miles from our drop zone. Led by Major Pearson, the detachment headed for its objective: the village of Amfreville. We picked up a few isolated paratroopers on our way. The radio operator tried and failed to make contact with the battalion. Pearson then decided he would have to use the regimental frequency to make contact with the staff. Later the voice of Colonel George Millett could be heard over set 300. He ordered Major Pearson to take our group to the regimental CP (command post). All day long, we picked up groups of paratroopers and joined battle many times, but we never located the CP. Later that afternoon, the major contacted Colonel Millett again and received fresh coordinates. We made a move at nightfall."

At dawn on **7 June**, our group was on the Gourbesville-Etienville road. Then I myself made contact with Colonel Millett who gave me new coordinates for his position. He told me he was sending out a guide to meet us. We found a sergeant at the edge of a wood who took us to the CP. There were a few officers around Colonel Millett, and 120 paratroopers. We then stayed in this position throughout the day and night under constant enemy fire. The following morning (**8 June**), Captain Taylor joined us with some officers and about a hundred men. We were running short of ammunition and rations. All the group had to eat were some rations we found in a German truck.

All day long, we defended our position against increasingly intense enemy attacks. Night fell and we began preparing to make a move. At that precise moment, I did not know what Colonel Millett was planning. I enquired from Major Pearson what our assignment was to be. I was told the division had ordered us to march towards the Merderet river to link up with another group commanded by Lieutenant-Colonel Shanley (508th). Our force set off just after midnight.

Lieutenant Roger Whiting and I brought up the rear. The column of about 250 Americans and 90 prisoners, moved south of the CP, turning north-west towards the Amfreville-Gourbesville road. Shortly afterwards, while Whiting and I were patrolling along the column of prisoners, we heard two MG 42s firing ahead of our group. We moved up the column to speak to Colonel Millett. He told me he was going to turn back and try another route. Whiting and I volunteered to fall back to the rear and cover the column as it retreated. While everyone fell back, we threw a few grenades and opened fire on the MG 42s to draw away the enemy gunners. Later we caught up with the detachment which had stopped to rest. After five minutes, seeing the column was making no move, and suspecting by then that something was up, I went up to the front of the group. The man who was supposed to be liaising between the front and the rear of the column had dozed off. So this put me, having the highest rank, in charge of about 150 men and the 90 prisoners with only a vague idea of what I had to do. I did know however that Colonel Millett had headed east for the Merderet. So I decided to carry on in that direction. A few hours later, I decided to organize a defensive perimeter in a field, until we could accurately locate our troops. We came under enemy fire before we had completely sealed off our perimeter. I gave orders to fall back south-east, staying parallel to the river. After a firefight lasting over an hour and 10% American casualties, I reorganized my detachment and sent out patrols, helped by some of the prisoners, to try and recover some containers. These were often booby-trapped and several prisoners were killed. I then tried to radio the Regiment over the emergency channel and I got through to Lieutenant-Colonel Maloney. I gave him our position and requested orders. He ordered me to stay where we were, pending further instructions. A few moments later, the lieutenant-colonel who was with Colonel Millett entered our perimeter with about thirty men. He informed us that Colonel Millett and his group had been captured and that a large German detachment was heading towards us. According to him, our only chance of survival was to cross the Merderet and link up with the US troops on the other side. I forcefully opposed this decision, saying that I was awaiting orders from Maloney, that our defensive perimeter only had to be defended on three sides as it backed up onto an inundated area, and that it could be defended even against a large force.

Also, I had heard the sound of fighting to the south-west, which meant that there were other Americans on this side of the river. I ended with the fact that the marshes were flooded for a kilometer all around, and that we were in danger of being wiped out by the Germans if we tried to cross them. I suggested to this lieutenant-colonel to cross the river with his group if he wished, except for the men of the 507th. As my superior officer, he decided to take over command and would not listen to my arguments. He ordered me to take 4 or 5 men and open up the way to cross the Merderet. I protested loudly against this order and said I would only be willing to obey it if he repeated it in front of two witnesses chosen by me. I then took 5 men and crossed the river under machine-gun fire. During the crossing, many prisoners were killed but luckily no Americans were killed.

*On dry land on the other side, I set up a defensive position with the help of Sergeant Hopkins. The lieutenant-colonel left us for the Divisional CP. I informed Colonel Maloney of my new position and took our prisoners (down to just 26) into a POW camp enclosure, and the wounded to the 508th aid station. We remained in this position all night and early the next morning **(9 June)**, we headed for the 507th's sector at the La Fière bridge…"*

The bridgeheads

In the 101st's sector, the bulk of the German defense rested with the 3rd Battalion of *Grenadier-Regt. 1058*, reinforced on 7 June by two companies of the 3rd Battalion of *Fallschirmjäger-Regt. 6*. Von der Heydte, the regiment's commander, personally led the defense. His 1st Battalion was swept aside by the paratroops of the 501st and 506th between Sainte-Marie-du-Mont and the Douve on **7 June**, and he had lost contact with his 2nd Battalion to the north, between Saint Côme and Sainte-Mère-Eglise.

Lacking reserves, von der Heydte decided to withdraw first westward then southward via the Carentan rail bridge. Fighting all the way to stop the 3rd Battalion, 501st (Ewell) on his right flank, and the 506th coming from the north and east, he extricated most of his men at about noon, leaving behind 40 truckloads of equipment. As they withdrew, the Germans blew up the main road bridge, which the Americans of the 101st were trying to do.

Thus, on the evening of **8 June**, the *101st Airborne Division* was able to carry on south for the next phase of the campaign. When on the afternoon of the 8th *General* Taylor informed *VII Corps commander General* Collins that Saint Côme and the north bank of the Douve had been mopped up, Collins merely answered: *"Very good; now take Carentan."*

Meanwhile, the *82d Airborne Division* held Sainte-Mère-Eglise, to the north as far as Neuville au Plain, to the south as far as Les Forges, and to the east on the banks of the Merderet between La Fière and Chef du Pont. Two large groups were cut off, one commanded by Lieutenant-Colonel Shanley of the *508th PIR* at Picauville on Hill 30 and the other commanded by Lieutenant-Colonel Timmes of the *507th PIR* in the Amfreville marshes. Their orders were now to loosen the grip at La Fière and to race towards Picauville, to open up the way inland for the troops piling up on the beaches.

Ed Jeziorski, *507th PIR, 82d Airborne Division*

One of the most dramatic assaults of the Battle of Normandy was the capture of the La Fière bridge on **9 June**. The bridge and the causeway covered several hundred yards with no cover and no way round,

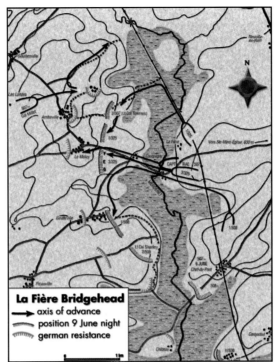
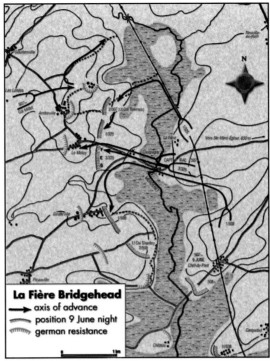

La Fière Bridgehead
→ axis of advance
position 9 June night
german resistance

1, 2, 3. Captain Paul Smith, his paratrooper's diploma and trench knife. (D.F coll.)

2

3

and so had to be taken and held so as to prevent enemy reinforcements getting through to attack *Utah Beach*. Several hundred paratroopers were east of the Merderet awaiting the assault. The *325th Glider Infantry Regiment* was assigned to lead the attack, but was forced back against superior numbers and artillery fire. In the end, a lone company of the *507th* contrived to push the enemy well back on the other side of the causeway. Ed Jeziorski was one of those men.

"We had been told that we were to be ready; we were the reserve for the 325th. If something happened to them, we were going to do it. [...] The 325th were in columns, and they were spaced correctly, and they were doing things the way they were supposed to. They kept as low as they could so not to make too good targets, but as they were moving they were just being knocked down right and left. There was no place to hide on the open causeway; a lot of men were getting killed. Their attack got bogged down.

At that point... a little second lieutenant, and he was a recent addition to our company, he yelled, 'Come on, you paratroopers, let's go!' That's when we went! There was a file of us on one side of the road and a file of us on the other side of the road; we were probably five yards apart, maybe even closer or wider. We started going, and it was just an unbroken line. It was just pouring in that much, that heavy [German artillery, mortar shells, machine gun fire]. This was the hottest day that I had ever been in.

As I crossed the bridge I had the machine gun on my right shoulder. After running several yards, the whole side of the road came up. It came up in a heck of a mass of dirt and right on top of me and knocked me down. I had to scramble to really get out from under the thing, but when I came out from under it, I looked and it looked like everybody was going the wrong way. I said, 'This way, guys.' They said, 'No, Jez, this way.' It could have been a heck of a round of artillery, but I don't know, it could have been a land mine. I didn't hear any noise, just the entire side of the road came up and came down on top of me.

Captain [Robert] Rae kept telling us to 'keep moving, keep moving, keep moving!' I was the only machine

Lieutenant-Colonel Arthur Maloney. (D.F.)

Captain Robert Rae in July 1944 near La Haye-du-Puits receiving his DSC following his action at La Fière. (D.F. Heirn-dal.)

gunner of the ninety or so in the company of us. [...] The little lieutenant was dropped and I never saw him again. I'm pretty sure he was nailed real well.

Guys were dropping, sure; how many of us got through, I don't know. [...] On the other side of the bridge, Boys [an assistant machine gunner] put the tripod down and I put the gun in the pod and we were working in the open, I was firing in the open. That's when Boys got hit. I had another guy come up, you had an ammo bearer always that was carrying a box of ammo, his name was Hine, and he was killed on D plus six. Hine was working the gun with me.

There was a 42 [MG 42], and he was throwing a lot of lead, just like they can do! As it was going over my head. I just held [the trigger] down on him until there was no more noise."

On **9 June**, Gavin completed a plan for a frontal attack to capture the village of Cauquigny from the La Fière causeway. The 3rd Battalion, *325th Glider Infantry Regiment* and 2nd Battalion, 401st, were assigned to lead the assault, with support from a few Sherman tanks of the *746th Tank Battalion*. Captain **Robert Rae's** company, holding the banks of the Merderet, was placed in reserve to back up in the event of the attack failing. It was planned for the artillery to soften up the area for fifteen minutes followed by smoke bombs to help the advancing assault troops. Starting orders were issued at 10.30, Rae provided what *machine-gun* support he could to the *325th* infantry who streamed out in whole columns from a wall of the Manoir de la Fière. The company commander, *Captain Sauls*, led the assault. The smoke bombs were not fired, Sauls orderd the assault from the manor, and crossed the bridge by now under a deluge of steel. On reaching the shelter of a tree Sauls turned round to discover he was alone, with his company pinned down and sustaining heavy losses.

A few dozen yards from the bridge on the high ground, Gavin realized that the assault was failing. With Lieutenant-Colonel Maloney, he joined Rae and ordered him to mount an assault. Rae divided his group of 90 men on either side of the causeway and raced screaming westward. Men fell, others got up again, seeing this officer whom nothing would stop. With all his weapons in support, the Germans stopped and suddenly fell back under heavy American fire in the face of this brave attack by the men of the 507th. Rae passed Cauquigny and his momentum carried him to Le Motey. The La Fière bridge was captured and was not recaptured. The Americans of the *82d Airborne Division* held onto their bridgehead.

The road to Cherbourg lay wide open.

Meanwhile, the *101st Airborne Division* held a straight line with the 502nd in the north between Chef-du-Pont, where it had linked up with the 82nd as far as

Houesville. The 506th stood astride the Carentan road, with forward elements at Le Pont-Douve. On its left, relieving Colonel Johnson's 501st and Captain Shettle's *3/506*, the *327th Glider Infantry Regiment* took up position on the locks at La Barquette and the bridges at Le Port. The 501st was held in reserve at Vierville.

During the lull, the battalions re-formed, gathering up their stray elements and those who had fought with regiments or even divisions they did not belong to.

The beach exits were now held by the 101st for the benefit of the *4th Division* which landed at *Utah Beach,* now reinforced by the *90th Infantry Division* whose leading elements (two battalions of the *359th Infantry Regiment*) came ashore at *Utah Beach* on D-day, the division reached full strength on 9 June. Their north and south flanks protected this path along which the *VII Corps* poured to cut the Cotentin in half and then swing round north towards Cherbourg. The 101st's airborne mission had run its full course. It now remained to win the Battle for Carentan.

Brigadier General Gavin. (D.F./Heimdal.)

Crest of the *507th PIR.*

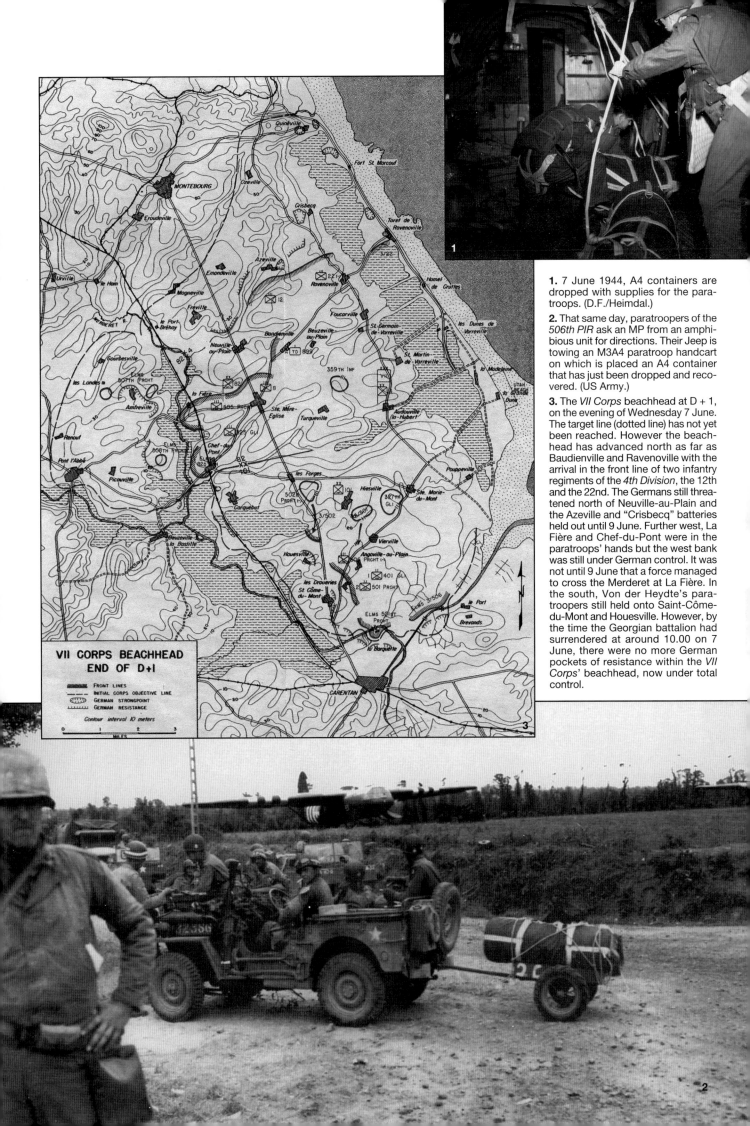

**VII CORPS BEACHHEAD
END OF D+I**

mmmmm FRONT LINES
———— INITIAL CORPS OBJECTIVE LINE
◯◯◯◯◯ GERMAN STRONGPOINT
mmmmm GERMAN RESISTANCE

Contour interval 10 meters

0   1   2
└───┴───┴───┴───┘
        MILES

1. 7 June 1944, A4 containers are dropped with supplies for the paratroops. (D.F./Heimdal.)

2. That same day, paratroopers of the *506th PIR* ask an MP from an amphibious unit for directions. Their Jeep is towing an M3A4 paratroop handcart on which is placed an A4 container that has just been dropped and recovered. (US Army.)

3. The *VII Corps* beachhead at D + 1, on the evening of Wednesday 7 June. The target line (dotted line) has not yet been reached. However the beachhead has advanced north as far as Baudienville and Ravenoville with the arrival in the front line of two infantry regiments of the *4th Division*, the 12th and the 22nd. The Germans still threatened north of Neuville-au-Plain and the Azeville and "Crisbecq" batteries held out until 9 June. Further west, La Fière and Chef-du-Pont were in the paratroops' hands but the west bank was still under German control. It was not until 9 June that a force managed to cross the Merderet at La Fière. In the south, Von der Heydte's paratroopers still held onto Saint-Côme-du-Mont and Houesville. However, by the time the Georgian battalion had surrendered at around 10.00 on 7 June, there were no more German pockets of resistance within the *VII Corps'* beachhead, now under total control.

2

1, 2 and **3.** An uninterrupted stream of equipment and vehicles arrived at *Utah Beach* and passed through Sainte-Mère-Eglise, a major crossroads on Highway 13. Notice again the signpost to the sea, 9.7 km, already seen with the horsemen.

7

8

9

10

11

Sainte-Mère-Eglise, from 8 to 12 June 1944.

4, 5 and **6.** We are still in the main street, near the cross-roads, looking north. We first see **(4)** Private Bishop patrolling the crossroads, with the Rue de la Gare on the left and the Rue Cap-de-Laine on the right. He has nothing to do for the time being. The damage caused by artillery fire can be seen on many of the houses. In the background, on the right, the same house can be seen as in photo **(7)**. A little later, army engineers lay telephone wires on the wall of the fire damaged hairdresser's shop **(5)**. (US Army and E.G./Heimdal.)

7 and **8.** This photo dating from 12 June shows a convoy of the 4th Infantry Division moving down south, probably returning from the front a little further along on a level with Montebourg. Notice in the foreground a Kettenkrad (tracked motorcycle used by German paratroops in this sector) recovered by US troops. The motorcycle is passing in front of the Town Hall, the entrance to which is on the right. This is where Milepost 0 of the Freedom Road was later set up (see photo **11**). Here we again see the house already seen in photos **4** and **6**. (US Army and E.G./Heimdal.)

9 and **10.** In the main street, this soldier meets two victims. Madame Jouan lost her husband Eugène, killed by a shell on 7 June. Her daughter Julienne lost her father. This photograph was taken by a *US Navy* photographer. (D.F. and E.G./Heimdal.)

11. Milepost 0 of the Freedom Road in front of the Town Hall. It stands in front of the monument to the civilian casualties, bearing, among others, the name of Eugène Jouan. (E.G./Heimdal.)

Sainte-Mère-Eglise from 9 to 12 June 1944.

1. On 9 June, the Renauds (the family of the mayor of Sainte-Mère-Eglise) were at the Simons, who took in some Americans, including Captain Arthur G. Kroos Jr., *Major General* Ridgway's aide de camp. From left to right: Alexandre Renaud (the mayor, only his hands are visible on the left), Henri-Jean Renaud (his son), M. Simon (with the hat), Alain Simon (hat), Arthur Kroos (seated), Paul Renaud, Jacqueline Simon, Madame Simon. (US Army.)

2. An MP of the *82d Airborne Division*, Private Bishop, directing traffic at the main crossroads. He warmly thanks an old lady who has just brought him a drink of cider, a beverage that always went down well. He is wearing a jacket, mustard trousers and a pair of jump boots. The MP armband indicates his job. The letters MP are also painted on his helmet which is here covered in camouflage netting. His divisional badge is sewn on his jacket. (US Army.)

3. Here we again see *Pvt.* Bishop, waiting for a convoy to arrive to do traffic duty. (US Army.)

8. Captain William G. Best, chief surgeon, 1st Battalion, *502d PIR*, visits Madame Bertot and her baby, Jean-Yves. From the earliest hours, this military surgeon operated a field dressing station in the Bertot family home where he treated the wounded. (US Army.)

4 and **5.** Madame Dijon is helped out of town by paratroopers sometime around 12 June. The dramatic situation had no effect on her legendary high spirits. (D.F./Heimdal.)

Today the neighborhood has a less countrified look to it. (E.G./Heimdal.)

6 and **7.** After the massive destructions and civilian losses, the survivors flee the highly exposed town. Here an old couple in the Rue Cap-de-Laine, on the corner of the gendarmerie, in 1944 and today. (Photos courtesy Heimdal coll.)

Utah Beach.

On the beach on 6 June **(1)**, infantrymen wait in foxholes in the sand. They are still wearing their inflatable life-jackets. Soon they will follow the troops advancing inland. The Sherman tanks on the beach have just landed and are still carrying their protective hoods. Two days later, on 8 June, a huge armada brought in an endless stream of troops and equipment **(2 and 3)**. Amphibious trucks, DUKWs, load equipment off the boats for transfer onto the beach. The 5 cm KwK gun **(2)** is still in its tobruk facing out to sea. Today **(4)** it is kept near what is now the museum. A Pak antitank gun is also facing seaward **(3)**. Various models of bulldozer are at work on the beach. Behind the sand dune **(5)**, equipment built up fast, with 22 323 men and 2 627 vehicles coming ashore on 7 and 8 June. A floating roadway was built, and what is left of it sometimes comes into view at low tide **(6 and 7)**. (Photos courtesy Heimdal coll. and E.G./Heimdal for the presentday photos.)

The Americans round up German prisoners on the beach. The bombardments caused heavy losses among the garrisons of some of the resistance nests. Barbed wire stretched across the beach provided makeshift POW cages, before the prisoners were shipped off to England. The photo at the foot of the page is an unusual color picture taken at Utah Beach in 1944. (Photos courtesy Heimdal coll.)

Achevé d'imprimer
sur les presses de l'imprimerie Ferré Olsina
pour le compte des Editions Heimdal
mai 2004